FROM ACORNS TO OAKS

MICHAEL HESELTINE

FROM ACORNS TO OAKS

AN URGENT AGENDA TO REBUILD BRITAIN

Biteback Publishing

First published in Great Britain in 2025 by
Biteback Publishing Ltd, London

ISBN 978-1-78590-980-1

10 9 8 7 6 5 4 3 2 1

A CIP catalogue record for this book is available from the British Library.

Set in Minion Pro and Trade Gothic

Printed and bound in Great Britain by
CPI Group (UK) Ltd, Croydon CR0 4YY

FSC
www.fsc.org
MIX
Paper | Supporting responsible forestry
FSC® C171272

CONTENTS

INTRODUCTION

This is not the book I had planned to write. My political career formally ended at the same time as the Conservative Party's resounding defeat in 1997. I had plenty to look forward to – going back to Haymarket, the company I had helped found in the 1950s, and an increasingly absorbing garden to develop. I had been in the political trenches since I joined the Conservative front bench in 1967 at the age of thirty-four.

I had written of my experiences up to that 1997 election in my autobiography, *Life in the Jungle*, which was published three years later in 2000. Then, after the passage of more time, I started writing again, curious to explore whether I had achieved anything of consequence throughout my political life. That book was to be entitled 'Building Blocks', as much of my work was focused on urban regeneration.

But in December 2005, David Cameron became leader of the Conservative Party and in the following March, he invited me to accompany him on a symbolic visit to Liverpool. He followed this up with an invitation to chair a policy group and work up some ideas for urban regeneration for inclusion in the forthcoming manifesto.

After spending eight years in retirement from frontline politics, I was gradually, but not altogether reluctantly, drawn back into the mainstream.

'Building Blocks' was permanently put on hold after the election of the coalition government in 2010 and my subsequent appointment to chair the Regional Growth Fund, set up to help mitigate the consequences of the public expenditure cuts. That was followed by an invitation to join Sir Terry Leahy, recently retired CEO of Tesco, and investigate how the city of Liverpool had evolved from the place I had first explored after the riots of 1981.

For seven years, I served in numerous government roles, produced five reports and chaired many committees. This second lease of political life was a fascinating and privileged return journey to the corridors of power, which only ended when I was summarily dismissed by Theresa May for voting in the Lords, against the government's wishes, for an amendment that would have given Parliament the final say on the historic disaster that is Brexit.

So, this book covers my brief return to private life, with the invitations that followed, the holidays we enjoyed, the obligations we took on and a feeling that the past is never really left far behind. I look at my return to the world of publishing, plus how I became deeply immersed in the development of the arboretum at our home in Thenford and the modernisation of our local village, which meant tackling, from the other side of the counter, planning and environmental regimes, many of which I had been responsible for introducing.

I also revisit my upbringing in Wales, and I reflect on what happened to all those important decisions I took in government, especially those which privatised more aspects of the public sector than any other minister.

This book also explores the long journey signposted by the phrases 'levelling up' and 'devolution', which began for me with the publication of the Redcliffe-Maud Report in 1969. Now half of England is governed locally by directly elected mayors and my report 'No Stone Unturned' can claim to be one of those signposts.

In 1981, I stood looking out over the River Mersey after the riots, wondering just how this grim series of events that ripped through the heart of the once-mighty city of Liverpool could have come about and what could be done about it. Here I have sought to revisit and re-examine my journey in striving to answer that question. From the streets of Toxteth to the banks of the River Thames, I devote a chapter each to our four great cities and the combined authority area Tees Valley, reflecting my conviction that transferring power from the monopolistic, poorly connected baronies of Whitehall to directly elected mayors is the only way to bring decisions closer to the voters who have to live with the consequences of them.

I have sought to look at a diverse range of policies, ranging from community gardening schemes to the establishment of the European Space Agency. Along the way, I steadily refined my understanding of the deep interrelationship between market and state and developed a distinctive analysis of what the state can – and cannot – achieve and what governments need to do to answer the biggest questions which still face our nation. How can we reinvigorate our once great provincial towns and cities, how can we re-energise our most deprived neighbourhoods and how can we rejuvenate our diminished industrial base?

Whatever economic dogmatists may claim, it is impossible to pretend that regeneration can be dissociated from industrial policy. I was determined not to allow my dismissal from government in 2017 to prevent me from participating in that crucial debate – not just about the nature of an industrial strategy but about whether such a strategy is at all credible – so I ultimately produced my own report.

I am, and always have been, a Conservative. I am deeply committed to the virtues and disciplines of competition. But the distinction between regeneration and industrial policy appears to me a stale and ultimately misleading dichotomy. I have learned that few viable markets can exist without the presence of the state and no modern state can excel without the dynamism of market activity. Technological innovation can often send entire city economies into soaring growth or a tailspin of decline.

Communities are also vulnerable to such vicious cycles. As indicators of dysfunction and instability rise, those that can afford to move away do so, further exacerbating the problem. But the actions of central government alone have, historically, rarely been successful in addressing these issues. All of these matters are examined in the chapters ahead.

There are some areas where I have been able to look further back. It is now nearly forty years since I resigned from Margaret Thatcher's Cabinet over issues associated with Westland Helicopters Ltd. Little by little, the truth has emerged, revealing ever more clearly the scandal behind those events. I bring the story up to date here.

It would be unfair to move on from such experiences and leave unstated my gratitude and appreciation for the people who turned theory into practice: civil servants. They can be easy targets, ruthlessly exploited by those anxious to cover their own tracks. But I want to record here how grateful I am to them.

There is one matter where I look forwards. I feel it is essential to explain my view about our future relationship with Europe – a *positive* and, in Tory terms, *contrary* view about Europe – which I do in the concluding chapters of this book.

I lived through the events after the Second World War, which inspired an end to a millennium of war in Europe. I grew up in the post-war world, where modern Europe was conceived, born and given substance. I took part in the 2016 referendum, the result of which left an empty chair at the table of European power and left an intellectual vacuum at the heart of Britain's government. I now have to listen to those responsible for this debacle scrabbling around to find excuses for their inability to honour their undeliverable promises, which I find most distasteful. The fightback is just beginning.

People often ask me whether I would go into politics again today if I was young. Many are surprised by the alacrity of my reply that I would, without hesitation. It has been a privilege beyond measure to be at the centre of the stage for over half a century and to witness the successes and failures, the ups and the downs. I hope that others may not have to start where I began, in the quest for effective regeneration of local economies and the creation of an industrial strategy.

We are a European power, and I have been privileged to support several Conservative Prime Ministers in the vision of ensuring conflict on our continent on the scale of the two world wars could never happen again. Thus, by joining a union of states who share that common belief, we acknowledge that, in a world of superpowers, sovereignty shared is not sovereignty lost but enhanced.

The dishonesty of the referendum and its consequences will continue to haunt my party until the younger generation restores this country's historic role at the centre of Europe. That is the mission for the future, but most of this book looks back at what I have experienced and learned over the last five decades.

Michael Heseltine

2024

PART I

OUTSIDE POLITICS

CHAPTER 1

OUT IN THE COLD

After stepping back from frontline politics following the 1997 general election, my autobiography, *Life in the Jungle*, was published in 2000. It concluded with the words I had used to end the pressure on me to stand for the leadership of the Conservative Party after the defeat of 1997: 'I won't do it.'

I have never regretted that decision. As I said at the time, I was looking forward to an executive role at Haymarket, which I had effectively left twenty-seven years before. There was the arboretum we wanted to develop and the book that my wife Anne and I had long talked of writing about its creation. These were exciting things to be done, and I had a clear view of how the rest of my life would work out.

From my childhood to the present day, I have enjoyed three careers that have interwoven as threads through my life: a love for the natural world, an entrepreneurial hunger and an ambition to become involved in politics. Life, of course, does not run on tram lines. A hotchpotch of unpredictable invitations and unconnected events were to take their place alongside my more predictable commercial activities and the development of the garden. The reader may find the way the narrative jumps from one subject to another in this chapter confusing. That reflects the way it happened. I have not tried to hide the lack of connection.

This begs the question of how to react to these events. Inevitably, someone of my age is often asked by young people for advice about their careers. It is an impossible question, as usually you know nothing about their talents, interests and background. But I do have an answer, drawn on my experience, that I use as a response: 'Do something that enables you to look forward to Monday morning.' It has been my single good fortune that, with the one exception of the eighteen months spent as an articled clerk at Peat, Marwick, Mitchell & Co. in 1955, every job I have had combined two or more of my three driving interests. The advice seems sensible, even directed at a very different generation than originally conceived.

My childhood was spent within easy reach of the Gower Peninsula in Wales, with its pristine beaches of Langland, Caswell, Three Cliffs, Horton and Rhossili. My grandfather walked me up the Clyne Valley while we watched the elvers battling their way upstream, and I was fascinated by the collection of canaries and British finches in Brynmill Park.

At about the age of eight, I was sent to the junior school of Bromsgrove situated in Llanwrtyd Wells. I hated my time there and ran away with another boy, Kellen Scott, intending to hitchhike the forty-eight miles over the Sugar Loaf mountain to Swansea and home. Unfortunately, the first car that stopped was driven by the headmaster – so I left and was sent to another preparatory school, Broughton Hall in Staffordshire. It was a magnificent black and white Tudor mansion situated in spacious grounds. The birdlife there was plentiful and I organised a club of budding ornithologists, which was called the Tit Club. I have guarded with my life the fact that every member was known by the name of one of the species, for fear that my designation as Great Tit would have provided endless material for merciless parody and ribaldry by political friend, foe and media alike.

The war was our ever-present backdrop. One of the house mistresses had a strong foreign accent – she was French, but the view gained currency that she was a German spy. Every night we would use Morse code to interpret the vocabulary of twits and twoos of the local owl population to produce evidence for our conviction. We meant no harm, but looking back, it was shameful and explicable only in the context of the time.

My hobby expanded significantly when I later became a student at Shrewsbury School. My friend Robert Wild and I spent hours luring unsuspecting blackbirds into traps so that we could put very light, numbered rings on one of their legs on behalf of the Royal Society for the Protection of Birds. I hand reared jackdaws and a magpie, collected from nests as they were about to fledge. My parents were left to look after a cage of forty budgerigars when I went back to school.

My sporting skills left everything to the imagination. As a high jumper, my height of 6ft 2in. gave me something of a head start, but I was nowhere to be seen on the cricket and football playing fields, which are so important in such a school. But the devil makes work for idle hands. I would buy large bottles of multi-flavoured lemonade from the local Post Office, then sell it on at a significant profit to my more strenuous colleagues as they returned from their physical endeavours.

Of course, these examples range from the trivial to the absurd, except that they reveal a lifelong love of the natural world and a restless entrepreneurial energy that was to characterise my adult life. When I left high office in 1997, there was no doubt what I would do. Not all my colleagues have such clarity or opportunity. Many of them made huge sacrifices to pursue a career in public service. Nothing infuriates me more than the slick generalisation that politicians are only in it for what they can get out of it. Margaret Thatcher, John Major, Geoffrey Howe and Douglas Hurd, to name four among many, could have enjoyed far bigger incomes outside politics.

My advice to anyone invited to serve in some prestigious sounding role in a national or international organisation is to read the small print. The chances are that you are being offered a high-sounding position without power, the sole purpose of which is to raise funds. There is nothing wrong with that but don't automatically assume that it is your intellectual ability and experienced decision-making that is being solicited. I was offered the chairmanship of the Royal Academy, which should not be confused with that of the president. What they really wanted was a fundraiser, and that was not for me.

Perhaps more predictable is the suggestion that you might write your autobiography after leaving politics. The money is often good but more important is to remember the thought expressed so clearly by Winston Churchill when he said that he knew what history would say about him because he intended to write it. So, get your side of your story into print because all of us in writing our autobiographies will be presenting our view of events rather than yours. You will not always be pleased when reading your colleagues' account of what 'happened' during events in which you were involved.

• • •

In 2003, I was deeply flattered to receive an invitation from Mary Soames to deliver a tribute to her father Sir Winston Churchill on the fiftieth anniversary of the Cold War summit he held in Bermuda in 1953.

Churchill had persuaded General Dwight D. Eisenhower, the newly elected President of the US, and the Prime Minister of France, Joseph Laniel, to attend a summit meeting in Bermuda, a British colony off the east coast of America. Of course, Churchill and Eisenhower knew each other well – Eisenhower having spent some time in England during the war preparing for the D-Day invasion in 1944, as the Supreme Allied Commander of the whole operation. The main purpose of the meeting was to discuss the desirability and possibility of a four-nation summit meeting to include the Soviet Union. Stalin had just died; little was known in the west about the possible intentions and actions of his successor.

After the Second World War, Berlin, the former capital of Nazi Germany, was divided into four occupation zones by the Allies, with the USSR controlling the east and the US, UK and France controlling the west. The division of Berlin was a key event in the Cold War and the city became a symbol of the division between east and west because it lay deep inside East Germany, which was occupied by the USSR.

A mere five years before the conference in Bermuda, the USSR had tried to regain control of all of Berlin. The right of access to the city by the western powers was by road, rail and air via three clearly defined narrow corridors through or above East Germany. Without warning, the Russians closed off the road and rail access by which most of the supplies to the isolated western part of the city were transported. This was an illegal and bellicose action that was only thwarted by the determination of the Allies, who instigated the Berlin Airlift. For over a year, US and UK forces supplied the western sector of the city by air from West Germany, enabling West

Berlin to survive until the Russians backed down. The world was in a very dangerous state – and there was much to discuss at the summit.

I had first met Mary and her husband, Lord Christopher Soames, when he was our ambassador in Paris and I was Minister for Aerospace and Shipping in 1972. I had been invited to dine with my opposite number in the French government and word must have reached Christopher. Undoubtedly anxious about the risk in allowing this unguarded young minister to be entertained by the French, Christopher scooped up the arrangements so that they were under his control and we were all taken to the theatre to see Marcel Marceau, the famous mime actor. My wife shares my vivid memory of our ambassador being greeted from all sides of the balcony as he waved and bowed to the distinguished French audience as we moved to our seats.

To compose a speech about Churchill confronts one with the most obvious dilemma. It has all been said a thousand times before and by historians with detailed knowledge far in excess of mine. There is a cartoon depicting him relaxing in the south of France with Prime Minister Asquith, in which he is asking whether there is any news from home. The reply makes my point: 'How can there be? You are here.' My friend Julian Critchley once described his early impressions of Churchill, as a newly elected Member of Parliament, in the division lobbies of the House of Commons: 'The usual chatting, animated mass of MPs stood apart to open a way through which the great man might pass. It was like watching history walk past.'

For my generation and many others, that is how we will always see him. I wanted to hear and see him speak in person and travelled to his Woodford constituency to listen to him address the annual general meeting of his local Conservative party in the late 1950s. I stood in Trafalgar Square in January 1965 to watch his cortege pass by. I have visited his grave in St Martin's Church, Bladon, near Woodstock, and his birthplace, Blenheim Palace. I have also delivered the annual speech in his memory at Harrow School, where he had been a pupil.

Churchill's conference in Bermuda perpetuates a memory of an extraordinary man whose life and influence are inseparable from an extraordinary century, a century that saw the zenith of British power and influence and in which he played a legendary role. Churchill had three great political passions: Britain's monarchy and empire, Britain's special relationship with the US and Britain's place in Europe. He brought his powers of oratory to celebrate the fact that such a diverse group of nations, forged in history by the military, economic and diplomatic interests of an island off the west coast of Europe, could see that it was in their own self-interest to remain bound by the bonds of Commonwealth. His famous phrase of 'To jaw-jaw is always better than to war-war' has its relevance in the evolution from empire to Commonwealth.

The bonds of language, law and democratic parliamentary government would be for him a lasting source of pride. He would proclaim that, despite the excesses and mistakes of imperial rule, our creation and leadership of the empire bequeathed a legacy where the balance between good and evil is heavily weighted on the side of virtue. His eyes would fill with tears as he reminded his grandchildren of those who joined so selflessly and sacrificed so much to keep alight one island of hope in mid-twentieth-century Europe. There were so many. Canadians and Rhodesians in the skies over south east England in the Battle of Britain; Australians and New Zealanders in the deserts of North Africa; Indians, Punjabis and

Gurkhas along the Irrawaddy River in Burma and at the frontiers of India itself; and many others.

Would Churchill recognise the US of today? It is no longer the world's only superpower and in many ways it is a very different country to the one he knew. It is so diverse, so interwoven with different interests and alliances. However, it is the fundamentals of politics, the rule of law, the love of freedom, the human rights of citizens and the ability to communicate in a common language that keep our countries so close.

As another Trump presidency raises questions about the cohesion of the US itself, as well as the NATO alliance, Churchill would remember the pressure exerted on President Roosevelt in 1940, which made him promise not to enter the Second World War. It was Hitler's fatal mistake in declaring war on the US that brought them into the war and ensured the ultimate liberation of Europe.

It has been my privilege to know something of Britain's relationship with the US. I was Secretary of State for Defence through the height of the tensions that surrounded the modernisation of NATO's nuclear weapons in the early 1980s. I don't believe any of us realised at the time that what was at stake was not just the right to maintain our deterrent capability but the future of the USSR itself. For seventy years, Pax Americana has served the US well, but it has served the world well too. The US has invariably looked to Britain for support where British interests and experience coincided with its own. Only once has that support been denied, when Harold Wilson rightly refused to send British troops to Vietnam. But, as every true friend would, I think Churchill would today use words of caution about what is perceived to be a recent – and coming – shift in American policy.

Churchill, above all else, was a man convinced by the need for international institutions to guide our international behaviour. A strong believer in the United Nations, as well as the need to draw the nation states of Europe into 'a kind of United States' and the need for the resolution of disputes everywhere by dialogue, he would, I think, have wondered at a range of decisions that seem to be differentiating the US of today not only from the US of yesterday but from much of the rest of the world. Of course, he would have respected the right of a rich, strong nation to pursue its own self-interest. No one understood better than he did the loneliness of great power. But the change over the years in the US's approach to various international accords such as the Paris Agreement, the Law of the Sea Conference, the ABM Treaty, the anti-personnel mines convention and, of course, the issue of Iraq seemed totally at odds with their past policies. The concern over a Trump presidency's approach to global warming is a recent example.

In my tribute to Churchill in 2003, I made clear my support for American policy – first in the joint decision, supported by United Nations resolutions, to eject Saddam Hussein's Iraq regime from Kuwait after his illegal invasion there in 1990 to try and grab Kuwait's oil fields. I also fully backed American policy in Afghanistan after the 9/11 attacks in New York in 2001, an act of shocking terrorism.

On the other hand, the decisions which led to our invasion of Iraq were of a different order. George Bush and Tony Blair, the two heads of government concerned, had, without the public or their governments being aware of it, made a decision that Saddam Hussein must be removed. This was at first a secret deal, which had momentous consequences.

To go to war in order to achieve regime change is not, apparently, against US law. But it is against the laws that cover the actions of

British forces, and Blair's agreement with Bush caused the Labour government to get into the most fearful muddle. The Attorney General had to be persuaded to change his initial advice to the Cabinet that British actions in the circumstances would be illegal; a document was produced, attempting to justify the proposed invasion, which contained matters that were untrue to say the least; and the arguments continue today as to the validity and legality of the actions that the two governments ultimately took.

The crucial question was whether Saddam had, or was attempting to develop, weapons of mass destruction. That he had chemical weapons was beyond doubt; he had used them on the Kurdish population in his own country. It was known that he was preparing to manufacture the materials to make nuclear weapons, but he had concealed whether, or how far, he had succeeded in this quest.

A resolution was passed in the United Nations ordering Saddam Hussein to allow UN inspectors into Iraq, with the freedom to examine all of the industrial facilities concerned with the production of enriched uranium. The weapons inspectors duly entered the country to start work. The US, backed by our government, complained to the UN that the inspectors were being prevented from doing their job by Iraqi intransigence and interference, and they presented a further resolution in the UN authorising the use of force.

This resolution was defeated, and it was then that the US and UK decided to proceed without the backing of a UN resolution. The UN inspectors left, their job incomplete, and the invasion took place. The rest, as they say, is history.

In the aftermath of the war, no weapons of mass destruction were ever found, but the overthrow of Saddam, and the way the consequences of the war were handled, upset the stability of the whole of the Middle East with unpredictable consequences for all.

Nations must be free to exercise their sovereign rights, but we must also ask the question: what is sovereignty in today's shrunken world?

We all know what it used to mean. It meant sending armies across frontiers or navies across oceans into conflicts with real or imaginary enemies. But nuclear deterrence, often aptly described as 'mutually assured destruction', has eliminated the concept of victory for anyone without unacceptable consequences.

In tomorrow's world, the greatest threats will not be those which need to be overcome by military might. Global warming, illegal production and distribution of drugs and the organised crime which controls that evil trade, international terrorism, tax evasion, cyber warfare; the regulation of global capitalism, the exhaustion of natural resources, population explosion, people trafficking and protectionism. All these problems can threaten every one of us, but they are also beyond the power of any one nation state to solve alone.

True sovereignty – the sovereignty that enhances security and power – will increasingly be a sovereignty that nations voluntarily share and enjoy collectively. Britain faces these issues most acutely in our relationship with our European neighbours. Churchill is often portrayed as a loner – his phrase 'Very well then, alone' created the famously defiant image of Britain in 1940 – but that was not an isolation of his choosing. No man was more proud of his country, its history, and the institutions and the relationships that bind us together. He was one of the first to advocate what he called 'a kind of United States of Europe'. Some seventy years later, the question remains as to what that means.

• • •

As I said earlier in this chapter, the reader will notice the seemingly random reminiscences which follow about my love of the countryside and country sports. I shot and fished for many years. I never actually hunted but fully supported those who did. The controversies that surround the issue of field sports continue to increase and I want to point out not just the influence that the countryside and its flora and fauna have had on me but how important it is that the balance between man and the environment in which we exist needs constant nurturing if both are to prosper.

After the Second World War, my father's return to civilian life in 1945 opened a quite different opportunity. His uncle Sam Stride, a prominent Swansea jeweller, and his father owned rights together over a stretch of the River Towy, where my father would take me to learn to fish. The thrill of choosing the appropriate fly, learning to cast or the jerk of a bite in a real river was of a different order of excitement from any that I had experienced during the war. I loved sitting on a stool alongside a pond, fixing maggots to a hook at a fishing competition in Brynmill Park. I won that early fishing competition but not due entirely to my skills with the rod and line. I had used up about half the time available with nothing yet in the net. There were plenty of bites, but cunning fish managed to devour the bread paste from my hook without being in danger of capture.

'Try one of these,' said a voice, as Mr Kiley, who worked for my grandfather, handed me a tin of wriggling maggots. When the whistle finally went, I had caught thirty-nine fish, a total of 11.75 ounces – enough to earn me a silver cup and seven shillings and sixpence, having outperformed the next competitor. I had hoped that after my father's death in 1957, this fishing beat would still be available to me and was deeply disappointed when Stride rejected my request.

My lifelong love of fishing has continued ever since. Over the years,

I have collected many unforgettable memories – including frequent visits to the River Tweed with Lord Ridley, nephew of my colleague Nicholas, and Sir Simon Day, a distinguished West Country politician, to the Rivers Naver and Helmsdale with Sir Max Hastings, a newspaper editor and historian, and as a guest on the River Test and the River Kennet.

In a class of its own must be the week I spent fishing one of Russia's great salmon rivers. In 2005, Sir Christopher Bland, chairman of the BBC, and Max Hastings took me to western Russia to two of the great salmon rivers, where a very comfortable but basic set of wooden huts provided the accommodation. It was a particular pleasure for me that they invited my son, Rupert, to join the party. The trip was organised by Roxtons and we were under the leadership of Charlie Wright. All seemed to be progressing smoothly until we approached Murmansk, our destination but also a centre of Russian nuclear activity.

The first intimation that something was wrong was the slowing and circling of our aircraft. Charlie came on the intercom to explain that there was a mistake in our flight particulars and that we did not have permission to land. We were escorted out of Russian airspace by two MiG fighters to an obscure provincial airport in Finland, where we landed amid some unfavourable local flooding. Charlie needed to get us back to Murmansk, which meant enduring one of the most uncomfortable journeys of my life in a tiny bus until 4 a.m.

Actually getting into Russia another way required some skill in itself as the frontier guards were quite unprepared for a party like ours. However, offerings of meat, drink and confectionery had an eloquent persuasiveness. We made it in time for our helicopter trip at the final stage of the journey, which took place in an ex-military aircraft that did not seem to be compatible with the threat about which I had been briefed all those years ago.

The Rivers Lower Varzuga and Kitza are huge and teeming with fish. In total, we caught 137 on the former and eighty-seven on the latter. I came bottom of the class with sixteen. They all had to be put back, as we were not allowed to keep what we caught. The competition was won by Major General Nick Ansell, who had figured out that the fish would seek the relatively less powerful flow close to the bank. He caught forty-four.

Naturally, I was interested to explore the views of my Russian ghillie. 'You must find your new freedoms more attractive?' I suggested. 'Communism was better,' came the reply from someone exposed for the first time to the workings and uncertainties of the market and unenchanted by the glasnost and perestroika that had brought it about.

If there was plenty to occupy my time, there was also the chance for holidays. One of the privileges that flowed from ministerial office, and indeed from executive responsibility for Haymarket, was the ability to combine political or business visits with the chance to explore the countries to which my career took me.

Visits to the Falkland Islands resulted in spectacular sights of the massive penguin colonies there. Selling tornado aircraft to Saudi Arabia took me deep into the deserts in search of birds of prey. Anne and I combined official trips with holidays in Barbados and Australia where we learned to scuba dive, first in Barbados, then off the Great Barrier Reef and then in the Red Sea, where the coral reefs were at their best and before the consequences of global warming caused the El Niño phenomenon to bleach them white. We also enjoyed a trip, again organised by Max Hastings, in a chartered yacht to the Galapagos Islands. Among the most famous birds to be seen there is the blue-footed booby. The name was immediately adopted for our party, which included Ken and Gillian Clarke, Douglas and

Judy Hurd, Anne and me, Jeremy and Gillian Isaacs and Caroline Waldegrave. Listening to Gillian Clarke singing music hall ditties or being instructed in the finer arts of bridge by Caroline are treasured memories.

We were not an undistinguished or irresponsible group, but we had a young German guide in her early twenties who insisted every morning that 'Ve vill haf ze briefing'. After two or three days of this, during which we were lined up like children at school, Ken Clarke was deputed to try to explain to her the depth of experience of her audience. The next morning, we waited with expectation. Nothing changed. 'Ve *vill* haf ze briefing,' she insisted.

Quite rightly, the conditions for such visits are tightly controlled and paths clearly marked because of the rare and fragile ecosystem there, but the experience of mixing with birds and seals who have no fear of humans is unforgettable. On one occasion, I was photographing the finches which Charles Darwin had made famous, but not to be outdone, one of them perched on my lens, thus posing the question as to who was watching whom.

• • •

My first shooting experience was with my father in 1943, when he was commanding a battalion of Royal Engineers based at Shotover House near Oxford. He had set himself the impossible task of firing a .22 rifle at the tiny wriggling heads of grass snakes in the lake.

Moving on from that childhood experience, I never had a lesson with a shotgun, but I started using them with my friend Simon Day in the mid-1960s and other invitations followed. I found it hard to understand that the essence of the sport is to swing the gun through the target before you fire and thus have a chance of hitting it. I was shooting at the bird and, of course, by the time I pulled the trigger the bird was no longer there. My colleagues, after each drive, would busy themselves collecting what they had shot. I was not one for hanging hopelessly around, so I devoted myself to collecting my spent cartridges. How it happened I will never know, but I did eventually hit a pheasant and proudly, at least to myself, I was able to record one bird for twenty-nine shots. Thus began a practice that remained with me to the end of my shooting career. While others would talk in general terms about the quality of each drive, I knew precisely my score. I was satisfied to maintain a record one bird for four shots in my last drive ever.

I was very fortunate to shoot with good friends at some of the best shoots in the country, over forty years or more – but you know when it is time to quit. That first stumble as you fire, or the cold of January, together with a growing sense of sympathy for the pheasant, increases the frequency with which you ask yourself, 'Why am I doing this?' So, I gave up in 2023 and have only one regret: Fred, our labrador, cannot understand why he is a gun dog no more.

I have from my earliest teenage days viewed horses with some suspicion. They are a long way from the ground, and while I respect – indeed, admire – people's ability to control these magnificent animals for their social and physical pleasure, I have long believed that God gave me feet to keep me firmly on the ground. Nevertheless, that in no way blinds me to the contribution of the hunting fraternity to the countryside and its people. The countryside is not a Walt Disney world. Foxes are vicious and cunning predators. They hunt not only to survive (farmyard chickens, ducks and newborn lambs are attractive items on their menu) but, unlike most other predators, they kill for pleasure, not just enough to feed their families.

The problem is that foxes have no natural predator and the issue, therefore, is how to control their numbers. There is no humane, gentle way to achieve that. Snares, poison and shooting can all inflict cruelty and pain. I spoke from the opposition benches in the House of Commons when we debated the Wild Mammals (Hunting with Dogs) Bill in November 1997 and again in 2000, where I made the case that the hunting ban was not about animals:

> The fact is that there are deep class resentments in the anti-hunting lobby. Let me make a simple point. Those who will suffer from the ban that the Labour Party wish to impose are not the rich, not the toffs. Those people's horses will go to Ireland or to France. There will be chartered aeroplanes to take them wherever the sport can be found, and given the growing affluence of which the Labour Party is so proud to speak, they will find ways of continuing. Those who will really suffer are ordinary people in rural communities – the people who stand and watch, and whose social life revolves around the hunt. It is they who will find that a great part of their lives has been removed from under them.

• • •

Let me now return for a moment to some special memories from my Oxford days – in particular, those of one of my oldest friends.

My friendship with Anthony Howard began when we both held office at the Oxford Union. Tony and I remained at opposite poles of the political spectrum, but I always admired the journey his career had taken him on. He started in journalism on the old *Reynold's News* before moving to *The Guardian*, the *Sunday Times* and then *The Observer*, where he served as Washington correspondent during the turbulent years of Lyndon Johnson's presidency. He then returned to London and moved to the *New Statesman*, which he edited for six years from 1972. A spell editing *The Listener* was followed by a return to *The Observer* as deputy editor. He moved to *The Times* in 1993 as obituaries editor. I shared his disappointment that he narrowly failed to edit *The Observer*, a post for which he was admirably suited.

When Tony died – far too early – at the age of seventy-six in 2010, I was anxious to provide a fitting tribute to his memory. Sir Jeremy Isaacs, another friend, contemporary and office holder in the Oxford Union, was an extremely successful television producer and executive at ITV, with credits including *The World at War*, before becoming the founding chief executive of Channel 4. During our Oxford days, both he and Tony Howard played a major part in helping to get me elected president of the union. These were friendships that transcended party politics; at the time Isaacs and Howard were chairman and chairman-elect of the Oxford University Labour Club respectively. Isaacs came up with the idea that Haymarket should create a unique award: an annual bursary of £25,000 for an aspiring journalist under the age of twenty-five, who wanted to write about politics and government. We hoped this would pay homage to Tony's innate ability to spot talent. In his time at the *New Statesman*, he recruited a dazzling roster of writers, including Martin Amis, Christopher Hitchens, Julian Barnes, James Fenton and Patrick Wintour.

I approached the editors of the three publications with which Tony was most closely associated – *The Times*, *The Observer* and the *New Statesman* – and they readily agreed to host the successful candidate in successive fourteen-week fellowships, working alongside their political staff in the Westminster lobby, where they would gain rare insight into Westminster, Whitehall and the workings of government. Applicants would be required to propose a political subject for in-depth enquiry and detail how they would go about their investigations. And remembering that Tony always valued sharp, lively copy ('Do me a flashy piece,' he would say to contributors), they would also need to provide a good example of their writing.

The award, which would run for five years, would be judged by a committee under Jeremy's chairmanship, consisting of the author and former political editor Robert Harris, the constitutional expert Peter Hennessy, the TV presenter Jeremy Paxman and the biographer Claire Tomalin. We were particularly fortunate to secure the services of *The Observer*'s Stephen Pritchard, who masterminded the process throughout, working his way through the numerous applications (averaging about 100 a year) to present the judges with a shortlist from which to choose candidates for interview.

One day it will be possible to chart the complete career journey of each winner, but already it is evident that the judges chose some notable young talent, all of whom are stars in British political journalism. Lucy Fisher, the first winner in 2013, set the bar high for later applicants. She went on to work as a political and defence correspondent at *The Times* and the *Daily Telegraph* and is now Whitehall editor at the *Financial Times*. Ashley Cowburn, our second winner, became a political correspondent at *The Mirror*. Henry Zeffman, who won in 2015, became the BBC's chief political correspondent after a lengthy spell at *The Times*. Patrick Maguire, the 2016 winner, returned to *The Times* after working as a political correspondent at the *New Statesman*, where he is now one of their star political columnists. Dulcie Lee, who won in 2017, is a senior journalist at the BBC. And in 2018, the final year of the award, Eleni Courea won and joined *The Guardian* as a political correspondent after working for *The Times* and Politico. Anthony would have been proud of all their work, continuing in his fine tradition of sparkling, enlightening political journalism.

Writing of Tony reminds me of the debt that I owe to Oxford University. I arrived as a typical product of the school system, middle class with a provincial background and a record of achievement that was best left undiscussed. I must have conveyed a certain confidence, nevertheless, as I was offered a place in Pembroke College, Oxford, and St John's College, Cambridge, on the basis of my school certificate results and an interview. I chose Oxford as I could take up their offer immediately, whereas Cambridge insisted that I should complete National Service first.

It was a new world for me, free of the regimentation of boarding school and made up of people from diverse backgrounds and with every shade of political opinion. It was up to you to pursue whatever opportunity appealed to you.

I spent most of my time in the Oxford Union. I once heard that George IV said of the Head Boy at Eton that you are greater now than ever I could make you. I quoted this remark in my last term as president of the Oxford Union during my retirement speech to explain how privileged I felt to have that position bestowed on me so young. I ultimately obtained a second in Politics, Philosophy and Economics at Oxford, described by my tutor as a great, but undeserved, triumph.

The renowned athlete Roger Bannister, the first person in the world to run a mile in under four minutes, later became master of Pembroke and conferred on me an honorary fellowship. A subsequent master, Giles Henderson, undertook a very large development of the college facilities, and I was particularly pleased to be able to endow two student bed-sitting rooms in memory of my parents.

In 2024, my wife and I joined the former Appeal Court judge Sir Ernest Ryder, who is now the master, to celebrate the 400th anniversary of the foundation of the college. Over the years, I have frequently returned to participate in debates in the Oxford Union, which are conducted very much to the pattern I remember. In November 2024, I was invited to propose the motion 'This house would rejoin the European Union'. Unfortunately, before the debate could begin, a point of order was raised under an arcane rule, which led to an interminable debate about union rules. After more than an hour of this, and with no prospect in sight of an early return to the main business of the day, I left. Behaviour of this sort, if repeated, will deter visiting speakers and a generation of undergraduates will lose the opportunity to listen to men and women who have served at the forefront of their profession.

In 1999, the House of Commons art fund commissioned a bronze bust of me for their collection. It was sculpted by Anne Curry, wife of David, a friend and colleague in the House. The Oxford Union now has one of the six copies which were cast, and we have another.

The Oxford Union celebrated its 200th anniversary in 2023. I was invited to speak at the dinner. Among the guests were many ex-presidents, including Theresa May and Jacob Rees-Mogg. It was with no small pleasure that I concluded my speech by saying that I hoped that this great centre of learning would be a leader in the fight to restore the country back to the heart of Europe, which was greeted with thunderous applause.

• • •

When I was first elected in Tavistock in 1966, we were aware that the constituency was likely to disappear in the forthcoming boundary changes. Sir Peter Mills was the incumbent in the neighbouring seat and was likely to want to contest the new, enlarged constituency. So I was aware that if I wanted a lengthy career in politics I should have to look elsewhere. I was selected for the Henley constituency in 1972, elected there in 1974, and Peter duly became the member for West Devon, which included much of my former seat. So that now identified broadly the area within which my wife and our family could settle. I was travelling by plane to Edinburgh when someone quite unknown to me, David Fleming, approached me to ask if I would like to buy his house, which he described as the ugliest house in England. We bought Soundess House in Nettlebed, Oxfordshire in 1972. It was wonderfully situated in the heart of the Chilterns and our purchase also offered the opportunity for my mother to move closer to her family. She sold her home in Swansea and moved to the Fairmile, just outside Henley.

From that time, my visits to Swansea became rare and always for some specific purpose. It was therefore with particular pleasure that in 2001, I received a letter from Robin Williams, vice-chancellor of the University of Wales, Swansea, inviting me to accept an honorary fellowship. It was a night of memories for me as I was able to invite my cousins, Gillian and Jimmy Pridmore. Robert Hastie, one of my oldest friends, attended the event in his capacity as Lord Lieutenant. I was equally pleased to be invited, in 2004, by the same university to give the annual lecture that had been established to honour Jim Callaghan, the former Labour Prime Minister.

I served in the Commons at the same time as Jim, but we were on opposite sides and he was of an older generation, which would normally have made for a somewhat distant and formal relationship. However, in this case, one event changed all that, as I was able to recount in my lecture. My daughter Alexandra, then aged eleven, had made an aggressive intervention in my political career. She had been so incensed by some comment she had read, which had been attributed to Jim, that without saying anything to her parents, she wrote a blistering letter to the Prime Minister. 'That Callaghan' had become a mortal foe as a consequence of what she thought was his totally unwarranted attack on her father. The response from No. 10 was immediate and electric: a letter of charm and courtesy that was followed some years later by an invitation to lunch in the House of Lords. Jim had won a lifetime admirer.

I also referred in the speech to one of Jim's less fortunate experiences. As Home Secretary, he was bound to put the findings of the Parliamentary Boundary Commission to Parliament. Its recommendations were unfavourable to the Labour Party and he was responsible for whipping his party into the lobby to vote down his own proposals. His letter to me following my lecture included an interesting comment about the event:

> You are kind in your comments about the 'political curiosity' of a Home Secretary voting down his own proposals. That was not the proudest moment in my political life. It arose from what happened in the 1945 Parliament, when Chuter Ede, with some gusto, set about redrawing the parliamentary constituencies. The redistribution was so sweeping that only eighty seats were left untouched and, on the Labour side, we thought we had been badly treated. The reverberations continued for many years and were at the root of what I did when I was Home Secretary and was determined not to repeat Chuter Ede's experience. That is an explanation not an excuse.

I was glad he was able to write about my lecture and say that he agreed with my analysis of the global situation. He was a good man who has a special place in our family.

• • •

These seemingly unconnected recollections have a habit of returning periodically to my connections with Wales, which go back right to the early days of my life. Fate has intervened on a number of occasions to take me back there – for very different reasons.

It is one of my few regrets that I was born with no musical talents at all – and that is an understatement. It was not for the want of trying. I attempted to learn the cornet and later the piano. I was the only boy ejected from a choir of the whole house of forty boys following a detailed audition by the music master. It was thus a special pleasure to be invited to become a patron of the Morriston Orpheus Choir. This honour has brought with it many happy memories, including their presence at Alexandra's wedding, the nostalgic evening in 2016 when we remembered one of the worst bombing attacks on Swansea seventy-five years earlier, and their singing at my ninetieth birthday party.

• • •

My ministerial career did not cover the devolved Welsh Principality, although I was delighted when my colleague Nicholas Edwards made good use of my ideas by establishing the Development Corporation in Cardiff's Tiger Bay and a garden festival in Ebbw Vale.

With the return of the Conservatives to government, leading the coalition from 2010, I gradually became more involved in the regeneration of rundown areas and the consequences of industrial decline. It was a particular pleasure to me, therefore, to receive an invitation from Alun Cairns, Secretary of State for Wales, in March 2017 to become involved in the project to redevelop Swansea Bay. I was fully briefed and presented with the detailed plans. A meeting was arranged for 8 March, where I was to accompany the ministerial team in holding extensive local consultation and explore the site. An agreement was reached about the role I was to play. But in the House of Lords the night before, I voted to give Parliament the final say on any Brexit deal. I was duly sacked and so ended my opportunity to play a meaningful role in Welsh affairs – or so I thought.

In 2019, the First Minister of Wales invited me to chair the external advisory group for a new National Forest for Wales, but with the looming Brexit chaos and the prospect of reaching the age of ninety, I had to acknowledge that I did not have the energy or the time for the task, so I reluctantly declined the offer.

In the spring of 2024, the troubles with steel production at Port Talbot made daily headlines. I was invited to see David T. C. Davies, then the Tory Secretary of State for Wales, for a discussion. I thought it wise to suggest they first clear the invitation with No. 10 in case there was any hangover from the past. All was well. Presumably my earlier regeneration experiences, particularly with the SSI steelworks in Teesside, influenced the invitation. The date and details were all in place when Rishi Sunak called the election. I was very sad not to be able to play what could have been one last useful and important role in the place of my birth.

However, now fate has once again intervened. I have been asked by Jonathan Reynolds, Secretary of State for Business and Trade in Keir Starmer's new government, to join him on a visit to the site. No date has yet been arranged, but I am thrilled at the prospect and it will resurrect memories of my visit there with my father in the 1950s.

CHAPTER 2

BACK TO HAYMARKET

Starting and developing a business from scratch is at the heart of the political philosophy of wealth creation for any Conservative. Of course, there is a natural attraction towards the benefits that success can bring, and certainly the sense of security and independence encouraged me as I contemplated the unpredictability of a political career.

There is, however, much more to it than that. The existence of a wide spread of independent wealth is an important counter to the extremes of state-based societies. Family-owned companies start and largely remain close to their local communities. Paternalism is out of fashion, but I think its critics lose sight of important relationships. Certainly, the closeness of the great landlords to their estates in this country saved us from the horrors of the guillotine spreading from revolutionary France over 200 years ago, but it did much more than that. Proximity encourages awareness – a sense of community, obligation and responsibility.

At their extreme, the family businesses of today – Sainsbury's, Morrisons and John Lewis – echo the great Quaker businesses (the Rowntrees and Cadburys) of Victorian England, but there are countless examples of many smaller companies providing outreach activities into their local communities. There is a stark contrast with the remoteness of the quoted company, often with their overseas management structures and shareholders. Investment companies often remunerate their managers with profit-related bonuses calculated on a quarterly basis. To them, the takeover is the ultimate prize.

I recognise the valuable role of these large, publicly quoted companies and the scale of community involvement in which many participate, but I remain firmly of the view that a large middle range of small and medium companies with their roots deep in the community is socially and politically important for a stable democratic society.

There is a strong entrepreneurial background to my family. In Victorian England, my father's grandfather was a partner in a well-known grocer, Heseltine, Kearley & Tonge, while my mother's father, James Pridmore, started his own business repairing machinery in the coal and oil industries. There were early indications that I inherited my instincts from them.

As a part of my drive to restore the finances of the Oxford Union, I had sublet a shed in the grounds to a fellow undergraduate, Clive Labovitch, who needed a place from where he could manage *Cherwell*, the university newspaper he had recently acquired. He invited me to become a director of the company and our friendship grew over long discussions in the president's office about our future lives. One evening in 1957, when I was standing by the switchboard of the New Court Hotel in Inverness Terrace, which another Oxford friend, Ian Josephs, and I had recently acquired, I received a call. It was no surprise to hear the news that Clive had bought a business and would welcome my advice. I caught a cab and listened as he described to me what he had bought.

Simply, it was a guide, on sale for two shillings and sixpence, for undergraduates newly arrived at Oxford, listing a range of valuable information such as hotels, restaurants, clubs and so on. Tucked into this was a forty-page booklet called the Directory of Opportunities for Graduates. Each page carried an advertisement from one of Britain's most distinguished companies, outlining the career opportunities they offered. The revenue arising from the forty adverts they had sold at £40 per page amounted to £1,600. I pointed out that it would be more relevant to undergraduates in their last year, not just at Oxford but at every other one of the country's universities.

Clive invited me to join him and that is where I began in publishing. Our next edition grossed £64,000 – £1.3 million in today's money. We expanded the series by adding two more editions: one for professionally qualified people and the other for school leavers. It became the golden egg of our goose within our various commercial projects – one of which, the sale of a long lease of a site on Mackennal Street in Regent's Park, provided the £10,000 we needed to buy a consumer magazine, *Man About Town*, that had been launched by the publishers of the trade magazine *Tailor and Cutter* to attract a new generation of customers to their Savile Row clientele. UK trade magazines at that time were of the lowest quality, but Clive masterminded the conversion of *Man About Town* into *Town* magazine, with Fleet Street editorial standards and world-class photography and layout. Tom Wolsey, the first art director, David Hughes, Nicholas Tomalin and Michael Parkinson, successive editors, and photographers David Bailey, Terence Donovan and Don McCullin all contributed to its world-class standards.

Town magazine, alongside Jocelyn Stevens's *Queen* magazine, completely transformed the glossy world of consumer publishing in the 1960s. We had lifted the downbeat drabness of post-war magazine publishing up to international standards.

Our *Town* magazine had, by then, penetrated deeply into the advertising market but was never to reach the circulation levels of *Playboy* and *Penthouse*. They offered centrefolds of full-frontal nudity as a basic ingredient of their editorial mix. I was quite clear that my political ambitions were not compatible with our attempting to compete with them, and in the end, the advertising followed the circulation and we gave up in 1968.

Shortly after the launch of *Town*, our printers, Keliher, Hudson & Kearns, offered to provide us with the cash to grow the business and thus feed their printing presses. A partnership was agreed in which we retained 60 per cent of the equity. Before the ink on the contracts was dry, Keliher had been acquired by Hazell, Watson & Viney, whose chairman Sir Geoffrey Crowther proposed a combination of Cornmarket Press, Clive's original company, and Hazell, Watson & Viney into today's Haymarket.

On the assumption that the cash would be available, I set about finding a use for it. My technique was not rocket science. There was a publication called *British Rate and Data*, which, among other things, listed the names of the chief executives of all the magazines published in the UK. I wrote to them all with a letter that was courteous to the extreme, expressing admiration for their product and setting out my view that we could cooperate and work together. I repeated this for the next few years and the upshot was that, as a result of my circular, we always bought a magazine.

The first round produced a response from A. E. Morgan, who explained that he had a medical publishing business, making a profit of £50,000 a year, that he was about to sell to the giant Thomsons for £250,000. He said he would much prefer the idea of selling to a small private company and that the deal was ours if we matched Roy Thomson's offer.

Haymarket's medical division is now the basis of our medical publishing business, which employs 350 people across the world and has a turnover of £70 million.

A subsequent mailing in 1965 enabled us to purchase *Amateur Tape Recorder* magazine. Simon Tindall, who was in charge of our consumer magazines, had its advertisers analysed, which revealed that a high proportion of them were offering hi-fi equipment. So we converted *Amateur Tape Recorder* into *WhatHi-Fi?*, a brand Simon Taylor, who went on to run the automotive section of Haymarket, had first created in 1973. We also launched *What Camera?*, although it was less successful.

At about this time, Clive Labovitch decided that the direction of travel of the company was not for him. I think he had been persuaded by his wife that he would be happier in the more rarefied world of book and literary publishing. We broke up the partnership without a cross word, a conclusion confirmed by Clive's loyalty to me over the years since that day, when the media tried many times without success to get him to comment adversely on events in my career. Clive and I split the partnership at the end of 1965. Our solicitor, Charles Corman, and our accountant, Jimmy Remnant, arbitrated a very amicable division of our activities. Our senior staff were given twenty-four hours to decide with which of us they wished to go. I was very fortunate that Lindsay Masters and Simon Tindall opted for me and were to become the colleagues who developed and grew the business while I was absent, making my way up the greasy pole which is politics.

Yet another recipient of my circular letter was the managing director of a weekly magazine, *The Accountant*, who invited me to his office I suspect more out of curiosity than serious thought of any relationship. He kept me waiting for about a quarter of an hour, during which time I flicked through a recent copy. I found myself counting the number of pages of recruitment advertising. The meeting began and I congratulated him on the excellence of his sales team's results. 'We don't sell the advertising,' he replied. 'It just comes through the post.'

I cut the meeting short as soon as politeness allowed and rushed back to tell Lindsay Masters that I had found a gold mine. *The Accountant* was selling some 15,000 subscriptions. We launched *Accountancy Age* weeks later and distributed it free of charge to a list helpfully provided by the Institute of Chartered Accountants of every one of their 60,000 members. It made a profit from its first issue and, together with a similar publication for computer staff, Lindsay and Simon sold it to VNU for £17 million in 1981.

By that time, I was a member of the government, so I thought I had better tell Margaret Thatcher before the news appeared in the press. I had the feeling that while a passionate advocate of the capitalist system, she might have had some anxieties when one of her colleagues became so conspicuous a beneficiary. Its runaway success was only eclipsed years later by the transfer of recruitment advertising online.

Hazell, Watson & Viney was acquired by the British Printing Corporation, which itself had six small publishing companies that, in aggregate, were about the size of Haymarket. In 1968, I negotiated a deal with John Pollock, one of their directors, to merge all of them into one company, thus doubling the size of Haymarket, in which we retained 40 per cent of the equity. This deal added two more brands to our portfolio that were to have profound, unexpected and exciting consequences – *Gardeners' Chronicle* and *World Press News*. *Gardeners' Chronicle* was the trade magazine of the Victorian garden. Its editorial was of high quality and its pages included a remarkable series of coloured prints. The illustrated advertisements would today give us a memorable reminder of the equipment of yesterday. By the time of our acquisition, the market had moved on and it had failed to keep up with the huge growth of local authority horticulture.

World Press News was the other relic. A public relations weekly, it was, in practice, little more than a bound copy of press releases covering the communications industry. Lindsay and I went to inspect our new acquisition in their offices near the Old Bailey. I have never conveyed so big an idea so briefly. I picked up a copy and handed it to Lindsay with the words 'Ad Age', a reference to the outstanding American magazine of that name. A couple of months later, after we had recruited an outstanding editor, Michael Jackson, and art director, Roland Schenk, to work under Lindsay's direction, *Campaign* was born and has remained central to our company ever since. Years later, I received an enquiry from Keith Crain, one of the owners of Ad Age, asking if he could buy *Campaign*, which presented me with one of the easier decisions of my commercial career. I said, 'No.'

This legacy continues to the present day, with our expanding global growth. An ambitious new strategy will see us further extending our footprint across the world through launches, acquisitions and partnerships. With the expansion of our brand into Canada, Germany and Indonesia this year, the *Campaign* portfolio now has eleven international editions, including the US, the Middle East, Asia and India. The overarching strategy of maintaining global content protects the integrity of the brand, meaning wherever people encounter *Campaign*, they can rely on getting the same experience, making the brand more relevant today than it ever was.

In the early 1960s, the opportunity arose to bid for the chance to produce *The Manager*, the magazine distributed to members of the British Institute of Managers. If there was a team that could win any bid, it was the one producing *Town* magazine. In the real world, however, I feared that the top brass of the institute would opt for a more establishment publisher. My solution was to ask Geoffrey Crowther, the former editor of *The Economist*, to join the bid. He agreed on the condition that we invited the *FT*. Their joint agreement gave us serious firepower.

I remembered an account by Donald Stokes, head of British Leyland, of a bid to supply buses to a Scandinavian transport company. He asked if, on the day that the competitors were to submit their bids, he could go last. The usual speeches, blueprints, technical data and illustrations occupied the time until it was his turn. 'Ladies and gentlemen,' he said, 'I would be grateful if you would follow me.' He led the committee outside, pointed to a sparkling new bus and explained that he thought that would meet their requirements. It was a killer punch and secured him the contract.

We copied his idea, and within a weekend we wrote, compiled, designed and printed a full magazine, the quality of *Town* magazine, called *Management Today*. We included a suitable profile of the institute's director as a frontispiece. The contract was ours, but it was dependent on free distribution to the institute's members. Years later, they decided that such a cost could not be borne by their subscription rates but agreed that we were free to publish on a standalone commercial basis. It remains a prestigious and influential brand, if nowhere near as profitable as it once was.

In the late 1960s, British Printing ran out of money and could no longer carry out their obligation to finance our expansion. They agreed to sell us their shares. We turned to David Shalit of the bank Charterhouse Japhet, who brought in Dick Strong from the development part of the bank. He devised a part equity, part loan stock arrangement, within which I retained 60 per cent of the equity with the rest divided between County Bank, Charterhouse Japhet and others.

We prepared the company for flotation in order to pay off the debts. At about this time, we encountered serious cash flow problems. We had far from effective control of our accounts department. British Printing shared my concern and their finance director, Chris Honeywell, recommended David Fraser as our new finance director, having known him when they worked together for Associated Iliffe Press. It proved a transformational appointment, although it was some years later before I learned that he was also my second cousin. He must have wondered about the wisdom of his decision when, within days of his arrival, bailiffs came to take away his desk as we were five months late paying our outstanding PAYE bills. The 1973 oil crisis rendered flotation unrealistic, which enabled us to persuade our City partners to abandon the idea. They lent us the money to buy them out, leaving the company with heavy debts. As a part of the negotiations, I arranged equity participation for the senior managers and set the terms on which I would eventually buy them out. The journey to a wholly owned private family business was in place.

It is now some sixty-seven years since Clive Labovitch, our secretary Thelma van Til and I sat in a top-floor office in Clive's family business in Lower James Street. We had not the first idea what the future held for us. That is the first lesson; you simply don't know how things will unfold. The second is understanding that some things just come down to luck (everyone hopes to get their share) and the third is to know which choice to grab (not everyone does). I had worked in a large firm as an articled clerk for eighteen months and then in a much smaller one. Instinctively, I knew it was not for me. I sought the financial independence that the creation of a successful business ensures. Those who have pioneered this journey know that there are very few straight lines. There are exhilarating summits, jagged peaks and the despair of the abyss. The trick is to come out on the right side. The final, and perhaps most important lesson, is finding the right people. Show me success and I will show you the person at the top – the leader. That philosophy has stood me in good stead.

I cannot fully express my gratitude for the ability and skill with which Lindsay, Simon and David managed the company over the years while I pursued a political career. I was elected to the House of Commons in 1966, gave up the role of chief executive in late 1969 and became a junior minister after the 1970 election. In 1970, Haymarket had an annual turnover approaching £4 million; by the time I returned in 1997, nearly thirty years later, the turnover had grown to over £100 million.

I had held some of the most senior ministerial portfolios that interfaced with the commercial world. I had operated internationally, negotiating with major companies and governments. I had a very different view of the world and the way that governments and the private sector interact. My colleagues had had some experience in overseas markets, particularly in France, Italy and Spain, but all that remained of our overseas business by 1997 was an American subsidiary based on our Monthly Index of Medical Specialties (MIMS) brand. My ministerial experience stimulated an interest in developing outside the UK. Looking back some twenty-seven years later, I can see the quixotic nature of that journey to a position where half of Haymarket is now based overseas. We grasped opportunities to replicate our activities either by acquisition, partnership or launch and, for the most part, we continued to run the acquisitions in the format that we acquired. There was often a tension between the UK team and managers thousands of miles away with their own priorities. Today we manage our brands and business more cohesively, albeit in a federated model. Gone is the turf and territory mentality, which has been replaced with collaboration. In short, we act globally but think locally.

During the 1980s, Haymarket had begun to try to replicate the success of our medical business in the UK in an American subsidiary. The healthcare provisions in the two markets were very different, but we thought we had found a formula. On my return, the US was the only overseas market in which we had a presence and it was struggling. Lindsay and Simon were fed up with its failure, and Lindsay had sent me a note shortly before I returned, outlining his fears that increasing government pressure on the pricing of drugs and pharmaceutical company profits would undermine the viability of our business model. They had put the American business up for sale and found a buyer. When I returned, I was in time to visit the US, meet the potential purchaser and knew at once what was wrong. He was a consummate salesman. I wanted to have another attempt and we sent William Pecover, one of our senior managers, to take over. Over the next two to three years, our footprint was more firmly established by the acquisition and launch of a number of specialist publications.

In 1998, I received a visit from Richard Edelman, a leading figure in the PR industry, who urged me to launch *PR Week* in America. Of particular help was Lord Chadlington, brother of my friend and colleague John Gummer (now Lord Deben), who had made a great success of his PR business, Shandwick. With introductions from him, I sought appointments with the CEOs of the largest PR companies in the US. I offered to launch *PR Week* in America at a cost of £1 million of our money if each of them would agree to take copies and advertise their job vacancies in the publication. It is perhaps characteristic of the American entrepreneurial ethic that, in a brief few days, I secured sufficient support to justify the launch. The venture established that I had not lost all the drive and enterprise that had helped start the company in the first place. My son Rupert had joined the company in 1994 and was then leading the UK sales team on *PR Week*. It made sense to send him to join the US team for the launch there.

Our business in America is now predominantly healthcare focused, with over 80 per cent of turnover coming from the sector. In 2001, we acquired medical publications from CPS Communications and the Cortland Group, which included publications such as *The Medical Pharmaceutical Marketers Directory*, *Clinical Advisor* and a special projects business that we later rebranded *PRI Healthcare* and *Long Term Care News*. We then added *Renal & Urology News* in 2002 and Haymarket Medical Education and *My CME* in 2008.

However, it would be a mistake to see the growth of the company happening as a result of acquisitions. Of course, this played a part in that it opened doors, but the real secret of the company's success was the development by the highly qualified and talented expert team of in-house employees. In recent years, organic development has been at the heart of our strategy with over 40 per cent of our turnover coming from brands we launched in the last five years.

I have bored my colleagues for years by repeating that a pill is a pill everywhere in the world. The argument runs that if you can serve two of the world's most advanced medical markets, there must be a hunger for our products much more widely. But my saying misrepresents the situation somewhat. We serve the pharmaceutical market by helping them promote their products for the marketplace either through the regulatory processes or to doctors once authorised. The various systems of healthcare provision are often quite different, opening marketing challenges arising from regulatory systems and drug names that are different. We are still wrestling with this challenge. The US is not only one of the world's largest and most competitive marketplaces, it is also one of the most litigious. We therefore deploy the highest standards of rigour to ensure our content is compliant using independent auditors and advisers to monitor our production. At the same time, we want to create an environment with every possible control in place, including the appointment of outside directors of impeccable repute.

By 1997, my three colleagues were reaching the point at which retirement was on the agenda. Lindsay in particular was anxious about the prospect of the tax policies of the possible Labour government. We had negotiated the terms of the buy-in of their shares in 1973, and I now had to implement the agreement. I therefore had to find £89 million to take back full ownership of Haymarket, which I duly did.

These were the days of easy money. At the turn of the century, the Royal Bank of Scotland had taken over our bank, the National Westminster, and was in an expansionist mood. We had moved our offices to Hammersmith in 1996 and after that had acquired, with some trepidation, a nearby nurses' hostel and experimental laboratory, which we turned into additional offices. More spectacularly, following a phone call from the liquidators Cork Gulley, we purchased an office block in Teddington and moved our consumer publishing magazines there. In 2004, we found another office site in Teddington on the banks of the River Thames. We bought the buildings subject to a sublease of fourteen years to Pinewood Studios. Some time later, Peel Holdings purchased Pinewood and asked if they could surrender what was left of their lease. I have written about luck; it does not often come by the bucketful, but this was one occasion when it did. Without the request to end the lease we would have had great difficulty in implementing any planning permission or we would have had to pay a substantial price to acquire it.

At this time, the collapse of Lehman Brothers in 2008, the Covid pandemic and the consequences of war in Ukraine were not even clouds on the horizon. The online revolution that was to change the nature of our business beyond measure had begun, but the pace and scale of it were not yet apparent. Of course, there were discussions within the company about it and it could be argued that I was too slow to embrace this new world. I was not alone. Our profile as it was at the turn of the century is almost unrecognisable today. The whole industry has gone through a revolution, which has probably not yet run its course.

• • •

I would like to pay tribute here to all the colleagues who worked with me through those exciting, sometimes turbulent times, but I have found no way of picking out just some from the hundreds involved. I treasure the memories: so much talent, so many laughs, but above all, the simple thought that without them the company could never have become what it is today.

Many have now left and others have emerged to run the company. The new global leadership team, which continues to be led by Kevin Costello, has now been in place since his appointment as CEO over a decade ago. He has worked for the company for most of his working life and has brought an inspirational spirit to the redefinition of the company's direction and scope. He has enjoyed the support of our finance director, Brian Freeman, who is also a long-serving member of the team, with such an encyclopaedic grasp of the detail that nothing gets past him unnoticed.

The vision and strategy which we have followed has transformed the business from a predominantly UK-based print publishing company into an international media, data and information group. This strategy was a deliberate choice, but it was also a necessity. We now live in a world where disruption is the new norm and we have to learn how to get used to the social, technological, commercial and environmental turbulence.

We are constantly facing unknowns, and as a business, we have had to change our approach to ensure we not only withstand those headwinds but capitalise and gain from them. Transformation comes at a price and we have repeatedly needed to raise cash. So we have sold the majority of our special interest consumer brands, including *FourFourTwo*, *Autosport* and *Stuff*.

And nothing illustrates these changes better than those we have made in our automobile business. We had acquired *Autocar* in 1985 and *Motor* in 1988 before merging them into *Autocar*, bringing together two of the oldest magazines in this field. We launched *What Car?* in 1973 to help car buyers make an informed decision. *Classic & Sports Car* was added in 1982. One of the biggest developments in this field was the creation by John Madejski of *Auto Trader*, which was a simple listing of second-hand cars for sale. Launched in print, it moved online and came to dominate that market and enjoy a pace-setting quoted company status. Hundreds of millions have been spent by would-be competitors, but no one has managed to diminish its prominence.

However, we have been less successful in our attempt to replicate this achievement in the second-hand market for that of new cars.

We have tried, at no little expense, various ways to insert ourselves into the online buying funnel for new and used cars, but we have now entered into a tremendously exciting commercial partnership with Auto Trader to drive our audience and leads into their platform.

The cars about which we were writing and photographing sold all over the world. In 1998, I visited Terry Mansfield, the chief executive of National Magazines, and on his office wall saw the covers of forty international editions of *Cosmopolitan*. This gave me the idea to license our magazines abroad. In a speech to our staff in 2005, I was able to report that we had eighty-four magazines under licence overseas. *F1 Racing* had twenty-six editions in nineteen languages, *Autocar* thirteen in ten languages and *Stuff* sixteen in fourteen. Two of those brands, *Stuff* and *F1 Racing*, were subsequently sold, leaving only *Autocar*, *What Car?* and *Classic & Sports Car* in our automobile stable. In its international journey, *Autocar* had a chequered career. Our venture into India proved a significant success. We got wind that one of India's most celebrated motor journalists was looking for the next step in his career. A German company Motor Presse Stuttgart had picked up the same rumour and we found ourselves in a bidding war to attract Hormazd Sorabjee. We won, but as part of the deal, we agreed to establish a partnership in which he would have editorial control.

Our partnership has developed within these constraints on a most friendly basis and, from both our differing points of view, has proved a triumph. We added *Campaign India* and *PrintWeek* to the stable, launched *WhatPackaging?* and continue to publish *Stuff* and *WhatHi-Fi?* under licence. In 2024, we divided the company, with the editorial excellence of *Autocar* being absorbed into Spinny, the market leader in web-based cars for sale, in a cash and share deal. Hormazd had been considering retirement but decided to take up a consultative role with that business while remaining a valued non-executive director of Haymarket India, our company there. Shortly after my return we formed a joint venture with the *South China Morning Post* to publish four brands, including two serving the automotive industry. With our wholly owned company in Asia, we acquired *Media and Marketing*, which was subsequently rebranded as *Campaign* in 2010.

In 2003, we moved into the financial sector with the acquisition of *FinanceAsia* and *PensionsAsia*. The latter was rebranded *AsianInvestor* and soon after we launched *CorporateTreasurer*. In 2008, we formed a joint venture with Cannes Lions to launch what today is known as APAC Lions, the festival of creativity for the region and sister event to Cannes.

The horticultural industry has been a latecomer to our overseas ambitions. *Gardeners' Chronicle* was acquired in the BPC merger of 1968 and we amalgamated it with a trade magazine to become *Horticulture Week*. In recent years, a young German entrepreneur, Alexander Kelm, the founder of Green Solutions, came to our attention as he promoted his new business to the readers of our German horticulture magazine, *TASPO*. He had become the dominant player in his market, and we decided to form a partnership to introduce his product into the UK market. A Dutch company, Garden Connect, had already acquired a significant share of the UK market with a similar product, but it was clear that the German platform offered a superior service. Together we bought the Dutch company and began the process of introducing the German platform, Green Solutions International, to their British clients. This process of international expansion has continued to accelerate; we have customers now in Canada, Ireland, Belgium, the United States, Estonia and France.

• • •

It is odd that so many things went wrong in the late 1990s. Governments overspent, companies overspent, people overspent. It reminded me of my early days in Langland Bay in Wales, catching the wave as one surfed to the beach. The power and the unstoppability of it and then, as you hit the shore, the crash.

But the crash hadn't yet come in the 1990s. The 'burn rate' became the measurement of investment success – the rate at which you could spend the capital you were investing became the substitute for the return that you could expect. 'Derivatives' was the respectable catch-phrase designed to cloak the fact that investors had no idea where their money was actually ending up. It was heady and exciting, but it was a delusion. We were all caught up in it. We were launching and acquiring businesses at home and abroad, buying the freehold of our offices and, by far our largest commitment, buying out the three shareholders who had masterminded the business in my ministerial absence.

But in the early 2000s, the bubble burst. Record profits of £12 million disappeared into a loss of £7 million. Haymarket still had huge debts following my decision to buy out my partners and to acquire the freeholds of our offices.

There was no escape. One part of our business, advertising recruitment vacancies largely in the public sector, collapsed overnight. £10 million of profit from the bottom line disappeared. If you add to that the burden of increased interest charges, you can see that crisis management became the order of the day.

Senior executives and I met on a frequent basis, and in order to try to get some balance into the meetings, I made it a rule that before anyone reported on recent trading, they had to produce a piece of good news. It was a stretching challenge. Our experience as a client of the Royal Bank of Scotland, where we were deep in the sin bin, was not a happy one. We were struggling to pay the interest costs of our borrowing, which, at its peak, came close to £145 million. It had to be drastically reduced and the easiest way to do that was to sell the freeholds of our offices. Fortunately, they were highly marketable and that, plus the sale of a number of titles, ended the crisis.

We moved into rented offices in Twickenham, remaining in the London Borough of Richmond. My personal relationship with the bank remained friendly and cordial throughout, but my colleagues at the coal face were bruised by the experience.

It is important to understand the context in which I considered all this. For the first time, I had the chance to turn the company into a wholly owned family business. The alternative would have been to go to the City looking for a short-term partner prior to a flotation. The option I chose was worth a few sleepless nights!

The background to all this turbulence was the internet revolution and transformation from print to digital, data and live events. Haymarket's success was born and nurtured in the days of print, but our enduring characteristic has been the quality of our editorial content. We produced magazines tailored for specific audiences and sold advertising pages to clients anxious to attract the attention of those audiences.

I remember in the early 1950s, one of the great advertising experts, as chairman of Schweppes, was Sir Frederic Hooper, who profoundly declared that half of his advertising was wasted. His problem was he didn't know which half. The coming of the internet has provided advertisers with an escape from that dilemma. They want details, names and eyeballs. They want them broken down into every manner of defined group so that they can target, with laser-like precision, their marketing budget. The pressures of these market changes have transformed the products of the company. It was important to realise that if we felt threatened, it was because someone else had seen an opportunity. We had to embrace change.

The need is for eternal vigilance, a continuous review of your business model and the flexibility to change before change is forced upon you. Whatever the immediate crisis, it is important to remember that the world is getting richer year by year, educational standards are rising and a prosperous middle class is one of the most important characteristics of the nation state. Publishers should either be able to find an opportunity in all of that or they should not be in the business at all. What we had to realise was the simple fact that our skills lay in the creation of content. If print and paper were being phased out as the method of conveying our content to the market, then we had to embrace whatever alternative vehicle became available. The internet and face-to-face events have become more effective means of distributing our content. What does not change is the philosophy of excellence in the creation of that content.

I have recognised that we may have been slow off the mark into the internet revolution, but it was not a black and white story. We were lucky to be able to climb the first step onto the bandwagon of early change when I received a phone call from Andrew Buxton, chairman of Barclays, in 1997. He told me he wanted to dispose of *Car Shop*, a digital car comparison site that allowed customers to compare cars prior to purchase. We acquired it and thus our print magazine, *What Car?*, gained an early toe hold in the new world of the internet with the launch of whatcar.com in 1998. The growth of specialist sites with their ability to offer more precise targeting of their audiences forced the move from print to online to continue. Recruitment platforms killed off many of the job listings, which had been an important revenue for us in the print media. News was now available in real time anywhere in the world. It was time to reassess and either sell, close or redesign our commercial model.

I have devoted many words here to the technologies that have so changed the nature of the business over a quarter of a century. There are two other factors that have exercised a profound influence on the business climate of today: the shift in employees' expectations and concern for the physical and social environment.

There is the story of a shipowner who was asked if he ever consulted the dockers. He is reported to have replied, 'Aye. We meet them on the quayside at 7.30 on Monday mornings. It doesn't last long.'

Today, such an attitude would close any company down. To that end, we stepped up our global sustainability efforts and launched Haymarket Impact in 2023. Impact encapsulates everything the business does environmentally, socially and governance-wise. We have focused our efforts where we can make a lasting impact to help the planet and its people, now and in the future. To reflect this, we redefined our overarching purpose to, 'Shaping a better future with remarkable content.' I believe we have a responsibility to help drive positive, meaningful change, as the consequences of climate change and global inequalities get worse. The world is behind schedule to meet 2030 targets in this current 'decade of action'. We can, and must, do more. Ultimately, as a media business, we are in a unique and privileged position to influence others with the content we create. It is crucial we use our voice to help shape a better future for all.

Those years I spent in the private sector were a roller coaster. Let me say it before anyone else: I made some serious mistakes. My only relief is that there was sufficient success on the other side of the ledger to compensate. I would never deny that the underlying motive was to make a profit, but this can be overemphasised. There is the challenge, the excitement, a sense of vision about what one is trying to create. A question asked at a board meeting sought to know why the company was bothering with struggling overseas subsidiaries. I paraphrased Edmund Hillary's famous answer about the conquest of Everest: 'Because they are there.' The strength of a private company is that there are no outside shareholders interested only in short-term returns, nor are there journalists poking around for bad news like blackbirds after worms.

It is now two years since I handed over the chairmanship of the company to my son Rupert, its chief executive Kevin Costello and finance director Brian Freeman. I have told them that I no longer want to run the company, but I still want to share the excitement. They more than satisfy my hopes with regular meetings and calls. My confidence in them is absolute, tinged only perhaps by a sense of envy. There is a whole world out there, so many opportunities on so many horizons that, with the talent they have at their command, everyday has its own excitement. I am not by nature a spectator, but I bow to the inevitable course of nature that has made me become one.

CHAPTER 3

TWO ENCOUNTERS IN CHINA

My first encounter with China came just after the start of my ministerial career. In 1973, Ted Heath was keen to increase our trading relationship with China and, as Minister for Aerospace and Shipping, I was added to the planeload of businesspeople who accompanied Peter Walker, Secretary of State for Trade and Industry, on an official visit eastward. The British embassy organised a massive display of products that it was hoped would attract a flow of orders. The customers came in large numbers, enquiring in great detail about the specifications and capabilities of individual examples of British expertise. I do not remember many actual orders being placed – it was said that more business was done on the flights to and from China than in the actual venue. Anne accompanied me, and for both of us it was a vivid and memorable visit. A few days spent in a country so large and complex as China can only scratch the surface of appreciation and understanding. Yet our impressions remain and are in the starkest contrast with later visits.

By western standards, China's economy was then largely a peasant one, with outdated and largely undeveloped industrialisation. Bicycles were the primary transport of Beijing and Shanghai. The air pollution was awful. Everyone wore uniform Mao suits with a simple choice of navy or grey. Most significant was the apparent subservience of people in the workplace. We were objects of curiosity, with people peeping round the corner to gain a glimpse. The sharpest contrast was in our meeting with Zhou Enlai, who ranks high among all the political leaders I have met for the sheer aura of power that surrounded him, remaining only half-hidden by the charm with which he greeted us.

Around the same time in 1973, I was asked by the Foreign Office to host a lunch for a visiting delegation from China. I was not pleased to be shouldered with a responsibility that should have been theirs rather than mine. They prevailed, and I rather tetchily sat down as the interpreters went to work. In the dialogue, words and phrases started to appear which had an unfamiliar ring: change, reform, opportunity, enterprise and opening up. I rang the Foreign Office immediately after lunch, explained that I was stone-cold sober and recounted the experience. I had been told of the revolution before it began and, as it had been forecast, so it happened. Even my far-sighted guests had not foreseen that the party would change its name, abandoning the word 'communist' in favour of calling itself the people's party.

Towards the end of my time in government, in the mid-1990s, I was due to meet President Jiang Zemin in Zhuhai. We landed at an airport of substantial size and drove along multi-carriageway roads into the centre. On our way we noticed that there was only a scattering of people and very few cars. This was a society where they planned ahead for future traffic patterns, of which there were few signs then. A very different approach from ours, where we wait until traffic is almost at a standstill before improving capacity.

The President had just returned from a visit to South Africa and, at dinner with the British Ambassador the night before, an official from his office appeared to ask whether we would understand if the meeting was cut to twenty minutes. Our ambassador rightly argued that I too had travelled a long way. Such meetings normally last for thirty minutes and anything less can rapidly attract the attention of the media, being perceived as a snub.

In the meeting, I kept my watch half-hidden but sighed silently with relief as the minute hand passed to twenty-five and then thirty minutes. After forty minutes the President announced, 'The meeting is over, now we will talk in English.' For another twenty minutes, he described to me the challenges China faced as it set about modernising its economies on the western coast while avoiding unemployment on the eastern seaboard.

Within days of becoming Secretary of State for Defence in 1983, I was briefed on the threat facing us from the Soviet Union. I surprised the assembled leaders of our military forces by asking them to return the next day and brief me as they might have done if they held their positions in the Soviet Union. The meeting never took place. Within a matter of years, the threat about which I had been so effectively persuaded had collapsed. It is not in the nature of politics to think through the situation from the point of view of the other side. In practice, it is likely to provoke charges of treachery or treason. If you are involved in the world of realpolitik, where you are faced with the tensions that are characteristic of international relationships, there is a delicate balance to be struck between understanding the other person's point of view while avoiding the disenchantment of your own supporters. Charged with such responsibility, it is wise to ask yourself how you, or we, or our friends might have reacted if faced with similar challenges ourselves?

One of the clearest examples is China's use of troops to end the demonstrations by students in Tiananmen Square in 1989. The event was greeted rightly with universal condemnation in the western world as an example of the worst consequence of communist dictatorship. But there is another side to the story. How did the students feel they had sufficient freedom to demonstrate in the first place? And why did it take so long for the authorities to bring in troops to stop the rioting? One explanation was the need to bring in troops from a long way from Beijing because the local soldiers would not have carried out orders to shoot citizens in a community where they lived, but I don't think that is a sufficient reason. I believe the students had been emboldened when the liberalising reforms began and felt they could get away with demonstrating, and the government was slow in responding because they did not realise how far the students were prepared to go. We shall never know.

Within the Chinese system, there are many debates which take place behind closed doors. There is a ruthless streak in the presidential power to decide, but I detect the same political alignment of the hard right opposed by the softer centre that characterises our parliamentary democracies. We have been governed within much the same disciplines for most of our history and certainly in the administration of our empire.

An example of the same debate with a very different outcome was my involvement in the handover ceremony transferring sovereignty of Hong Kong back to China. Chris Patten, a former Cabinet minister and now Lord Patten, was the last governor of Hong Kong. He was apprehensive, quite rightly as it turned out, that China would not tolerate the freedom of speech that existed under his administration. He had introduced legislation to protect such freedoms with the strength of law. This had adversely affected his relationship with mainland China, leading to an impasse over the arrangements for the handover ceremony itself. We wanted a proper public occasion while the Chinese wanted to ship their troops into their new barracks, unnoticed, late at night. It was agreed that I should visit Premier Li Peng to discuss the arrangements. I explained our pride in the legacy that we were about to leave behind and that I had been a member of the Cabinet team that had, fourteen years ago, agreed the terms of the negotiations for the transfer of power. The hope I had felt at the time was for a new and enduring relationship. I concluded by pointing out that the eyes of the world would be focused on the occasion. We were leaving with pride in the over 150 years of our administration and, in particular, pride that reunification was taking place peacefully and within the terms of the original agreement.

There was little discussion but simple agreement to proceed as I suggested. This was to provide me with the haunting memory of the unique military command 'Battalion will leave Hong Kong' as the Union Jack was lowered and Prince Charles embarked on HMY *Britannia* to sail into another world. For me, this all concluded by my getting lost in a packed crowd of local citizens. I simply remember finding myself separated from the royal party, my wife and the governor looking out over a dense sea of black hair. I was about a foot taller than everyone else. Inexplicably, I missed the quayside nostalgia of watching the departing yacht sail off into history.

Another major encounter with China came after I had stepped back from frontline politics. In 1998, I returned to China as chairman of Haymarket to explore the possibility of launching magazines there. I visited Beijing and asked the embassy to fix an appointment with Vice Premier Li Lanqing, with whom I had enjoyed a personal relationship while I was President of the Board of

Trade. He generously agreed to see me at very short notice, a fact observed by the powers that be.

At about the same time, Tony Blair visited China. He agreed to establish an Anglo-Chinese Forum to further relationships between the two countries. I was invited to be the co-chair with Dr Song Jian. By the time of the second meeting in 2000, we had gathered support from Blair, Deputy Prime Minister John Prescott and China's Vice Premier Wu Yi. In my opening remarks, I reflected on the importance of this forum:

> When we started on this new venture last year, we could not be sure how the forum would turn out. Certainly, it had an auspicious conception announced, as Mr Prescott said, by Prime Minister Blair and Premier Zhu. Its birth was no less remarkable when President Jiang Zemin and Tony Blair opened the first meeting in London. And its growth and development this year is a true indication of the enormous importance these different interests, industry, finance, media, environment, culture, education and law attach to the bilateral relationship between our two countries. The size of my delegation and the Chinese side is impressive. Much has gone on between our two countries in the intervening period – visits by ministers, trade negotiations, cultural exchange to name but a very, very few. Whilst the forum itself may not have been directly responsible for all these events, nonetheless I firmly believe the fact that we met last October and that both our reports went into our respective Prime Minister's offices will have played no small part. The relationship between Britain and China, I believe, is in excellent shape. The forum has contributed to that.

I noted that there was a 'tremendous challenge' between the expectations and requirements of both sides, as the forum did not exist in a vacuum and we existed to complement work done by others. The forum looked at ways to help China develop an educational software industry, together with a new generation of IT-literate teachers. The forum has also helped them to explore new ways of developing collaborative research programmes and private–public training partnerships.

In the fields of environment, science and technology, we identified six priorities for working together, including promotion of waste recycling and environmental best practice. In finance and industry, we emphasised the importance of London as a key financial centre and explored the opportunities for more direct investment in both our domestic markets.

The lawyers identified specific opportunities for cooperation on environmental law and intellectual property rights. Colleagues from the media industry not only explored opportunities for closer cooperation in the provision of business services, film and TV production and personnel exchanges but also concerns about freedom of speech in China in an open and constructive spirit.

I do not think that Song Jian or I will look back and feel that we achieved momentous events with the forum, but it provided me, without doubt, access to informal dialogues and a continuing place as a spectator of the China that was emerging onto the world stage. The contrast between my first visit in 1973 and the forum meeting in 2000 was extraordinary. There was an informality, a dialogue and an openness of expression which would never have been possible in 1973. I recall, one evening in Beijing, turning to my host, who had expressed views that seemed to me far to the right of anything to which I would subscribe and observed, jokingly, that I thought in some ways he was worse than Mrs Thatcher. This was not seen as an insult. The fact that such informality could characterise our relationship was indicative of the change that had taken place.

In the same vein, my meeting with Li Lanqing had been arranged with speed and courtesy. In response to my request about the possibility of launching our magazines in China, he quoted Confucius – 'Every journey needs a first step' – and I was directed to some obscure part of the government machine.

This was not as negative as it first appeared. We obtained a licence and subsequently launched *Autocar* in China. The mechanism consisted of a licence being vested in the editor, who had to be a Chinese citizen. There was no way he would listen to us and we were effectively without the power to run the business, so we closed it down. Rupert Murdoch went through a similar experience during a meeting with President Xi, who would have known that Murdoch had given up his Australian citizenship and become American in order to publish in the US. The President is said to have smiled and enquired politely if Mr Murdoch was now proposing to become a Chinese citizen.

• • •

Both my political and commercial interests made me a natural recruit to The 48 Group Club, known appropriately as the Icebreakers, which had been founded in the 1950s after the initiative by Lord Boyd Orr, in association with such British Hong Kong giants as Jardines and Swires, to open up trade with China. Jack Perry, the first chairman of the club, did so much to further relationships and trade between Britain and China that when he died, he became the first foreigner ever to be accorded a memorial meeting in the Great Hall of the People in Beijing.

The organisation was an important point of contact with the Chinese government and its agencies. On Jack's death, his son Stephen became chairman and later invited me to speak to the 48 Group's annual dinner in February 2007. I asked him to suggest a topic. 'Oh,' he said, 'why don't you talk about China? You've got seven minutes.' I saw this as an opportunity rather than a threat, as it sharpened the mind.

In that speech, I set out how China had changed from an ineffective, backward and largely agricultural economy to a world-class manufacturing – and increasingly, service – industry-based economy so quickly and so comprehensively. The phenomenon that struck me most was the vision that inspired and drove China's successive governments. I pointed out that we have to recognise and acknowledge that China has a planned economy, in which an intricate system of priorities, licences and joint ventures give structure to the initial vision. In looking at what was to come, I noted that there were three factors that reinforce China's emergence as a serious player in world politics: job creating exports and financial stability, the need for western technology and the search for energy.

China needs international stability, but it would be naïve to think that its foreign policy will be driven by western interests any more than ours will be driven by Chinese interests. There are no easy reconciliations between our view of human rights and the treatment of minorities. I recalled that the retreat of nationalist forces in Taiwan under General Chiang Kai-shek created inevitable tension that was hugely increased by the existence of some 150 other islands, many claimed by other powers. Those of us who watched the transfer of sovereignty over Hong Kong and Macau can only hope that an ultimate accord will be reached and that diplomatic skills will prevent a conflagration, with unpredictable consequences, in the meantime. I concluded my speech:

> Of course, the west must and will continue to press the case of oppressed minorities and to argue for the freedoms of liberal democracy. If history is any guide, the increasing spread of private wealth, advancing education standards and, above all, access to world communication networks and an international Chinese diaspora will take that country along a journey familiar to anyone with a knowledge of our own history. Disraeli gave working men the vote 157 years ago. Women got the vote ninety-six years ago, and in my adult lifetime we have been acknowledging Prime Ministers and Presidents who were seen as terrorists in our former empire.

I returned to China for several future meetings of the forum, addressing the fourth meeting in October 2003. At that time, I noted that, as the single largest European investor in China, the UK has an important role to play in China's economic transformation. I added that we hoped Chinese companies would increasingly see the UK as a stepping stone to Europe and increase the level of investment in the UK. Chinese students had already taken that step – they now form the largest single group of foreign students at UK higher education institutions. In 2004, marking the fiftieth anniversary of the 48 Group, Haymarket produced a celebratory book to serve as a history of the past fifty years of trade between UK and China, a memento of the anniversary and a look ahead to the next fifty years. I invited members of the group to contribute to the book.

During the 2004 meeting, I observed that one cannot 'fail to be impressed by the changes that have already taken place and by the palpable sense of enormous change still to come', noting the technological developments that allowed China to leapfrog the development of western democracies. Communications is a prime example of the change and challenges China is facing – it becomes increasingly hard to control the flow of information when 1.4 billion people have unfettered access to it. I argued:

> There is also no way that any government can seek to control this medium effectively – technology will always outpace the means of control and whilst this is undoubtedly a challenge to those in power, the advantages of these communication tools to economic and social development must be acknowledged and embraced.

Although much has changed since this speech, I highlighted the fact that China showed some commitment to joining a number of multilateral bodies, both economic and political, and signed a number of key treaties, such as the Non-Proliferation Treaty and the Comprehensive Nuclear Test Ban Treaty, as well as the UN International Covenant on cultural, social and economic rights. Winning the bid for the Beijing Olympics in 2008 was a significant moment but, I warned, 'Joining the world stage is not a one-way process and China cannot avoid the scrutiny that this membership brings.'

In that speech, I said joining the World Trade Organization (WTO) presented a huge challenge for China, providing unprecedented competition for China's domestic industries, and that the benefits may not always be apparent. The requirements of joining the WTO in terms of corporate governance, transparency and reliable and enforceable laws, while producing some pain in the short term, would no doubt be part of the way in which economic growth can be encouraged and sustained.

The already extraordinary feat of China's economic development has not come without protest at and dissatisfaction with unemployment and growing inequality. The economic differences between the eastern seaboard and the western provinces, between urban and rural communities, cannot be underestimated. Economic growth is an absolute imperative.

Even in 2004, it was clear that China was receiving a high degree of attention from the world for its human rights record. It was an area that is clearly a challenge for China's leaders but one where more understanding is required by those outside China – more understanding, that is, of the existing developments in the rule of law, of the practical considerations in ensuring the necessary standards and legal processes operate from Qinghai to Shanghai, from Inner Mongolia to Hainan. Many training programmes and exchanges were being run with China's legal professionals; this is to be encouraged, as is the agreement to work together on some key issues such as human rights and police training, something that no country can afford to be complacent about. But, as I pointed out, 'It is unrealistic to expect the rule of law and constitutional government to take root overnight and replace centuries of the rule of man.'

The other area in which China showed it was then keen to engage with the rest of the world is the environment. China has contributed to, and engaged with, many international forums on environmental matters and has signalled a responsible and mature attitude to its environmental responsibilities. The environment is clearly a world issue and one on which developing and developed economies need to work closely together. The statistics of what economic growth has done to the environment in China made it clear that the air quality in a number of Chinese cities falls below internationally accepted standards. It was also clear that deforestation was a primary cause of the recent terrible floods and that many of China's rivers were and are badly polluted. But we also know that this is a problem recognised by China, and just as in the west, much of the pressure for change is coming from within through an increasingly strong and articulate environmental lobby expressed through the press and the work of domestic NGOs, as well as through the strengthening of the State Environmental Protection Agency, which has growing powers of enforcement. China does not need the world to tell her what the problems are. Summing up, I set the tone of how I hoped China could develop:

> We can hope that China will choose to leapfrog some of the disastrous mistakes countries like my own have made in its industrial development by taking advantage of new technologies – for example, for clean fuels and for power generation. Which brings me to Hong Kong and the role that it can play in China's development. I do not see an eclipse of Hong Kong by Shanghai but rather that Hong Kong will become the financial centre for the southern part of China in much the same way that the City of London services Europe and New York services North and South America. In addition, I believe that there is the opportunity for China to make use of the enormous intellectual pool existing in Hong Kong – something which we see is already happening in legal exchanges and in the fight against corruption – both areas where Hong Kong has a long tradition of well-tried and tested systems.

I last returned to Hong Kong to celebrate the twenty-fifth anniversary of Haymarket's presence in October 2023. Driving from the airport, I passed endless cranes associated with new development, while the centre remained as I remembered. I stayed in the Mandarin Hotel, as I always had, and here the change was immediate and profound. The expats were gone. On my previous, pre-handover visits, there would have been some Chinese guests, but only around one in ten of the hotel's customers would have been Chinese. This time, the ratios were reversed, indicating a wider social change in the composition of Hong Kong society.

When Haymarket was first set up in Hong Kong, we had acquired magazines owned by Australians and Americans. Our managers were a mixture of those we acquired and those that were sent out from the UK. Today there are few Brits working in our company, which is almost entirely staffed by local citizens. The same process has transformed our Singapore office. Together, they are spearheading an expansion across Asia, the scale of which is exciting. Yet we are fully aware of the political changes that have curtailed the freedoms of the local people. As a believer in parliamentary democracy, I cannot approve of this. I faced a simple decision as to whether to transfer our activities or accept that for the people themselves there are limits to their freedoms to protest and criticise. But I do not believe we would serve any local interests and certainly not those of our very talented employees by leaving. My responsibility was to maintain the wider discussions with China that I have conducted constructively on many other occasions since.

In 2004, I said that there is no doubt that the twenty-first century will be China's century, but we should not underestimate the very real challenges China faces in turning round various aspects of life there – the economy, the legal system, government, human rights issues and others – in a relatively short space of time. More developed countries have sometimes had centuries in which to adjust and reform.

No one outside China can dictate the pace of change there, but nor can China be oblivious to the opinions and views expressed by those she seeks to join in the world outside. These are all questions for China herself. Countries such as the UK can engage and debate and help as required, but China has the ultimate responsibility. Any analysis of China in the last twenty years can only conclude that an enormous amount has already been achieved – the standard of living, the quality of life and China's role in the world have all developed immeasurably. I had hoped that engagement with the outside world, together with the various programmes of exchange on economic issues, the environment, the law or even political philosophy, would enable us all to come to understand China better and help China to realise that constructive criticism is not a sign of betrayal but rather an indication of a more mature and meaningful relationship.

Events since then, however, have shown that China is taking a different course, and my optimism in those early days when China began to engage with the western world may have been overstated.

What is clear is that the new Labour government has decided to attempt to improve relations with China. It is impossible to predict how events not far ahead will facilitate or impede their endeavours. President Trump's trade policy may force this country to choose between American protectionism and our dependence on Europe, our largest trading partner.

Certainly, there will remain serious disagreements, particularly over competition policy and human rights, Taiwan and Hong Kong. However, there are also issues where we have clear common interests, particularly around global warming and investment policy.

In the end, there will always be the critical question about which approach is most likely to produce at least a working relationship if not a solution to our present disagreements. On that basis, my instinct will be to encourage those who continue to talk.

CHAPTER 4

MODERNISING AN ENGLISH VILLAGE

My selection as the Conservative candidate for Henley made it possible for Anne and me to begin the search for a permanent home in the country. We assured the Henley selection committee that we would live in or within easy reach of the constituency if I were chosen. And so it was that the search began. We had the clearest idea of what we wanted. Our ideal would be an outstanding example of eighteenth-century architecture, which would house the pictures and furniture we had already started to collect. Even before our marriage we toured the antique shops of the Cotswolds. We shared a very similar appreciation of what we liked, helped by Anne's experience as an aide to Andras Kalman in his Knightsbridge art gallery.

I would describe our search as professional – others may be less charitable and use the word 'ruthless'. Every technique was deployed, including the use of helicopters to seek out targets. We were prepared to drive through the imposing gates of a walled estate to look. That nearly ended in tears. Our excuse was well prepared. We would ask anyone who questioned us whether Mr Wilkinson was there. Of course, he never was, and we would depart with appropriate apologies. Then one day, he was! We fled with no semblance of dignity.

The breakthrough came when on holiday in Portugal. We met a young girl who told us her relative Sir Spencer Summers, the former MP for Aylesbury, had just died and his home in Thenford, Northamptonshire, was about to come onto the market. My wife had seen it while hunting with the Bicester.

When we returned from holiday, I crept up the back drive. It was our dream. We were invited to meet Lady Summers, who liked the idea of a family similar to hers becoming the new owners. We offered to pay the asking price and so the property never came onto the market.

I have stressed that it was the quality of the house that mattered to us. Thenford was then Grade II listed, although it has subsequently been changed to Grade I. We had assumed there would be a garden, but I had no concept of what that would mean. In practice, we had bought a home, a working farm of over 400 hundred acres, with the associated buildings, and a number of village cottages. The garden around the house was an undistinguished two acres. I was engaged in the political responsibilities of shadow Secretary of State for the Environment, together with my involvement in Haymarket Publishing. I had no knowledge of farming.

It made financial sense for us to buy the house and its immediate surroundings, with the help of a £25,000 mortgage, while Haymarket purchased the commercial activities and associated property.

One other event completes the background to Thenford. In 1972, as a minister of state under Peter Walker in the Department for the Environment, my wife and I visited Heveningham Hall in Suffolk, a magnificent mansion designed by Robert Taylor with much interior work by James Wyatt. The house and its grounds, designed by

Capability Brown, had been offered to the nation for £300,000 in 1965 by Margite Wheeler, a member of the Vanneck family, when she was faced with impossible running costs. We fell head over heels in love with it. Tavistock, my constituency at the time, was facing major changes and I needed to seek pastures new. There were plenty of Conservative seats in that part of the world, so I decided to take my chance. I agreed with Peter Walker that I would reimburse the government for the money it had laid out on the acquisition. The deal was agreed. Champagne was consumed with our friends Mark (now Lord Marlesford) and Gabriella Schreiber who had introduced us to the property.

However, Peter Walker moved to the Department of Trade and Industry in 1972 and his place was taken by Geoffrey Rippon. Officials said the papers needed to go to the new Secretary of State. He had no problem with the plan, but suggested the papers should go to the Prime Minister. I was already having doubts by then, but whatever the facts, the thought of my personal arrangements being subjected to prime ministerial scrutiny was the last straw.

We withdrew and the property remained in the ownership of the government. When I became Secretary of State for the Environment in 1979, Ian Gilmour, who was also in Cabinet as Lord Privy Seal and spokesman in the Commons for foreign affairs – because Lord Carrington, the Foreign Secretary, sat in the House of Lords – persuaded me to sell the property to Abdul Amir Al-Ghazzi, an Iraqi businessman. Much expenditure on essential modernisation followed, but a serious fire caused significant damage. The property changed hands and was purchased by Jon Hunt, who had created Foxtons, the estate agency business. The result of my decision to return the property to private ownership is that it has been modernised with essential services and facilities, its garden restored to its former glory at no cost to the taxpayer, and it is open to the public. I learned lessons here, particularly with reference to the National Trust.

The National Trust is rightly highly regarded by the British public. From its creation in 1895, it has preserved important parts of our heritage and often taken over responsibility where private ownership could no longer cope. High personal taxation and inflation were the recruiting sergeants for the trust. But there was no provision for a transfer back to private ownership, even to owners later able to assume the financial responsibilities. An unintended consequence was to impose a time warp on many historic buildings. Private owners would often have modernised their homes and buildings as new services and technologies became available and would have been able to offer the public a better historical and horticultural experience. I had demonstrated the discipline required to protect the public interest when I transferred Heveningham out of public ownership. I can see no reason why the same process should not be followed with some of their properties. There will be many who oppose such a programme, and they will advance the argument in one form or another about responsibility to preserve the past. But, increasingly, the trust is now doing the exact opposite.

For example, many former owners would be appalled by the decision, taken by the trust some years ago, to ban hunting on their land. A particularly clear example is the land previously belonging to the Aclands in Exmoor, which came into trust ownership with the express condition that hunting should continue.

On the other hand, there is the example I came across as the MP for Tavistock, where trust land was protected from a bypass proposal because of the rules in their constitution. A further, more recent example is that the role of slavery in a property's history has raised questions about the suitability of some of its contents for display. I share the general abhorrence at this vile practice from past centuries and take some comfort from this country's leading role in its abolition.

What emerges from these examples is that the trust, when it wants to, can claim the status quo must be maintained in order to block what may be necessary change because their constitution allows them to. But in response to pressure either from its members or from the public, they can be as flexible as they wish. This is not a satisfactory state of affairs.

There is overwhelming evidence that properly regulated ownership can offer the public the chance to visit and enjoy such properties if they are in private hands. Sensitive custodianship by a caring family, living in the house with the resources to maintain and improve it, can be as effective a guarantor of our heritage as managers that are answerable to a remote bureaucracy. Recently, I read that the Royal Society for the Protection of Birds is disposing of parts of its estate. I have no doubt they will ensure any new owners maintain their standards of care.

• • •

By 1979, I was the ultimate custodian of British heritage and its flora and fauna as the Secretary of State at the Department for the Environment. I was also responsible for the regulatory regime, governing the rules necessary for their protection.

I could not have foreseen that years later, particularly after we had lost office in 1997, that I would find myself coping with the bureaucratic jungle that I had helped to create with the Wildlife and Countryside Act of 1981. I remember very well the conversation I had with the Royal Society for the Protection of Birds shortly after the 1979 election. 'What do you want?' I asked them, explaining that they were unlikely ever to have another Secretary of State so willing to introduce more protection for the birds they loved. At much the same time, I won the quango hunt by closing or privatising more similar organisations than my colleague, Sir Keith Joseph, the Secretary of State for Industry. In 1984, I accepted with enthusiasm the proposal from my officials to merge two bodies, the Ancient Monuments Board for England and the Historic Buildings Council for England, to form one quango: English Heritage. It made sense but also added one more to my score!

A quarter of a century later, I was invited to celebrate the organisation's twenty-fifth birthday in Blackpool. The speech I made was entitled 'Worm's-Eye View' and within it, I set out to explain what it was like to live in a world I had myself partially created.

'I once helped, as Secretary of State, to create the legal framework for Britain's heritage and environment,' I told the audience. 'Times have changed. I am back as a private citizen. I am now forced to take the worm's-eye view. I am at the receiving end of the system.'

Increasingly, I feel more sympathy for the worm. I have no time for the 'bonfire of forms' brigade. I am a preservationist and environmentalist and will oppose any suggestion that the law of the jungle or laissez-faire capitalism can be trusted with such a precious and essential part of the country. But I also think there are simpler, cheaper ways to enable the private sector to play a bigger role in securing the same objectives and thus avoid much of the delay and cost of the present system.

Let us examine the legislative process from its beginnings. The need to legislate can originate from many sources: manifesto promises, pressure groups, the consequences of a new international treaty, official advice that changing circumstances need to be recognised in law and, perhaps more rarely, a personal experience or conviction. Officials will produce the pros and cons, ministers decide the priorities, Whitehall and a wider world will be consulted, agreement to legislate achieved and parliamentary procedures put in place.

Invariably, the legislation will prescribe what the Secretary of State may or must determine. The ultimate delusion lies, of course, in those words. It is quite unrealistic to believe that down the line, at the end of an administrative and executive chain, the Secretary of State will decide anything. To define the number and composition of these chains would need a work of encyclopaedic scale, but the reader will get the message. The law, once passed, will inevitably transfer power to an arm of local government, a quango or other regulatory body. Whitehall does not easily lose control. With the apparent transfer of power will come circulars outlining how the transferred powers are to be exercised. With the churn of ministers now the norm, it is unlikely that the minister or official who initiated the legislation will still be around to scrutinise any secondary legislation or consequential circular.

Thus, constrained within Whitehall's straitjacket, power devolves to lesser bodies. Each will have its own executive with teams of lesser officials, each presided over by a committee of councillors, charged to determine local versions of the relevant policy. Up to this stage, any individual likely to be affected by a particular policy will have played little or no part in its formulation. The private citizen comes face to face with the bureaucratic machine when they need to seek permission under the provision of the legislation.

I have particular experience of the planning machine, having presided over the appeals procedure for five years and been involved in the property market all my adult life. In proposing a development that requires permission, you inevitably have to engage professional advice to prepare the necessary documents. You will be advised of the hurdles to be jumped to achieve that end. You have a choice between preparing the detailed plans and submitting an application or seeking a pre-application interview with an official from the planning department. The risk built into the first option is that you waste time and money preparing plans that never had a chance of approval. The risk that comes with the interview option is that you again waste time and still run the risk of failure. At the moment, our local authorities are under such pressure that, in our case, only applications for more than 200 houses qualify for pre-application discussion.

The problem at the heart of the system is that no individual official can make a decision. Behind the official deputed to offer guidance are others in specialist departments – highways or the environment, to name just two. Worse, each of these officials can change during the course of your application. I have been through the process where such a change led to different guidance, although I must point out that our protest led to the restoration of the original advice. Our application to convert derelict farm buildings into two adjacent bungalows was threatened by a tree preservation order, listing a particularly bad specimen of our common oak. We argued, correctly, that a heavy branch falling might endanger any inhabitants and the right decision was to fell the tree, but faced with more delay and expense, we accepted the council's decision. The country lost another home.

I think that a twin planning system, combined with an appeals system, could cope with many of the complaints about the present system. I outlined my ideas in the speech I made for English Heritage in Blackpool in 2005:

> It would be possible for private sector firms to act in conservation matters as a one-stop shop. The firm would be licenced and would have to demonstrate expertise to obtain such a licence. The local authority would have reserve powers, tightly defined, to intervene. There would be an appeal system, but this would be two-staged. An outside arbitration would arrange a site meeting within a prescribed period, in an attempt to resolve disputes. The firm would be at risk if a prescribed national body felt it was behaving in an unprofessional manner.
>
> Second, it would be possible for an individual owner – property or land – to obtain a licence to manage their property within agreed guidelines. Failure to comply with their licence could restore the full panoply of the present system. A vital part of the success of such a system is the fear by either firm or owner that careless or wanton behaviour would risk licence revocation. The terms of such licences would be crucial. As Secretary of State, I would approve the general provisions and the ability to impose conditions myself. Any delegation of such powers to the bureaucracy would effectively lead to a replication of the present system.

Following on from this, licences would be issued to specialist companies. They would almost certainly be existing agencies, who would already possess or rapidly acquire the necessary knowledge and expertise. The conditions upon which they were issued would be meticulously observed, for fear that revocation would threaten their business. They would be able to propose detailed planning proposals for submission. Planning authorities would have a month to grant permission or to call the application in for detailed examination, but after a limited time, they would have to pay for the delay caused. There would be a right of appeal by the local authority against such a price mechanism if they could show they had behaved with good cause. Application under these new arrangements would preclude anti-social or non-conforming use and would largely relate to domestic housing. It is a small step to widen this system to landowners, who would apply for licences prescribing the working practises and environmental standards they would adopt in the management of their estates. Again, the value of such licences would be much treasured. Any development on such an estate would require the support of a specialist and licenced company as outlined here. A partnership between the two licences would free the estate owner from more intrusive interference by public bodies. The same appeals procedure would apply.

An interesting point arising from this examination of complication and cost in the wider planning system is the much vaunted but incorrect claim that the public sector does not create wealth. The planning machinery is living proof of the extent to which the public sector does create jobs. The Town and Country Planning Act of 1948 is a fundamental pillar of our modern society. The debate should concentrate not on the need or otherwise for regulation but on the most effective and cost-effective way to achieve the necessary standards.

Here is one more example of excess that the system creates. A common feature of any planning permission is a condition to commission specialist advice about the site, its history, its environment and anything else of concern. The experts know that their opinion is open to challenge in the courts. Every backside has to be protected, which demands a level of detail sufficient to resist the most searching judicial review. A simple letter does not offer protection. Bulk becomes a substitute for relevance. As someone who had to pay the fees, I felt I was being taken for a ride. The issue here is not one of doctrine or dogma. It is about the most cost-effective way of securing the objective.

• • •

The year 1976 was a pivotal one in my life. Margaret Thatcher was reported in *The Economist* as being intent on sacking Peter Walker, Paul Channon and me. I was saved because on the day of execution, I was not only scheduled to appear with her at a rally of small businesses but was then later to open the opposition case from the Commons front bench. The enthusiastic response to my speech at the party conference that followed secured my position in the shadow Cabinet. Outside of politics, as well as being chief executive of Haymarket, I was the owner of our new home, a working farm and much of the village of Thenford.

The farm we acquired was typical of many of its size, family owned, run by a manager (if not the owner or tenant) and drawing income from a wide range of activities. Bullocks were bought in to be fattened, sheep lived on the pasture, the arable crops included wheat, barley and potatoes, and there were a few chickens and perhaps a pig or two.

In our case, timber, although originally producing income of significance, had been discontinued and the woodlands left to nature in an early foretaste of what rewilding would look like. There was a range of outbuildings, varying from ancient stone-built barns matching the village houses to the modern prefabricated storage facilities. Cattle yards were often interspersed with occupied houses. Our original purchase from the Summers family was further enhanced by the acquisition from the Goodwin family of their home and a number of redundant barns close to the site of the original manor house. Without stretching the imagination too far, it was possible to see that some of the stone used in the construction of these barns was cut too finely for such buildings and it was probably reused when the manor was demolished and replaced by our house in the late eighteenth century. Certainly, the top floor of our house has rooms lined with panelling from the manor. The only record that exists to help date precisely the era in which much of the present Thenford village was built is a plaque built into a building called Post Office Cottage, inscribed 'TW1694'. Thomas Woodhull was the grandfather of the Woodhull who built our house.

The story of the past almost fifty years since we arrived is a tale which has been repeated in many parts of rural England. A revolution has taken place in farming practices, enhanced property values have driven a much-needed modernisation of living conditions and, in our case, the derelict woodlands have developed into the arboretum. The arboretum is open to the public on selected dates but is available every day to those who live in the village. Yet there was no plan to do this from the start. Our concern was to find a house for our family of period and quality. Everything else flowed from challenges that were consequential to that.

Originally, we bought with the house thirteen habitable buildings, all of which needed modernisation. Included in those buildings was a former cottage used as a potato store, the remains of the village smithy and a site which the Ordnance Survey map of 1871 revealed two cottages had once stood on.

We now farm over 1,400 acres, including some seventy acres of arboretum and woodland, as Haymarket purchased two neighbouring farms in Stanwell and Chacombe, together with a succession of individual parcels of land as they came onto the market. We have set out to modernise the cottages and to build only where there is clear evidence of earlier construction. We preserved the original character of the village and even, in a number of cases, restored thatched rooves in place of slate. With hindsight this was a mistake, as we are already having to restore the first thatch at considerable expense. The potato store has now become two detached houses, an imposing house in the centre of the village is now on the site of the smithy and Quinlan Terry has designed two attached cottages, named Woodhull Cottages, for the derelict site.

The farming activity undertaken today is of a quite different scale to that when we arrived. To secure the advantages and economies of modern farming, the company has entered a farm-sharing scheme with the Goodwin family. This new arrangement requires buildings and equipment of a size and scale to cope with the larger equipment and the bigger harvests. The consequence is the opportunity to convert the old farm buildings into accommodation and a visitor centre, in order to serve the public visiting the arboretum.

When we moved to Thenford in 1976, the village had twenty-four homes. The completion of our existing plans will increase that to forty-two, of which ten are owner-occupied, seven are occupied by staff and twenty-five are let to tenants. Only three have been newly built, as opposed to conversions, and all of these are on plots that were originally developed either as houses or the village smithy.

As owners of a substantial part of the village, there have also been opportunities to improve its environment. In the 1970s, the centre of Thenford village had its own spaghetti junction of telephone and electricity cables crisscrossing the open space. Alec Bond, who lived in the village, prepared a scheme to re-lay these cables underground. The cost was shared equally between the district council, the county council and ourselves.

In the south-west corner of the village there had been a classic village pond, fed by a stream that crossed the road into medieval fish ponds, which we had restored. The pond had long since silted up and overgrown with willows, poplars and the usual marsh land growth. John Atkinson, the local contractor helping us with the garden, was diverted to the restoration of the pond. We bought two large weeping willows and planted a conifer windbreak of *Abies grandis* and *Metasequoia glyptostroboides*.

My wife explored the history of Thenford as part of a project she undertook while on a course with Christie's. Much helpful information came from the county archives in Northampton. The thirteenth-century St Mary's Church is the responsibility of the Parochial Church Council. It sits on land surrounded by ours. Nearby there were the remains of the medieval manor, the home of the Woodhull family. Michael Woodhull replaced it with our house, a mile to the north-east and on higher ground, to create a drier environment for his renowned library. We have no further details of the composition of the village before that. Presumably it housed the families that worked on and served the farm at the time. The survey map of 1851 indicated the location of three fish ponds that would have provided a source of food at the time. These have now been restored: they were heavily silted up and had been joined at either end to create islands which are now ornamental and home to a pair of swans.

A mile away, close to the walled garden Michael Woodhull built when he was constructing our house, the remains of a Roman settlement were excavated in 1971. There is some evidence that the church may have been built on a Roman burial ground, following the discovery of an urn when digging a grave in the churchyard. Other Roman relics were found in the neighbouring fields, including a medal of the Emperor Constantine. The dig that took place in 1971, under the expert supervision of Ian Saunders working with the Oxford University Archaeology Society, revealed that a habitation was built in the fourth century AD and it is thought to have been part of a larger complex, though this is yet to be established. The most exciting discovery was undoubtedly the mosaic pavement, which was subsequently removed and laid down in our house, where it remains today. The excavation took place over three years, after which the site was buried once more and returned, undisturbed to this day, to cultivation.

Woodhull had no heirs, having been predeceased by his wife and children, who died in an epidemic. The ownership of the estate passed to the Severne family on his death in 1816. The Summers family then became tenants before the Second World War, moved out on its declaration and then acquired the property on their return after the war. They sold it to us in 1976. We are fortunate to have been given a collection of photographs taken by W. H. Dupe, the family butler, around the end of the nineteenth century. These provide a fascinating snapshot of the village community of the time – including the carriage and stable staff, housekeeper, school children, gardeners and other villagers. Framed versions now hang in our visitor centre. The question remains over the construction date of the bathing pond, the name given to the lake that was here when we arrived. Supplied by a canal fed from one of the northernmost fish ponds, it is situated immediately to the east of the churchyard and the site of the two old manor houses. We do not know who built them or when.

God is not a great gardener. We arrived after a long period in which the environment had determined its own destiny. There may be those who wish we had left well alone. We will leave an inheritance, about which others will make a judgement. We can only leave our view, for the record, that given the choice, we would do it all over again.

CHAPTER 5

A KEEN GARDENER

I remember where it all began. In my father's absence during the war, we lived with my grandparents in the Uplands district of Swansea. The tiny lawn was a home to daisies, and my grandfather had a lever on a long handle, which, if inserted under the daisy leaves, facilitated the plant's removal. Later, in the war, at the age of nine, I went to a prep school, Broughton Hall in Staffordshire. The headmaster, Kenneth Thompson, gave every new boy a square of mud and a packet of Virginia Stock seeds. I spread mine carefully. Six weeks later I had a sea of colour, and I was hooked. It was these experiences that encouraged me, after my parents bought a house with a two-acre garden after the war, into gardening. I organised two friends – David Davies and Peter Bevan – into a team called Hesdavan, which I hired to my father for five shillings an hour to assist with the necessary tidying.

My political career began first fighting Labour-held seats, then I won a Conservative seat that was promptly listed for dissolution. Most of our early married life was therefore spent renting other people's houses and gardens. No roots were put down until 1976, when we bought our present home in Thenford – and we knew that this was the fulfilment of a dream.

It was ideal for us: a classic example of eighteenth-century architecture. The estate had shrunk to 440 acres of working farmland, with a small area of domestic garden. There were woodlands, buildings and several cottages. Anne and I bought the house and its immediate surrounding garden. There was a difficult moment before the contract was signed. Martin Summers, the son of the owner, Sir Spencer Summers, whose parliamentary career overlapped with my first four years in the House of Commons, explained that his mother was deeply upset at the loss of woodland around her house, which stood within the estate and where she proposed to move. They would quite understand if we did not wish to conclude the deal, but Lady Summers wanted to keep the twenty-five acres involved. Good sense prevailed. She retained the land, granting us the right to acquire it when she left or died. There was a downside to this: the land included a two-acre lake, which was an important part of the view from our house. I was able to reassure my wife that we would create a new lake by damming the stream below our house. This we duly did.

By the time we moved in in 1976, as we listened to Red Rum come second in the Grand National, I was deeply involved in the shadow Cabinet which left me little time for anything but the immediate garden. We did, however, create a fence around two acres and fulfilled another lifetime obsession by filling it with swans, geese, duck and pheasant. Webbed feet and horticulture do not mix, in my experience; they tread down the pond margins. But a worse problem was the Reeves's pheasant, who would lie in wait for me before attacking me with the vicious spurs on the back of his legs.

Some lasting memories survive. We began work on the area close to the house soon after our arrival. Not far from our front door lay several piles of rubbish – old pots, broken bottles and an accumulation of household waste from times past. We knew that when this was cleared away, there would be a somewhat bleak, empty area.

We needed professional help, and secured the services of Lanning Roper, the distinguished garden columnist at the *Sunday Times*. My first request in 1978 met with a brisk refusal: 'I am sorry but I am too busy. Ring me in a year's time.' To the day, I did just that and thus began a most happy relationship. Lanning's extensive interests in music and the arts created a great bond with my wife, Anne. I had much to learn. My knowledge of trees and plants was minimal, best illustrated by my belief that a hornbeam was something they danced in the Georgian navy. I made many efforts to urge him on but then heeded his oft-repeated advice about the patience required by gardeners. Very sadly, Lanning was not in good health and he died in 1983.

In retrospect, the most significant event was an introduction by Charlie Shelburne, now the Marquis of Lansdowne, to Sir Harold Hillier. Harold was one of the great nurserymen of the twentieth century and founded the Hillier Arboretum in Hampshire. He responded to our request to discover what would grow best in our soil by spending a couple of days at Thenford. He produced a voluminous list of hundreds of suitable trees and shrubs. Perhaps characteristic of my impetuosity, which Lanning so deplored, I bought the lot.

When we moved in, the two-acre walled garden had been turned over to grass and used to rear lambs, thus protecting them from the ever-present foxes. We returned it to its original pattern of paths on the advice of Quinlan Terry, the well-known architect. The next step was to arrange the consignment from Hillier in lines in the walled garden, until we had time to clear and plant the derelict woodland.

At this point, we had not realised that Harold Hillier had sold us the basis of a collection. Instead of the ordinary *Fagus sylvatica* – the common European beech – we had seven or eight beeches from different parts of the world. This was also true of dozens of genera, including species and hybrids. The whole saga nearly ended in disaster: faithfully carrying out instructions to line out the new arrivals in the walled garden, the gardener had done just that, but the new arrivals were still in their pots! Just in time, drooping branches and piles of leaves on the ground alerted us to the impending crisis.

Quinlan Terry also solved a problem with our children. They had grown up in Devon with a wonderful beach at the bottom of the garden, then moved to a house near Henley where we had built a nice swimming pool – but now they were at Thenford with no water at all. Quinlan designed a new pool, alongside a spacious pool house in superb Palladian style. Our children forgave us!

Lanning Roper's death left a serious gap, but we were fortunate enough to persuade Roy Lancaster, then director of Sir Harold Hillier Gardens, to fill it. Roy combined many talents: an encyclopaedic knowledge of plants, a remarkable familiarity with their places of origin and a boundless energy and enthusiasm. We had begun the process of restoring the woodland, which included the damming of a stream to create six small ponds down the eastern side of the woodland horseshoe that surrounded the house. The collection in the walled garden was slowly transferred to their permanent sites.

The biggest project was to devote some two acres to plants that had their origins in China. Roy had travelled there extensively and could recount in detail the origins of the plants in the wild. In 1986, the two of us laid out the area, which was predictably called Chinatown. Until this point, we had always mixed plants without any reference to their geographical origins, which still remains our policy. The experience of working with Roy over the years had given me the confidence and at least the basic knowledge to take over the design myself. There was no masterplan. Each area, as it became available, was treated as an individual room. The concept was well illustrated at Hidcote in the Cotswolds.

In 1997, we embarked upon some exciting new ventures. Firstly, George Carter redesigned the walled garden. He did a remarkable job and transformed the interior, with its new paths, into a sleek, formal garden. All the somewhat scruffy glasshouses were replaced by Alitex greenhouses, there is a magnificent water sculpture by William Pye and the garden is planted out in a series of lawns and flower beds. A large aviary offers an intimate relationship with a selection of parakeets, chosen and supplied by the president of the Parrot Society, Les Rance, a local bird breeder.

About ten years after we moved into Thenford, Martin Summers told me that his mother was now content to let us have the final twenty-five acres, which included the site of the old Manor House, the fish ponds and the canal built to service the original lake. Most of the area was a jungle. The fish ponds were just indentations, totally silted up and overgrown. Their locations had to be verified with the aid of a map from 1851.

John Atkinson – a local contractor who was a master with earth-moving equipment and had an infinite capacity to take care – was working at Stowe at the time and we were fortunate enough to persuade him to join us, bringing his heavy excavation equipment with him. He methodically excavated the fish ponds, restoring them to their Victorian design, which was not quite the same as their original structure. Originally, the fish ponds would have been rectangular in shape and, in our case, five in total. The Victorians had chopped the ends off two of ours in order to create islands. The Royal

Environmental Commission, having inspected ours, said that the Victorians had ruined their authenticity and that there were much better examples in Northamptonshire. They advised us to restore the Victorian legacy. This meant accepting the island concept, and we invited a local architect, Robert Adams, to design three bridges to allow access to the islands. The colour of the bridges – red, blue and green – came to identify the islands themselves.

In 2016, my wife and I recorded these remarkable experiences in our book *Thenford: The Creation of an English Garden*, published by Head of Zeus. We made many mistakes. Indeed, we were so aware of this, that we tried to persuade the publishers to accept the title 'Mistake by Mistake: The Creation of an English Garden'. We were told that no book with such a depressing title would sell. We gave in – although both of us still think we should have stood firm. Every gardener would have recognised the reality implied in that proposed title.

The book covers the development of the walled garden, a sculpture garden, a trough garden, a fountain garden and a 100-metre herbaceous double border outside the south-facing wall of the walled garden. Another stream was dammed to create a water garden, headed by a rill with nine rectangular ponds. The idea for this was inspired by a photograph of a rill in Canada. We showed the photo to George Carter and asked him to design one for us. We had chosen George, who did so much of the design work, after seeing an exhibit made by him at the Chelsea Flower Show. It consisted of an Etruscan boar on a plinth at the head of a long rectangular sheet of water, bordered by pleached lime trees. We had two sculptures that we wanted to see reflected in mirror pools in the walled garden and we thought George would be the person to achieve this for us.

Gardens are living entities. There have been three significant changes since we published our book. We have now driven a path through the middle of the Chinese area that Roy Lancaster helped to design in 1986, to open up two new vistas along that path. The first lake we excavated could only be approached by a grassy path to its southern edge. Its western and northern edges were enclosed by pasture for sheep and occasionally bullocks, while the east side was planted in a way that rapidly became impassable. We have now cleared a lakeside path along the eastern edge, using trees and shrubs chosen for their autumn colours. They are *Cornus* 'Midwinter Fire', *Liquidambar* and *Nyssa*. Both these changes are too recent to produce exciting photographs but will, one day, do just that.

As Lanning Roper kept telling me – patience is a virtue!

The third big change brought results almost overnight. Over twenty years ago, our head gardener Darren Webster pointed out the potential of the south-facing wall bordering the field outside the walled garden. With Beech Alley at Hidcote as our inspiration, we had created a five-metre-wide herbaceous border, divided into four subsections and demarcated by yew buttresses topped with round balls. A wide grass strip and a beech hedge to match the wall completed the design.

One evening in September 2018, it struck me that we should create a second border by moving the beech hedge five metres out into the field. I argued that we should transplant the existing twelve-foot hedge, but I was persuaded that it would be wiser to start with saplings, which would not require heavy staking. The project was ready for planting by the following spring and success was underpinned by generous additions of horse manure. The original borders were divided into hot and cool colours and the new borders were zigzagged to locate hot opposite cool and cool opposite hot. It had taken years to grow the pom-pom balls on the yew buttresses of the original border. To speed up the progress for the new border, we bought nine-foot yew cones, each with a central stem. We then pruned these to the approximate shape of the original and within a year or two, we had the desired effect. Two marble urns on matching columns were found in the *marché aux puces* in Paris. At the southern end of the new borders, we planted a yew circle. To the east side, a gate designed by Jim Horrobin led to the new entrance to the walled garden. We commissioned a matching gate from Jim for the southern end of the borders and were fortunate to purchase a magnificent pair of Coade stone urns on their own bases from Simon Phillips, Britain's leading antique dealer.

We had a problem with the land level, which slopes significantly. George Carter designed an attractive solution in the form of a pair of double steps, leading left and right off a brick platform, on which we placed a Haddonstone bench of classical design. A semi-circular yew hedge hid the back of the bench and enclosed a magnificent *Magnolia* 'Star Wars' tree and a bronze sculpture by Lucy Kinsella named 'Rolling Horse'. We took the opportunity to design and plant the surrounding area as an extension of the original orchard.

We had not planned to create a specific type of garden. It was uncharted territory, but by the time I was free of government responsibility, it became clear to us that what had emerged would likely be of public interest.

So, a fundamental question emerged: should we open the garden to the public? Inevitably there are tensions associated with opening one's garden; it is rather like living over the shop. Many questions need to be answered first. Where does home life end and commercial activity begin? What priority should be given to tidiness for the benefit of the public at the expense of the detail of the collection?

How can one ever be sure that one has complied with a duty of care for visitors?

There are serious advantages too – not just the cash flow that opening would create for us, but the income it would generate for the local people who work to make it possible in the visitor centre and elsewhere.

We began by introducing a practice associated with big estates in the eighteenth century – that of allowing access to our fellow villagers. This has material benefits beyond the enjoyment they derive. There is a sense of shared ownership and community that can act as a serious deterrent to trespassers.

We never envisaged that this would be the logical conclusion of the journey we began nearly fifty years ago, but there is no turning back. We decided to open and we hope our visitors enjoy the garden and arboretum as much as we do. Our visitors are most appreciative and many bring specialist knowledge of great interest.

Equally unpredictable has been the march of technology. I still have the loose-leaf folders and original card index system in which we recorded the collection. Our trees and shrubs have to be labelled; we purchased the first engraved labels, but I soon bought our own engraving machine and did it myself. It was crude in the extreme, requiring a tray of letters that had to be screwed into racks, which enabled a lever to guide a drill onto blank plates. Now our 'gravograph' computer-controlled drill does it all for me. The card index has long been replaced by a computer catalogue, within which we can match pictures of the individual plants themselves. The camera in my mobile phone produces pictures of a quality better than those I used to take with more serious equipment and then downloads them automatically. In addition to all this, we now register our plants through a geostationary satellite process that can locate any item in the collection to the nearest square metre. Our website provides the public with an increasing range of detail about the arboretum while simultaneously acting as the booking and cash collection system for public open days. Virtual tours for online visitors in any part of the world are just around the corner.

We have recently converted redundant farm buildings to the north of the village into residential accommodation and a new visitor centre, which can cater comfortably for over a hundred people. In recognition of Haymarket's wider horticultural activities and in celebration of the company's relationship with Germany's giant horticultural exhibition, IPM Essen, the Lord Mayor of Essen donated and planted an eighteen-foot *Acer rubrum* 'Redpointe' at the gateway.

The arboretum is now a major habitat and source of food for wildlife. We have a record of the eighty different species of birds seen here and we were fortunate to have two botanists as tenants, who presented us with a list of insects they have recorded. Property conversions required bat surveys, providing an informed record of which species live here. We have introduced hedgehog hotels, which were given to us as presents.

More controversial is our squirrel policy. We have zero tolerance of them. The moment of decision came when I was informed that out of forty nesting boxes scattered around the trees and buildings, thirty-eight had been attacked by grey squirrels. This and the all too evident damage they do to trees, often rare species, led to the instruction to cull. Within six months, 400 were shot over the seventy acres. By the beginning of each breeding season, there are very few left. However, about 150 young ones come from neighbouring farms every year, demonstrating the need to maintain the policy. Despite our control over squirrels, we see fewer different bird species today, which reflects the environmental pressures adversely affecting birds.

There had been no evidence of human activity in the arboretum since the 1920s, when one of the Severne family, the previous owners of the estate, told us that his father had given him a bundle of ash saplings and told him to plant them nine yards apart. Apart from that, no account or evidence exists since the records of Michael Woodhull's book *Revenue from Woodland* in the late eighteenth century. Where trees died or fell, they remained. The invasive birch, thorn and brambles became part of the covert for the pheasants in a small family shoot. A leaking cesspit did little for the environment.

My wife is a keen sculpture collector and, assisted by Robert Adams, designed a sculpture garden. Here there are significant works by Lynn Chadwick, Michael Ayrton, Elisabeth Frink, Ronald Rae and Philip Jackson, among others. But the most conspicuous sculpture – the one that all the visitors comment upon – is a bust of Vladimir Lenin. This is a monumental work of Russian art. A British man in Latvia after the collapse of the Soviet Union in 1991 spotted this massive statue of the man who had led Russia from 1917 to 1924 lying on the ground. It had been removed from outside what we were told was a KGB building. The man asked some officials what was going to happen to it, whether it was for sale and, if so, how much they wanted for it?

'Hold on!' he said when he received a positive answer. He picked up his phone and rang a friend who ran Summers Place Auctions in Sussex.

'I'm in Latvia, and there's this bust of Lenin,' he said. 'It's quite big and they want to get rid of it. How much should I pay?'

The answer came back: 'What's it made of?'

'Bronze.'

'How heavy is it?'

'About ten tonnes.'

'I'll ring you back.'

Moments later the friend did, saying, 'I've checked the scrap value – offer them £10,000.'

When the statue came up for sale in an auction of garden statuary in Sussex, we bought it for £20,000. Heaven knows what a Russian oligarch might have paid. It was only years later that a visitor to a Thenford open day alerted us to the fact that he was in touch with Dzintra Regina Janson, who had sculpted it as a young artist soon after graduating from the Latvian Academy of Arts. We established contact and she was able to send us a picture of the statue's unveiling ceremony. The bust was placed on a substantial plinth outside what is now the district council building in the town of Preiļi. The ceremony, which took place 4 November 1987, was presided over by Anatolijs Gorbunovs, Secretary of the Central Committee of the Communist Party of Latvia, who went on to become Deputy Prime Minister in the Latvian Way Party after Latvia became a parliamentary democracy.

The story has an unhappy ending. After Latvia gained independence from the Soviet Union in 1991, Russian sculptures there were torn down and disposed of – in contrast to neighbouring Lithuania, where they were collected and preserved. Dzintra was treated as a traitor and for the rest of her life was only able to get work designing tombstones.

In researching the background of the sculpture, we had reason to make an enquiry of the British Embassy in Latvia. We learned that our ambassador, Paul Brummell, was planning a visit to Preiļi, and he was able to add to the information we had after a few local conversations.

The building behind the sculpture was erected on a greenfield site in 1961 to house the local government office. A standing sculpture of Lenin was created in 1964, but it was of inferior quality and by the mid-1980s, a decision was taken to replace it for the celebration of the seventieth anniversary of the October Revolution in 1987. The architects responsible were Juris Ārgalis and Peteris Birulis.

When the Berlin Wall came down, a group of local people led by Edgars Mukans, a local PE teacher and leader of the local branch of the People's Front, demolished the monument in 1991. There had been some subsequent expressions of concern at the loss of so outstanding an example of cultural history.

The trough garden was another example of how unpredictable new ventures can be. In the 1980s, we were staying with friends in Cornwall, Richard and Mary Carew-Pole, who lived in a beautiful house, Antony. In their garden I saw a wisteria growing in a trough – one of those troughs they used in medieval England to provide water for the cattle. I had thought that it was a lovely idea, but we had never done anything about it until we were at the Hampton Court Flower Show about twenty years ago, when we discovered a young dealer with a dozen troughs.

Anne said to me, 'For God's sake, get on with it – you've been banging on about it for years!' So, we bought seven; eighteen months later, we had collected the forty troughs that now make up our trough garden. It is now an alpine garden – we do not know of another and we believe it to be unique. A year or so ago, we went back to Antony and told Richard and Mary about our project and its origins. 'A wisteria in a trough?' they said. 'We don't have anything like that.' I said, 'Of course you do! Forty years ago, I saw it.' So, we went back to see my dream trough. There it was and there, planted about ten feet behind it, was the wisteria. My dream had been misconceived. But the reality justifies the mistake!

The last curiosity, the gift of collections, was one which we could never have foreseen. Over decades, we had gradually built up our own collections – 300 viburnums, 300 magnolias and 350 oak trees. The unexpected development arose from the wish of enthusiasts to share or, more usually, dispose of collections for which they wanted a new home. My first such experience came during a visit to a garden centre in Somerset, where I saw pots of box plants. 'What are those?' I said. The owner explained that they had been left there by the collector, who had expressed little recent interest. We got on the telephone and I said, 'Yes, I'll take them.'

By far the biggest of our collections is the national collection of snowdrops. Carolyn Elwes of Colesbourne encouraged us to start collecting in the early days after we came to live at Thenford in the 1970s. We began in a small way, adding a dozen or so each year. By 2013, we had recruited Emma Thick, a *Galanthus* enthusiast, to our garden staff and the collection had grown to about 300. Out of the blue, David and Margaret MacLennan, keen gardeners and owners of one of the UK's largest snowdrop collections, phoned and asked if we would be interested in joining the list of public gardens to which they distributed surplus bulbs from their collection every year. Eight or ten years later, they told us they were reviewing their collection, which by then had been awarded scientific status, and that they would like to duplicate it with us. Over the next year or so, they would transfer bulbs from their collection so that we would have a replica. Around 300 pots arrived in August 2023, taking our total number of species to 900. Another large gift came in 2024 and there are more to come.

That year, I also received a message from Tom Mitchell, who I had first met when he transferred his collection of epimediums to us. He had moved to Europe due to his wife's employment with the

European Medical Agency, which had left the UK as a consequence of Brexit.

He was an authority on snowdrops and had visited the natural environment of virtually every known species. He had also built up his own collection, numbering hundreds of varieties, which were housed at his mother's house. His mother's house was now up for sale and he wanted to find a place for his bulb collection. It consisted largely of snowdrops, but there were also some *Narcissi*. Would we like them? I could not believe my luck. Here, at last, was a real benefit from Brexit, and I grabbed it. Whether my gratification makes up for the loss of jobs and the loss of the UK's influence internationally is another matter, which I shall come to later. We collected some ninety trays, containing 2,000 pots, before their house was sold in May 2024.

Our collection now numbers 1,200 varieties and we are delighted that it has been recognised as a national collection by Plant Heritage, the world's leading garden plant conservation and research charity.

In researching this chapter, I came across a speech I was proud to make as vice-president of the Royal Horticultural Society on the occasion of the 2017 Chelsea Flower Show. The society enjoys world renown, together with Kew, Edinburgh and the many great parks and gardens that make up the British horticultural inheritance. I was struck by the simple thought that what we had been doing at Thenford in our small way had been done before, countless times over many generations, by private citizens and public initiatives. I spoke of how agriculture and horticulture were developed side by side, while a consequence of the Industrial Revolution had brought the concept of gardening to the ever-expanding middle classes, as well as the public realm:

> The need to protect commons enjoyed public support – Hampstead Heath, Clapham and Wimbledon remain today. William Pitt, in 1808, is credited with the description of the parks as the lungs of London. In 1842, more London public parks were added: Victoria Park in Hackney, Battersea Park and Finsbury Park. The Public Health Act of 1875 introduced loans to acquire land for recreation. You can walk the three miles from Parliament to Olympia through parks that are part of London's 1,700.
>
> Ebenezer Howard, post-1898, ensured horticulture was central to the garden city movement and planning of the new towns. Professor [Patrick] Abercrombie's wartime work anticipated the reconstruction that peace would enable. I have referred frequently to the changes as they affected London, but similar changes were to be found throughout the United Kingdom's towns and cities. Nearly one fifth of the land in our towns and cities are parks and gardens. There is nothing new in politics. The garden festivals of 1979 mirrored earlier initiatives. It is a shame the idea disappeared. The RHS Bridgewater Garden project in Salford, Greater Manchester, is a glowing example of imaginative urban renewal.

In that speech, I argued that Britain is truly a nation of gardeners. But I stressed that it goes much beyond public and private estates, beyond flats with balconies and window boxes:

> In whichever form, gardens are expressions of ourselves. They are statements of pride and responsibility. They are definable spaces, often requiring easily acquired skills. They provide talking points for communication with neighbours. They impose a year-round discipline. They provide a therapeutic escape from daily pressures.
>
> Since 1964, the RHS's Britain in Bloom competitions have

> involved different communities across the UK creating greener and more beautiful surroundings and a growing sense of community pride. Over 200 communities participate in the RHS's 'It's your neighbourhood', a community gardening project helping people to make lasting improvements to their local environment, whether that's the street they live in or a small patch of communal land. And their latest campaign, Greening Grey Britain, is doing much to encourage others to turn paved over gardens and derelict land into beautiful green spaces.

My efforts to achieve urban regeneration had some occasional crossover with gardening. In 1981, it was my privilege to help with the launch of Groundwork in St Helens, Liverpool. Groundwork had plans for allotments in Speke, a suburb of Liverpool, as part of their programme of over 2,500 projects to help urban communities make better use of their environment.

In my address to the RHS, I named some of the local organisations that provide access to gardens – from the Scotswood Natural Community Garden in Newcastle to OrganicLea in London's East End. All these organisations recognise the creative and therapeutic capacity of horticulture to stimulate interest, energy and commitment for countless of our less privileged citizens. There is a huge opportunity here, but it is a journey half completed. It is an example of how our structure of government relies too much on the functional monopoly of Whitehall departments. For example, when it comes to tackling the problem of deprived urban communities, horticulture is sponsored by the Department for Environment, Food and Rural Affairs; the Home Office deals with drugs and crime; the Department of Health and Social Care deals with mental health; the Department for Communities and Local Government deals with local government matters; and the Department for Work and Pensions with unemployment.

There are two gaps here. First, insufficient attention is given to the challenge of living in a deprived community as a problem in the first instance. Second, little attempt is made to involve the local people themselves in plans to improve their lives and livelihoods.

I ended my RHS lecture by expressing this sentiment:

> We know the pleasure we get from gardening. We also know the therapeutic sense of purpose and personal satisfaction and the pride of achievement we derive. If it does so much to enrich our lives, imagine what it could do for others.

It has certainly done so much for mine.

PART II

REFLECTIONS

CHAPTER 6

REGENERATION: DID IT WORK?

There is little difficulty in finding agreement on what constitutes good urban policy. Typically, better housing, improved transport, the clearing out of dereliction and neglect, and the creation of infrastructure to encourage the creation of jobs feature high on any list – not to mention more school places in more modern facilities and an improved capacity for healthcare at all levels, from GP practices to general hospitals. However, where the difficulty, and controversy starts is when you ask how these necessary improvements can be made in practice. My belief has always been that the answer lies in the public sector working closely with private enterprise. I came into politics from a commercial background and experienced the rocky journey that started with three of us crammed in a small office and ended with my signing off wages bills for several hundred people every month. No one should underestimate the discipline of that monthly payroll.

Throughout my career, I have been involved in several different types of regeneration efforts. Initially, there was a steady shift from the private to the public sector following the Second World War. The process of change, however, that began in the 1980s and 1990s was of a different scale and of a more enduring character. It started a revolution in thinking that had profound and lasting consequences for our economy. There were many different aspects, but one theme ran through them all: privatisation. Despite what some critics said, putting assets into the hands of the private sector was always a means to an end, not an end in itself. Each case required careful examination to ensure the proposed structure would deliver a wider spread of wealth in a more competitive environment. Judged against the above criteria, it can be argued that water privatisation failed both of these tests, for example.

With decades of personal experience of urban regeneration, I look back at what worked and why. But these lessons do not apply only to urban deprivation; they apply to cooperation between all the state institutions and the private sector too. I can claim to have privatised more aspects of the public sector than any other minister. I will plead guilty to the charge that I was too doctrinal in some decisions I took while I was in office, but I will always argue from my first principle, which is that there are inherent characteristics within the private sector that have advantages over the public sector.

One other question has been forced upon me when confronting complex situations and that is to ask, 'Who is in charge?' That question is much easier to answer in the private sector, with its managerial pyramid, profit centres and much simpler – but stricter – disciplines. By contrast, the public sector has a complexity of contradictions, usually associated with too many hands on the tiller as a result of overlapping responsibilities, scarcely relevant committees and independent quangos. I faced all this in 1981 when trying to identify the causes of the riots in Liverpool. It rapidly emerged that no one was in overall charge. Thus began my long journey in support of directly elected mayors and devolved authorities and to make it clear that they are accountable for their efforts to solve the knottiest of problems.

URBAN DEVELOPMENT CORPORATIONS

The Urban Development Corporation concept owed its origins to the creation of the new towns, which were an imaginative response to the slum clearance needed and the huge demand for housing after the Second World War. Each new town had its own chairman, commission, planning powers and resources for the task. I thought this could be replicated on a smaller scale.

During my first time at the Department for the Environment in the early 1970s, I was looking for a solution to untangle the piecemeal development of London's South Bank, which was being regenerated with absolutely no coherence. The result was, and remains, a hotchpotch of unrelated and often ugly construction. I asked officials to prepare plans for a body that had essentially the same planning and other powers as the commissions and which would be appropriate to that part of London.

Before I could properly respond to their proposal, I was moved to be Minister for Aerospace and Shipping. (I have often wondered if rumours of my intentions were in part responsible for my being promoted.) In 1979, when the Conservatives returned to government, I was faced with some 6,000 acres of largely derelict land in east London and I asked officials to dig out the earlier papers. I realised the potential to use the concept of an Urban Development Corporation for large-scale urban regeneration.

The idea was, however, to prove an unpopular one. Officials in my department objected on the grounds that it rode roughshod over the responsibilities of local government. Geoffrey Howe, now Chancellor, objected on the grounds that it would require additional public spending and that we should rely on tax incentives to create a more limited enterprise zone. Keith Joseph, the then keeper of the party's Conservative right-wing conscience, objected on the grounds that this was another example of the interventionalism we had been elected to stop and that the market should be left to deal with the problem. Margaret Thatcher summoned the three of us to No. 10 to settle the matter.

How on earth could I win the argument against two of the most powerful members of the government? Fortunately, before making my case to the Prime Minister, I had consulted Reg Prentice, the Conservative member for Daventry but previously the Labour MP for East Ham North. His solution was simple: 'Tell the PM the councillors are all communists down there.' It worked. Thatcher supported my view that, while incentives were valuable, the private sector would not clear the detritus of yesteryear while there were cheaper options available to them to build on greenfield sites. In addition, no serious investor would be interested in working on a project with an inhospitable climate for their staff.

GARDEN FESTIVALS

Garden festivals were a proven concept developed in Europe to restore derelict, often war-damaged sites. The concept was simple: use public money to clean up these sites and then organise a garden festival to demonstrate their viability and availability. Thus, they became attractive to private developers once the festival concluded. The first example in the UK opened on the banks of the Mersey in 1984 and attracted over 3 million visitors. There was considerable scepticism as the work proceeded. 'Give us jobs, not trees,' was the cry on the streets.

However, the result was a site so popular that there was public resistance to moving forward with the original purpose of the exercise – namely, to create jobs, housing and commercial development. Consequently, it took far too long for that development to take place. A second festival took place in Stoke-on-Trent in 1986 followed by three more at two-year intervals in Glasgow, Gateshead and Ebbw Vale. There remain many places with urban squalor that could be transformed in this way.

Just before the 2024 election, I was invited by Lord Johnson, a minister in the Welsh office, to accompany him on a visit to Port Talbot where the local steelworks were facing closure. The journey would take me past the Ebbw Vale garden festival site, and I decided to visit it as part of the research for this book. The election ended up preventing such a ministerial visit, so my detour never took place. However, in the final days of preparing this text, I attended the funeral of Ruth Dashwood, a well-known and much-respected local lady where, at the reception that followed, there occurred a coincidence that is almost beyond belief.

I was approached by Celia Warde-Aldam who, under her maiden name Celia Cleverden, had completed a thesis as part of an honours degree course at Bath University, which earned her a second-class award, on the subject of the five garden festivals. Her thesis was finished in June 1989, which precluded any possibility that she could have summarised the development consequences, particularly as two of the festivals had not yet taken place. But for me, it was interesting as a lesson on how history is written. She had, of course, explored the original concept within which they had been established in Europe. They had been promoted to serve the interests of the horticultural industry and its products and to give an opportunity for innovative design in the area of public green space. She referred to a paper that had been prepared in my department as a result of an initiative from the Joint Council for Landscape Industries. As a result of this research, she became aware of the original purpose of the festivals and thus was able to make judgements about the consequences. In her note to me accompanying the thesis, she warned that it was not very flattering! She had conducted detailed conversations with the Liverpool local authority, which had fed into her assessment. She could not have known my side of the story, which was not published until a year later.

I had first heard of these festivals from a parliamentary colleague, Philip Goodhart, MP for Beckenham, in the months preceding the 1979 general election. I knew nothing of the promotional organisation of the horticultural industry. He simply told me of this German idea to reclaim bombed sites for regeneration by organising garden festivals on them as a short-term process that would persuade the private sector to then develop there.

I had commandeered this land from one of the local authorities, who had had their own ideas as to what to do about it. They were furious that I had taken the toy from their pram. Officials organised a competition to choose a site for an international garden festival. Stoke-on-Trent submitted the better proposal, but I had special responsibility for Liverpool and decided that they should have a second festival two years after the first. At that stage, there was much cynicism and open hostility. I can more than understand the comments Celia would have received from her consultation. But the outcome was quite different. Such was the success of the festival that public opinion demanded that the rejuvenated park be maintained as a public facility. It was years, during which the maintenance was quite inadequate, before the original concept could be activated.

Stoke-on-Trent hosted the second festival from May to October 1986. It was opened by Queen Elizabeth II and located on a site formerly occupied by the Shelton Bar steelworks. After its closure, parts of the garden planting were preserved as public spaces, known as Festival Park, while most of the development was driven by St. Modwen Properties. A wide variety of uses of the site have emerged, with one common characteristic: none of them could have been predicted as the concept developed. Today, a retail park, a wide range of offices and sporting facilities, a marina for narrow boats and a four-star hotel are located there. It is reported that the cost of reclaiming the site amounted to £5 million and that the festival cost another £17 million to run.

The third in the series was based in Glasgow and was the only one to be based in Scotland. Under the leadership of the Scottish Development Agency, it occupied 120 acres of largely redundant dock land on the north bank of the River Clyde and was opened by Prince Charles and Princess Diana on 29 April 1988. It attracted over 4 million visitors, easily exceeding any of the other four. The agency then developed the site after its use, which included the small Festival Park, the Glasgow Science Centre and, close by, the headquarters of BBC Scotland and Scottish Television, together with other hotels and offices. This event, together with the European Capital of Culture Award in 1990, provided a welcome shop window for the city.

Gateshead was the fourth site chosen for a festival between May and October 1990 and attracted some three million visitors. In practice it was organised over four different sites, covering 200 acres formerly occupied by a gas works, a coal depot and a coking plant, which necessitated interconnections, including a ferry across the Tyne. It was reported to have cost £37 million to reclaim and redevelop the land, which later was used largely for housing.

Finally, the last site was on land used by former steel and tin works owned by British Steel in Ebbw Vale, South Wales, from May to October 1992. It attracted over 2 million visitors, a lower figure than the other four, which is easily explained by its relative remoteness when compared with them. Festival Park remains as a seventy-acre legacy, with a lake and owl sanctuary. The development of housing and a retail park was only partially successful, as the latter fell into disuse and is currently being reconfigured as industrial units.

There will be those who point to the costs involved in the process and question the use of public money for such a purpose. The question that they avoid is what would they have done with sites such as these? I am appalled by the thought that they would still be as they were all those years later. Equally, I would be the first to admit that it is not possible to predict what use the private sector will find for the reclaimed land. In that sense, it is a gamble based on reasonable but unpredictable consequences. Certainly, any renewal of such schemes should recognise that there are maintenance costs associated with the preservation of the garden features, which are likely to fall to the public purse. That may well be desirable in the overall rejuvenation of a locality, as a glance at the role of our many treasured public parks demonstrates, but that requires a decision and not just the hope that something will turn up as the gardens are left to deteriorate.

GROUNDWORK

During my time in Liverpool, I was invited to a meeting of officials in St Helens which led – after a hiccup or two – to the establishment of Groundwork, a charitable organisation set up to help communities help themselves in improving the environment in which they live. A group of public servants were looking for solutions to the all-too-familiar problems of squalor on the fringes of urban areas, where it was easy for fly-tippers to dump old mattresses, broken household appliances and other rubbish. The officials were talking of recruiting an army of volunteers to clean up the mess.

As Secretary of State for the Environment, I could only be totally enthused by the proposal. Here was a project to be run by volunteers, with no public expenditure implication! I set off for the meeting with a light step, but the reality was very different. Around a table with some twenty people, it rapidly transpired that they were not volunteers at all. They were being paid to carry out a particular function in the context of reclaiming the urban fringe. So, of course, there were executives, consultants, advisers and specialists, all in one way or another dependent on public expenditure for their livelihoods. The meeting came to an early and disappointing conclusion, which can be summarised as 'brilliant idea, rotten execution'. Nevertheless, I left them with a note of optimism: 'If you come back to me with a genuine volunteer concept, I will certainly be interested and will do my best to give you the necessary support.' Thankfully the lesson was learned and eventually proposals emerged which were much closer to what I had originally understood.

Although Groundwork was born on Merseyside, it relates widely to our whole country. It is no surprise to me that the Groundwork organisation has evolved into a significant national asset. Today the Federation of Groundwork Trusts is a national network of charities employing 1,300 people and generating £100 million a year in charitable funds to invest in local communities, the delivery of environmental enhancement, green skills and urban regeneration. This includes connecting people with nature on their doorstep, helping young people access green jobs and supporting communities to prepare for the impacts of extreme weather.

In a typical year, Groundwork is linked with more than 7,000 community groups, helping more than 10,000 young people and planting some 40,000 trees. All of the sites which Groundwork has worked on over the years are now valuable community assets – former colliery sites turned into natural country parks and redundant local authority land and buildings reborn as thriving community hubs. The original idea was simple and will be familiar to anyone who cares to glance at those areas that separate the urban from the rural landscape. There is often a rather grubby hinterland. There will be discarded bicycles, the odd pram or supermarket trolley, litter and a general feeling of neglect. The idea that was put to me was that volunteers should be encouraged to come together to reclaim this damaged and neglected environment and restore it to its pristine, natural condition.

STOCKBRIDGE VILLAGE

Cantril Farm Estate, halfway between the two civic centres of Knowsley and Huyton & Kirby, had been designed on the Radburn principle and consisted of 3,000 properties split equally between houses, maisonettes or walk-up and multi-storey flats. In addition, there were extensive areas of open space. The management of the estate was poor and the tenants had a deep mistrust of the council. Over 10 per cent of the properties were vacant, there was a huge backlog of day-to-day repairs, there was no structured capital replacement programme and the estate had become a dumping ground for homeless families who had no connection with the area and no real desire to live there. This was the slum that I first visited in 1981. By the time of the 1981 Toxteth riots, male unemployment was 49 per cent and youth unemployment 90 per cent. Decline had taken hold, with the police struggling and residents and businesses fleeing the area. Two thirds of its residents were in rent arrears and just 1 per cent had exercised their Right to Buy.

The then Labour leader of Knowsley Council, Jim Lloyd, was in despair and asked for my help. I agreed to do so with one condition: he would not object to any solution that I proposed because the private sector might be involved. He responded, 'We've tried everything else, I agree.'

During my initial visit, I identified three problems: the soulless design of the estate that was inimical to community development, the unbalanced social mix and types of tenure, and poor management.

Tom Baron, who I had persuaded to take a leave of absence from his managerial role with the builders Christian Salvesen to become my special adviser, came up with a plan, prescribing 'major surgery'. He worked with local colleagues, Vernon Jackson and Dave Coates, and three weeks later brought back two sides of A4 paper outlining their ideas.

The whole image had to be changed and the estate renamed. Stockbridge Village was to become a place where people would choose to live, rather than being forced to live there due to their economic circumstances. The estate was to be sold to Stockbridge Village Trust, a private limited company whose sole aim and objective was its regeneration. A dedicated team of officers would be based on the estate to establish a relationship of trust with the residents and to introduce excellent management practices. Community development required a robust day-to-day maintenance and capital replacement programme. The physical environment had to become more attractive to create a much more balanced pattern between owner and tenant.

As part of my attempt to create awareness and seek solutions to the unacceptable living conditions to be found in parts of our cities, I had invited the chairmen of thirty of the largest institutions in the city to join me in a bus tour of deprived areas of Liverpool. I knew of no precedent for this and at one stage it looked as though I was facing the humiliation of an empty bus. Every day I asked David Edmonds, my private secretary, about the responses. The news was not good, until one day he reported a phone call from an uninvited chairman. The question he asked was simple: 'I understand that the Secretary of State has invited some of my competitors to join him on a tour of Liverpool. Why have I not been invited?' The word had got around.

I was also particularly fortunate in that Tim Sainsbury, my parliamentary private secretary and effectively my right-hand man, knew Robin Leigh-Pemberton, then the chairman of the National Westminster Bank. We filled the bus and at the end of the tour, I invited them all to tea in the Adelphi Hotel. They sat in rows, eyes cast down as I got up to speak.

'I don't want your money,' were the words that transformed the atmosphere; suddenly there were thirty smiling faces. I invited them to second a bright young manager to join a research team to seek reforms that might attract financial institutions to help.

We were able to establish a Financial Institutions Group (FIG), which produced an interesting report. Included on the tour were Clive Thornton, general manager of the Abbey National Building Society, and Owen Rout, general manager of Barclays Bank. I negotiated with them to create a public–private partnership to rescue the Cantril Farm Estate. The challenge was to persuade them that there was sufficient equity in the estate against which to secure their investment and to structure the new arrangements to ensure the project would be effectively managed. At no stage was it suggested that they should make anything other than a prudent, if unusual, investment.

These proposals were presented to a meeting of Knowsley Council in August 1982 and were agreed, subject to the assent of the residents. The public consultation meeting was held in December 1982 at Cantril High School and was attended by approximately 600 residents. They overwhelmingly agreed with the proposal, with only five votes being registered against.

Three undertakings secured this support. First, Tom Baron agreed to become part-time chairman of Stockbridge Village. Second, Lawrie Barratt agreed that his well-regarded house building company, Barratt Developments, would develop the adjacent land with low-cost housing, including rental homes. Third, I was able to commit substantial funds from my departmental budgets to improve the environment and rebuild some of the worst parts of the estate.

The Abbey National Building Society committed £3 million and Barclays £4 million, of which £2 million would be in the form of long-term mortgages. Knowsley Council would retain the balance of £3 million when the estate was sold to Stockbridge Village Trust on 6 April 1983, some ten months after the bus tour.

Many of the high-rise buildings containing flats and maisonettes were demolished, while almost 2,000 existing flats were redesigned to make them more accessible. Large sections of unused land were sold to Barratt Homes for new private house building. We built a new shopping and community centre, leisure facilities and a police station. We introduced new on-site management and eliminated the unpopular separation between pedestrians and vehicles.

Within a year, the backlog of repairs had been cleared. By 1985,

15 per cent of the estate was owner-occupied and residents began to move in. But the regeneration was not without hiccups: the Right to Buy sales were initially lower than expected and twenty-two of the new homes we built sold more slowly and at lower prices than expected.

With interest rates rising, the Department for the Environment ordered a review before committing further funds. A deal was struck in which more public sector cash and lower interest rate payments were agreed. By 1987, the project was back on track, helped by the government allowing capital funding to be committed over a longer period instead of the normal system of an annual grant. This greatly encouraged private sector investment.

In 2013, I returned to visit Stockbridge Village and saw how much had changed. Challenges remained but the transformation was dramatic and a shining example of what can be achieved in the most difficult of circumstances, where the public and private sector work together to rebuild trust.

Since then, the work to build further on this trust has continued – with Knowsley Council working with private and public sector partners to invest approximately £20 million to maintain and further transform the area. In recent years, the provision of a revamped neighbourhood shopping centre, more local sports facilities, better education provision and an extra modern housing scheme for those who need care has continued to carry out the promises made to the community.

This coincided with the implementation of the Community Energy Saving Programme in Stockbridge Village. The scheme targeted particular lower super output areas and properties there that had been built in a way which meant they suffered from poor insulation. The main way this was made more energy efficient was through external wall insulation, although additional measures such as loft insulation and boiler replacements were available to residents within the scheme.

British Gas contributed £7 million to the Community Energy Saving Programme. The project helped improve more than 1,000 properties and will eventually save over 350,000 tonnes of CO_2 emissions over twenty-five years.

This collective and continuing commitment to make Stockbridge a success is an instructive example as to what can be achieved through pragmatic partnership working – delivering positive social and economic outcomes for the inhabitants in an area which was all but 'written off' by many people. In recent years, the population has grown by 80 per cent to almost 11,000 and local employment and residents' skill levels have significantly increased at the same time. Home-ownership levels have steadily grown; only around 45 per cent of the area's 4,700 households now live in social housing.

I have no doubt that Tom Baron brought a decisiveness that owed more to his private sector experience than to the traditional public sector caution. His pragmatism and agility was instructive – it encouraged the trust and its staff to move more quickly and with more sensitivity to the benefit of residents.

There is no escape from the tensions that exist at the extremes of human deprivation. It is all too easy to dump problem families on difficult estates, but the consequence will be more anti-social behaviour and violence, ensuring that anyone who can do so moves away. The problems multiply and trying to manage such tenants is difficult in itself – never mind the consequent challenge of persuading socially aware tenants or owner occupiers to take their place. This whole process was in its early stages in 1983 when I was moved to become Secretary of State for Defence.

SOMERSET HOUSE

Standing on the Strand, Somerset House has an imposing facade. But nothing can prepare you for the magnificence and grandeur of the courtyard within. Designed by Sir William Chambers and built in the last quarter of the eighteenth century, it was intended to house government departments and learned societies such as the Royal Academy, the Royal Society and the Society of Antiquaries.

My first experience of it came about when I was approached by Nicholas Goodison on behalf of the Courtauld Institute with a proposal that part of their art collection should be moved to empty rooms in the north-west corner of Somerset House. This coincided with the wider concept suggested by Simon Jenkins, former editor of *The Times* and a noted commentator on and advocate for matters of heritage, that the whole site should be opened up for wider public use rather than used as government offices.

In the early 1990s, I was approached by Lord Rothschild, chairman of the Heritage Lottery Fund, to ask for my support in a negotiation he was conducting with Arthur Gilbert, a British-born philanthropist who had made a considerable fortune in real estate development in California, to persuade him that his collection of silver, micro-mosaics and gold boxes should be moved from its present location in the Los Angeles Museum of Art to London. A critical part of the negotiation was the home that could be on offer in London. Arthur had already been offered the Queen's House in Greenwich, but this had not provided sufficient inducement and Lord Rothschild wanted to up the prize. He was successful and his fund provided some $30 million to convert that part of Somerset House into a suitable museum. Sir Arthur was knighted in 1999 and his collection, worth a reputed $300 million, was opened in 2000 by the then Queen Mother. However, it did not provide the level of public attraction that was hoped for and, after 2008, it was moved to the Victoria & Albert Museum in South Kensington.

Being attracted by the idea, to enable all this to happen I persuaded James Mackay, then the Lord Chancellor, to move his officials elsewhere and free up the necessary space. I reached the same agreement with Norman Lamont, the Chancellor of the Exchequer, to move tax officials from a neighbouring block, but the Treasury fought like demons and delayed that part of the process. In the end, they gave in. I was pleased that Tim Sainsbury agreed to take charge of a trust to which the government would transfer its ownership and thus complete the conversion of Somerset House into a centre for culture and education. Tim assembled a formidable group of trustees, including Simon Jenkins and my old university friend, Jeremy Isaacs. He acquired a Portakabin, from which the project could be directed. Tim has outlined the problems he faced in his own autobiography, not least that it took him years to get the Treasury officials out and release the space for the cultural purposes intended.

Despite these early problems, the original vision has more than proved its validity. Somerset House is now a significant arts and community attraction. I have wrestled to find a way to expand on such a statement, but as there are over 600 organisations consisting of small business, creative enterprises, charities and studios, it is impossible to give a clear outline of what this actually means. The limited space available indicates that it provides shared facilities and accommodation for a creative, energetic and talented group of people. The scale and diversity must, of itself, stimulate a culture in which talent is inspired and flourishes. The central area now features a popular ice rink, financed by Jacob's and Tim's charitable foundations, and a magnificent central display of fountains provided by the Edmond J. Safra Foundation. Regular concerts attract some 3 million visitors a year. Tim and those who took on from him are entitled to a sense of great pride that they have achieved such a magnificent transformation of what had previously been just a car park for the tax officials of HMRC and a handful of lawyers.

THE DERELICT LAND GRANT

In 1990, I returned to the Department for the Environment for the third time. In the 1980s, I had devoted much of my time there to the reclamation of derelict land, much helped by the availability of a Derelict Land Grant mechanism that Peter Walker had introduced in the 1970s, in order to clear up coal and other mining tips and thus restore the countryside. By the 1980s, the job was complete and I was able to use the grant to clean up urban dereliction.

One example was the Wavertree Industrial Park in Liverpool, a substantial piece of contaminated land owned by Plesseys and British Rail. By that time, I had introduced new conditions for grants, which required the recipient to show an after use that led to additional expenditure by the private sector. This concept of 'gearing' became a common feature in my use of public funds and is at the heart of my proposals to re-energise the British economy today. The inclusion of the concept into City Challenge, the use of funds by the Millennium Commission and later the allocation of grants under the Regional Growth Fund not only generated huge sums of private investment but forged personal relationships between people from the public and the private sector, who would not normally work together.

CITY CHALLENGE

In the 1980s, my approach had been targeted largely at derelict land. In the 1990s, encouraged by the success of the Stockbridge

Village Trust, I turned to the more complex challenge of urban slums. There were large-scale opportunities for redevelopment, with the Urban Development Corporation (UDC) stretching over 6,000 acres and across five East End boroughs in London or, in a smaller example, 600 acres on the banks of the Mersey. Many of the projects were much smaller still, but the central theme was the same: a partnership between the public and private sector. Central government provided the grant funding to eliminate the historic contamination and make such sites competitive in a marketplace where private investment was an essential factor in the necessary rebalancing. I was careful to ensure that local interests were fully involved by appointing the local councillors to make up a minority on the boards of the UDCs.

I was aware that a far bigger and more ambitious challenge lay ahead. The country was covered by concentrations of acute poverty, high unemployment and low (if any) ambition, characterised by a vicious circle of decline. The transformation of Stockbridge Village Trust provided me with an example of how to achieve the conviction that something must be done.

On the back benches from 1986 to 1990, I had the opportunity to learn something of the way other countries set about satisfying the challenge and aspirations of local communities. My idea was called the 'City Challenge', whereby we would invite local authorities where such slums existed to design a plan involving the community itself and bring about change.

It attempted to bring a whole new approach to regeneration, moving beyond the reclamation of derelict land and towards the rejuvenation of destitute communities. Instead of initiatives arising from the functional departments of local authorities, whether they be housing or transport or social welfare, City Challenge rested on the concept of a whole community designed around a particular place, with the active support and participation of its residents. Urban authorities that contained areas of acute deprivation would be invited to make a bid for funding for a programme designed to transform a particular area. This element of competition was fundamental to its success. In order to succeed, local departmental officials had to put forward a plan that was comprehensive and strategic in its approach and show that it had been developed, and would be delivered, with the full support of the local community. Without the support of residents – the local chief constable or the head teacher of the local school – the plans would be meaningless. I have learned that you can't change a whole place unless you have the help of the whole place.

In 1991, I introduced a competitive system offering thirty local authorities the chance to receive £35 million in the form of £7 million a year for five years. Only ten would win – though ultimately we awarded eleven grants. A proposal put to City Challenge also had to include a discrete organisation to manage that proposal and its implementation, with a designated chairman. We had to be persuaded not only by what was proposed but that it would actually happen. In order to make the challenge work effectively, we had to provide a vehicle to coordinate several central government departments. We created local offices of government, staffed with officials from the relevant spending departments, under the chairmanship of a senior civil service, in order to ensure effective communication with the City Challenge team.

In total, some twenty authorities received over £750 million after the second round in 1992. Involving a competitive process to tackle social problems was a revolution in the use of public money. Despite the outcry, we held a second round. The losers went to the winners to find out how they had changed their approach to raise their standards. This was an important change because it made local authorities coordinate their approaches – and it made local authorities consult stakeholders in their area such as universities, public bodies, council tenants and the private sector before putting their schemes forward.

Distributing money in this manner did, of course, prove highly controversial. The press labelled it 'Tarzan's Tombola' and there were complaints that allocations would be unduly influenced by party-political considerations. As it turned out, all the winners except one in the first round were from Labour authorities. The exception was Conservative-controlled Stockton. The losers were offered the chance to bid in another round the following year, and one of the most gratifying outcomes of the competition was the speed with which first-year losers sought out the standards that had separated them from success in the first round. The competitive process forced the different strands of local government to work together.

One of the more intriguing questions is how such a successful scheme could vanish apparently without trace. Two colleagues, who were friends of mine, took my place in the Department for the Environment following my move to President of the Board of Trade – Michael Howard (now Lord Howard of Lympne) and John Gummer (now Lord Deben). During the 1990s, they replaced each other. The question should have been asked about the possibility of a third round of City Challenge, but neither of them has any memory of such a question being asked. My immediate suspicion is that the Treasury would have been only too happy to simply let the moment pass. This may be unfair, but I know these two colleagues so well that it is simply unthinkable that they would have told me anything but the truth.

City Challenge was not a straightforwardly localist policy. Instead, it was designed to get the best out of both levels of government. Whitehall set minimal conditions – it decided the localities, including residents and service providers, designed the solutions and allocated funding based on the merits of each project. It recognised that the problems faced by particular places could only be solved by local efforts but also that central government has a unique ability to catalyse and draw together local players to do so.

Without the competitive element, additional funding would simply have become a handout, incorporated as a marginal increase in existing budgets and channelled through the path of least resistance – existing local authority schemes. The competitive element motivated councillors and local authority officers to go that extra mile in putting together the broad social coalitions and thinking from first principles about how the money could be most effectively spent. It also catalysed public–private partnership by motivating local authorities to look for the projects with the highest potential to lever in private sector money. If you can go to a minister with evidence that their £35 million will secure £100 million of investment, you have a very strong bid. Challenge funding isn't just a different method of allocating money. It ensures that money is seen, and spent, in a totally different way.

DAVID CAMERON'S 100 ESTATES

This scheme was announced in January 2016. David Cameron explained his ambition in an article in the *Sunday Times*:

> So what's our plan? Today I am announcing that we will work with 100 housing estates in Britain, aiming to transform them. A

> new Advisory Panel will help galvanise our efforts and their first job will be to build a list of post-war estates across the country that are ripe for re-development, and work with up to 100,000 residents to put together regeneration plans. For some, this will simply mean knocking them down and starting again. For others, it might mean changes to layout, upgrading facilities and improving local road and transport links. The panel will also establish a set of binding guarantees for tenants and homeowners so that they are protected. To finance this, we'll establish a new £140 million fund that will pump-prime the planning process, temporary rehousing and early construction costs.

I was asked to chair the official team responsible for the initiative, but from the outset, I knew that such a limited sum would need imaginative administration to get anywhere near success.

The money available had to be used for the most effective leverage of additional funds from other sources. The private house builders, housing corporations and local authorities were obvious targets, but packages would have to be agreed in detail before any work could start. Micromanagement was the order of the day, and I personally presided over meetings to be sure what I agreed to deliver for the Prime Minister was based on realism – not just generalised good intentions. My confidence was not boosted when I returned from a holiday in the Caribbean to find that the department had distributed £34 million in order to use up its public expenditure budget and prevent the Treasury capturing the underspend at the end of the financial year. Any responsibility I had was removed when I was abruptly sacked by Theresa May in March 2017. To the best of my knowledge, the steam went out of the scheme with my departure and it withered on the vine.

USE OF THE PRIVATE SECTOR

When the draft Right to Buy legislation was first put to me after the 1979 election, I realised that Labour councils would apply the closest scrutiny in their attempt to lessen its effectiveness. One tiny flaw and a judicial review would seek it out. I would be held responsible by unhappy backbenchers who were anxious to see the legislation passed. I therefore instructed officials to take the draft to a prominent silk at the Bar with the order to imagine that he had been instructed by a council with limitless resources and the determination to block its success. Sure enough, the advice came back that such a fault had been found, together with the necessary advice on how to correct it. The legislation survived all scrutiny and was implemented after Norwich Council lost just such a test in court.

Later on, when I returned to government after John Major became Prime Minister in 1990, I was responsible for the replacement of the poll tax. This had been an ill-thought-out and clumsy attempt to replace the outdated rating system of raising local government revenue, which was largely driven by right-wing dogma. It had played no small part in the downfall of Margaret Thatcher. Officials pointed out that with the manpower constraints of the public sector, it would take a decade to complete the revaluation of all houses that would be necessary to introduce my new proposals. But I was well aware that local estate agents in the private sector knew the approximate value of every house in their area, and all we had to do was conscript this readily available resource to do the valuations for us. We built in safeguards for anyone who thought their property had been overvalued by giving them a right of appeal. Little use was ultimately made of this safeguard, and the abolition of the poll tax and its replacement by the council tax – effectively a more progressive rate – was a material contributor to the Conservative's 1992 election victory. We need similar thinking about the planning system, which is now a serious impediment to the UK's economic growth – upon which our prosperity depends.

ENTERPRISE AGENCIES

As a consequence of my involvement in the regeneration of Liverpool after the riots in 1981, I came across an initiative developed by Bill Humphrey of Pilkington, the giant, world-class glass manufacturing company. The company had had to lay off a significant number of its employees, and Bill set out to provide an advisory service, to help as many of them as possible into meaningful jobs. The psychological approach that he adopted made sense. He was not offering a ritzy consultancy in a wall-to-wall carpeted, glass-panelled office. He was located up a dingy staircase in a small room at the back of a Pilkington's building. He was prepared to do his best to advise his former fellow employees about anything he could that would help them find a job or create employment. Here was a gem of an idea that had a much wider application than simply in St Helens on Merseyside.

Unemployment was a major national issue at the time, and there was an urgent need for the sort of helping hand that Bill had developed. The spread of the concept of enterprise agencies was timely. A parliamentary answer by Secretary of State for Employment Norman Tebbit, in November 1983, set out the government's view of the progress that had been made here. The principal support took the form of tax deductibility for contributions donated to them by companies. A government grant of £75,000 was made available to the organisation Business in the Community to help establish and sponsor them, and they were encouraged to make use of the small business services and other government departments.

In 1992, on returning to the Department of Trade and Industry, I became deeply involved in an analysis of the UK's competitiveness. I did not believe that a few simple headlines about a number of new government initiatives added up to a coherent response to the question of our competitiveness. To even stand still compared with our European competitors, Germany and France, we had to perform at least as well as them in a very large range of factors that affect the process of wealth creation. Capturing such an agenda involved a more inclusive view of both government and private sector, uncharacteristic of public administration in this country. One facet of such a review was the need to provide advice for small and medium enterprises, particularly in exports.

In theory, the Chambers of Commerce should have been able to provide a first-class service of this sort to their members, as was commonplace on the continent, but the lack of expertise and experience of the staff in many chambers precluded this. There had been opportunities to strengthen the chambers, for example by incorporating them into the Manpower Services Commission, with all its resources, and thus increasing the potential strength that could have enabled the chambers to raise their game. But the chambers were not up to it and I decided, therefore, to implement a discrete organisation, Business Link. This new government-funded business advice service merged other government services, each of which distributed information of value to small companies. Ultimately, Business Link was among the first casualties of the austerity measures implemented by the Conservatives on their return to government in 2010. This was not a good decision and I set about reversing it when I became chairman of the Regional Growth Fund.

CHAPTER 7

PRIVATISATION

It is part of the folklore of non-interventionism that the alternative involves soft choices, subsidised failures and public ownership. But the reality is that it is impossible to point to any of the UK's competitor economies that do not intervene persistently and effectively in their own affairs – yet this is often dismissed as irrelevant to our own experience.

I can claim to have privatised more parts of the public sector than any other minister and to have abolished more quangos even than the leading advocate of non-intervention in the 1980s, Sir Keith Joseph. Looking back on it all some thirty or forty years later, the consequences of some of the decisions I took are there for all to see – and perhaps it is useful to take another look, in order to remember and learn some more lessons.

COUNCIL HOUSE SALES

There is nothing new in politics. I have a pre-war political poster from an election in the 1920s showing a working couple looking at their farm animals with the message in bold type, 'Our own smallholding. Thanks to the Unionist Party.' The same messages are often repeated in different circumstances. Conservative councils in the 1970s pioneered the sale of council houses to their tenants alongside the drive to encourage the private sector to build new homes. By contrast, Labour-controlled councils refused point-blank to have anything to do with sales purely for doctrinal reasons.

After we narrowly lost the election in February 1974, Peter Walker persuaded Ted Heath to develop our council house sale policy, which was announced by Margaret Thatcher, the shadow minister responsible, in the run-up to the October 1974 election. When the Conservative Party returned to power in 1979, it fell to me to carry through the policy. It was, beyond doubt, one of the greatest social reforms of modern times, the effects of which have been thoroughly documented.

One caveat remains, however, which arises from the deal I did with the Treasury at the time. We agreed that 75 per cent of the capital receipts from the sales would be recycled into new social housing. The present shortage of social housing can, in part, be attributed to the decision, taken after I had left the department, to divert the promised funds into their wider budget. This is so often the way HM Treasury moves to regain control.

HYDRAULICS RESEARCH STATION

In 1982, I transferred the Hydraulics Research Station, a government research laboratory on the margins of my constituency in Oxfordshire, to a private company limited by guarantee, now called HR Wallingford Ltd. The move proved a significant success. It allowed the company to grow and develop into a globally significant organisation in its specialist areas, while retaining its fundamental research credentials and activities. The number of people employed was 250 in 1982. Today there are 350 staff employed globally, with

70 per cent of its commercial work coming from outside the UK. Over the same period, its turnover has risen from £10 million to £32 million.

The organisation has transformed from being mostly reliant on the UK public sector to being immersed in global markets, primarily funded by international commercial activities and funding agencies, working on exciting, innovative projects. These include playing a leading role in the development of marine facilities for gas export and import, supporting energy transitions and the development of fixed and floating offshore wind in the marine environment, national climate change and flood risk assessments in the UK and globally, prediction of water availability, the spread of dengue fever in Southeast Asia, and leading on satellite-assisted dam safety techniques in Latin America.

THE AUDIT COMMISSION

Auditing of public sector accounts was undertaken within the public sector itself, and I could see no reason why this function could not be carried out by private sector firms. So in 1982, I introduced legislation to create the Audit Commission, which was established in 1983 to bring this about.

The commission became responsible for appointing auditors from the private sector to audit all local authority accounts. It also collected information from each local authority on the cost of its services and was thus able to publish comparative statistics that would expose best and worst practice. The intention was to enable a local electorate and a wider public to ask why the cost of emptying dustbins, for example, varies from one authority to another.

However, following the 2010 general election, the new Secretary of State for Communities and Local Government, Eric (now Lord)

Pickles, announced the coalition government's plans to disband the Audit Commission and grant authorities the freedom to appoint independent external auditors from a more competitive and open market. The Audit Commission had apparently lost its way. Pickles argued that, rather than being a watchdog championing taxpayers' interests, it had become Whitehall's poodle. However, having the ability to compare and contrast performance within the public realm had been a significant boost. It put the laggards under pressure to liven up or outsource where possible. In turn, that prevented the wheel being reinvented hundreds of times across the country. It was not a good decision, and they ended up having to recreate it under a different name.

To redress this balance, it was claimed, Pickles's new arrangements would create an army of armchair auditors: local people holding local bodies to account for how their tax pounds were spent and what that money is delivering. The new arrangements came into effect when the Audit Commission closed in March 2015 and was replaced by Public Sector Audit Appointments, the National Audit Office, the Financial Reporting Council and the Cabinet Office. A new local audit framework came into effect from April that year. The unfortunate consequences of this decision were highlighted in an article by Michael Goodier and Patrick Butler, which appeared in *The Guardian* in November 2023. They wrote:

> The early warning system designed to identify English councils in serious financial difficulty is in crisis, with hundreds of local authorities failing to meet the legal deadline to publish audited accounts covering £100bn of public spending.

The authors added that the vast majority of English councils failed to have their accounts signed off by the deadline, and some ten public bodies effectively declared bankruptcy. The article acknowledged that Rob Whiteman, chief executive of the Chartered Institute of Public Finance and Accountancy, described the situation as a 'public administration disaster' and pointed to the scrapping of the Audit Commission as the key issue.

Not all privatisation works. A briefing note by the House of Commons Library in February 2024 set out the position clearly: 'Since 2010, the concept of best value has had a residuary existence. There are no regular assessments or performance metrics used to determine whether or not an authority is meeting its duty of best value.'

In June 2022, Michael Gove told the Local Government Association annual conference that a new body, the Office for Local Government, would 'shine a light on how local authorities are performing and delivering' by bringing together existing data. Gove declared that 'taxpayers will be able to see which councils are going the furthest on the environment, which are pioneering transformative children's services, and which are providing best value for money'. Thus, the Audit Commission was reinvented.

ROYAL ORDNANCE FACTORIES

Royal Ordnance Factories were built and run by the government as part of the rearmament demanded by the Second World War. When I arrived at the Ministry of Defence in 1983, there were sixteen different units employing 19,000 people throughout the country. I could see no reason why this should be a state-owned industry and, in preparation for a sale, transferred them to a company, Royal Ordnance PLC. This company was bought by British Aerospace in 1987. Under the new ownership there were mergers, acquisitions, closures and rationalisations, which make it impossible to track the detail of what happened. But I can record that BAE Systems is now one of the world's largest contractors in this field.

CONTRACTORISATION IN THE MINISTRY OF DEFENCE

In 1983, this form of privatisation was introduced by Peter Levene, an industrialist whom I brought into the Ministry of Defence (MoD) first as my special adviser and subsequently as chief of defence procurement. The Royal Dockyard at Devonport was a role model for the worst examples of public ownership. Absenteeism, strikes and time devoted to personal kit production were at unacceptable levels. Peter found Devonport making wooden crates at great expense, rather than buying them in much more cheaply. Whereas industry does 'just in time', the MoD too often does 'just in case'.

I announced a consultative process about a structure for the future in a statement to the House of Commons in April 1985, which led, in 1987, to the appointment of a private sector contractor to manage the workforce. The improvements secured were sufficient to lead, in 1997, to a full privatisation of the dockyards at both Devonport and Rosyth. The effort that went into buying warships, not on the basis of value for money but to eke out orders to keep double the number of shipyards and dockyards that were needed in work, was indefensible.

Officials in the MoD saw their military colleagues as partners, but if you are working on the basis of partnership, the private sector is going to outclass you every time when it comes to money. There was a curious logic behind the partnership approach. The military knew that, in war, the front line's ability to fight depends on the supply chain, which is no stronger than its weakest link.

The official advice submitted to me accepted this approach and opposed the appointment of contractors after a competitive process.

I rejected this advice, which led to the only time in my ministerial career that, at the end of yet another meeting on the subject, I dictated the words that were to be the conclusion of the meeting.

We eventually succeeded in insisting on competitive tendering for many more contracts than had been the norm until then, and regular reports were produced showing the percentage of contracts let by competition. Yet there still remains too little competition in defence procurement. There are too few contractors and not enough cooperation between the public and private sector, which results in delayed and underperforming projects.

Peter Levene's appointment as chief of defence procurement was challenged by the Civil Service Commission on the grounds that it was announced without a competition, so I asked for and secured Thatcher's support to overrule them. Another objection was that Peter was to be paid £30,000 more than the previous incumbent, which simply reflected the fact that he had taken a significant pay cut to work for the public sector. I think Peter saved the best part of £1 billion in his first year in the position, so more than earned his extra £30,000.

Here is a charming illustration of this change of attitude that occurred during Peter's first week in the job. A senior official came to him for a routine decision: 'This is the best and final offer for a contract we are seeking to let. After going through the whole competition process, this company has won. If you will sign it off, I will tell the chairman that the contract is his.'

'How much is the contract for?' asked Peter.

'£3.1 million,' replied the official.

Peter said, 'Tell the chairman he can have the contract for £3 million.'

The official responded, 'But I can't do that. "Best" and "final" mean just that and we have been through the whole process properly.'

Peter reached for the telephone. 'Very well then, I'll tell him.'

The official, who was by now thoroughly flustered, said, 'Er… hang on just a minute and I will see what I can do.'

Shortly afterwards, the official returned and announced that the deal had been concluded at the price of £3 million. Peter had saved over half his annual salary in his first week in office!

Peter went on to sort out problems in Canary Wharf and the Jubilee line before he left the public sector to take charge of Lloyd's of London and, later, serve as Lord Mayor of London. He richly deserved his elevation to the House of Lords in 1997.

ROYAL PARKS

With hindsight, I may have taken the wrong decision when I replaced the in-house teams looking after these important parts of London's heritage with private contractors, but I have spoken to Michael Fitt, a park superintendent at the time, which provided some fascinating snapshots about the atmosphere surrounding the decision-making process.

The gardeners were worried that outsourcing skills would lower standards of maintenance and the quality of horticulture. I had hoped that the Royal Parks would be an exemplar for the contracting industry, while recognising that an important objective was to cut costs. Ultimately, the Royal Parks retained their senior management team and maintained a close relationship with the contracted gardening teams, who continued to think of themselves as Royal Parks staff. But Fitt told me that he believed that many of the traditional gardening skills, specialist training, plant collection curation and personal touches may have suffered as a result.

He reminded me of the occasion when we first met, after the Pavarotti concert in Hyde Park in July 1991, which was attended by

Princess Diana. It was at the reception that followed that Fitt told one of his colleagues of his intention to tell me of his forebodings about privatisation and how the parks were changing, only to be reminded that it wasn't his place to speak to the Secretary of State.

Undeterred, he persisted, came up to me and asked me if I would visit Richmond Park, for which he was responsible. I agreed and the visit went into the diary, but not before he had been interrogated by the senior official at the parks and palaces division, who had been horrified by his impertinence in speaking to me. He received a lecture on how to behave in front of a Secretary of State, instructions to prepare papers for me to read on arrival and to have all the staff there, in order of rank, to meet me. He had decided that my tour should be conducted by Bill Cathcart, his deputy and tree expert. On my arrival, I was presented with papers and staff, as he had been instructed. Fitt recalled my arrival and remembered my resulting remark: 'I'm not here to read papers. I'm here to see you and the park which you asked me to visit.'

To the apparent dismay of my entourage, Bill and I headed off in a Land Rover to view the park – especially the Isabella Plantation, with its magnificent collection of azaleas, rhododendrons and ancient oak trees. Fitt's intention was to enable me to see the park unaccompanied by officials. He would follow a little later with my 'minders'.

There was panic when they arrived at the plantation because I was nowhere to be seen. Bill and I were found with our arms stretched around an ancient oak tree, measuring its girth to ascertain its age. Officials were perturbed that the press might get hold of a picture of me hugging trees.

In his earlier instructions, Fitt had been told to only offer me a cup of tea at the end of the tour – nothing extravagant because my time was limited and I had to be away by 1 p.m., with speeches to prepare for a forthcoming Tory conference.

Following instructions, he had arranged a short stop with a cup of tea at Pembroke Lodge. The caterer discovered it was the Secretary of State arriving and, wanting to impress, laid on not just a cup of tea but sandwiches, a glass of wine and all the trimmings. To the consternation of my team, I said this was very welcome and settled down to lunch.

Commenting on the quality of the building, I asked Fitt if it would work as a visitor centre. He had told me such a facility was on his wish list, which he mentioned as we walked round the park. The building was used as a cafe, but much of it was derelict and in urgent need of repair, for which no funds were available. As a consequence, the Royal Parks were handing the lodge and gardens back to the Crown Estate to be converted into a private residence. A small part of the garden was to be retained, with a cafe incorporated.

During lunch, I expressed my determination to find a way to maintain the lodge as a public facility. Attempts by officials to persuade me to read the papers before I made such a decision were of no avail and I made it clear that the building was to be kept in the park. I delivered, finding several hundred thousand pounds to supplement monies from Royal Parks to stabilise the building. It was later restored as a successful cafe/restaurant, with a separate wedding facility.

Michael Fitt had asked if there was any possibility that he and his fellow superintendents could visit the arboretum at Thenford. I had agreed, of course, and not long afterwards a phone call from the parks and palaces division of the department set the ball rolling. He was informed that they would choose which staff would accompany him as they didn't want anybody who wouldn't be respectful, pointing out they would be visiting the Secretary of State in his own home. They should leave at lunchtime and not bother the family.

On a rather wet day they arrived, bearing a gift of unusual shrubs to add to our collection. Lunchtime duly arrived and Fitt was set to leave. He was amazed by my reaction when he explained his instructions. Apparently, I asked if he was man or mouse and told him to go if he liked but the other lads were staying!

They all enjoyed both the family lunch and a further tour that afternoon. Never one to miss an opportunity, I used the chance to demonstrate my view that they did not need a layer of civil servants to help them run the parks, and I remember that, at the time, they saw my point.

The Royal Parks became an executive agency in 1993 with an advisory board, giving the Royal Parks more autonomy. In 2017 it became a charity, with the Prince of Wales as its patron and a board of trustees, which created the opportunity to bring some of the gardening back in-house. My own experience persuaded me that there is a very personal connection between gardeners and the gardens they manage, which cannot be replicated by the transfer of that relationship to outside contractors.

BRITISH COAL

This is a sad story, but one that must be told. Within days of my return to the Department for Trade and Industry in 1992, I was presented with the worst problem of my career. At the time of electricity privatisation, contracts had been signed by the former Secretary of State for Energy committing the newly privatised companies to buy from British Coal for five years. The five years were almost up and the companies would soon be free to buy coal more competitively on world markets. The directors of those companies had a duty to their shareholders to buy competitively and there was also a clear public interest in keeping electricity prices low.

In discussions with the directors of the electricity companies, they presented me with their dilemma. In their position, I would have done the same. It would have been wrong to expect the taxpayer to shoulder the enormous burden of subsidising British Coal, even if I could have devised an economic or industrial case for doing so. There was no other choice than to proceed with pit closures.

At about that time, I was in the north east of England and saw a headline in a local newspaper that forecast this. It made me realise that the miners knew only too well what was afoot. It was party conference season and I set off to make John Major aware of the storm that was coming. I was told that he was involved in preparing his conference speech. I shrugged my shoulders, with the thought that it was my job anyway, and decided not to bother him. In the event, it was not the miners that created the storm but the Tory voters of middle England, who might have railed against the clique that ran the National Union of Mineworkers but who also had a real sympathy for the miners themselves. John was not pleased and I had a rough time at an emergency Cabinet meeting on a Monday morning before I had to make a statement to the Commons.

The interval between Cabinet and the statement in the Commons was of particular importance to me. I had been invited to speak at Peter Jenkins's memorial service. He was not only a distinguished journalist but one of my oldest friends, dating from our childhood experiences in Langland Bay, near Swansea. I was determined to fulfil that commitment.

In the end, I was able to sell ten of the mines to RJB Mining, which went on to become UK Coal, but had no choice other than to close the rest and make 30,000 people redundant. I persuaded the Treasury to make generous redundancy terms of about £30,000 per miner and brought back Peter Walker to head up a task force charged with seeking alternative employment in the areas affected. The only upside was that in future years, this dangerous and unhealthy industry would no longer cause death and injury to miners and ruin their health.

It is striking that, in 2019, quite a few of these areas voted Conservative. But that was based on the deceptions of the Brexit campaign, designed to address their legitimate feelings of being left behind and forgotten by fanning the flames of immigration and the idea of 'control' by Brussels.

NUCLEAR ENERGY

In May 1995, as President of the Board of Trade, I was responsible for the division of the nuclear industry between the old Magnox nuclear plants, run by British Nuclear Fuels, and the eight remaining nuclear plants that were run by a new company, British Energy. The old plants had ongoing safety liabilities that made them unsuitable for commercial valuation, but British Energy, containing the more modern reactors, was to be privatised. That remained the reality until 2009, when BE was taken over by the nationalised company Électricité de France (EDF).

There are few more potent examples of the UK's short-termism. For years and years, successive British governments have prevaricated, postponed and stuttered their way to a position where our nuclear reactors are old and less efficient than our competitors, while we have in fact achieved nothing but talk towards their replacement.

Contrast this with the French who, having looked at the need for clean energy in the years ahead with a strategic perspective, simply got on and built the power stations that were required. As a result, over 60 per cent of the electricity they produce is by nuclear power and they are net exporters to the rest of Europe – much of it to us. Our national grid has no less than six interconnectors with nuclear power from France, where 15 per cent of our energy requirement comes from. The election manifesto of the Labour Party in 2024 promised to create a new state-owned company, Great British Energy, that would focus on the production of renewable energy – particularly offshore wind. The new Labour government has also pledged to continue Conservative plans for building a new generation of nuclear power stations and these will be developed in the private sector, so they say. We shall see.

THE ADVISORY AGRICULTURE SERVICE

The Advisory Agriculture Service (ADAS) can trace its origins back to 1915, when the government had established War Agricultural Committees in each county of the UK; these were revived in 1939. They then had wide powers to instruct farmers as to what they should grow and how they should grow it on a field-by-field basis. In the extreme, they had the power to take over the land. Agriculture in the 1930s was so unattractive an industry that much arable land had reverted to pasture. There existed a range of consultancy services, run by local authorities and universities, but they were uncoordinated and ill-prepared to face the urgent challenge to increase food production. Under the new leadership, over 1.5 million acres of productive land were brought back into use following the outbreak of the Second World War.

After the war, the National Agricultural Advisory Service was enshrined in law to coordinate the various advisory services and extend their availability widely throughout the farming community.

The new name ADAS followed a reorganisation in 1971. By the mid-1970s, the organisation employed some 5,000 people. Changes, disposals and closures continued, including our accession to the European market with its very different system of agricultural support. The introduction of new technology and the rationalisation of offices led to considerable redundancies, and the scrutiny to which all such organisations were subjected after the election of the Conservative government in 1979 had led to the introduction of charges for the use of their services, a programme of full cost recovery and its conversion into an executive agency in April 1992, operating within rules closer to the market. I became involved when I was Deputy Prime Minister in 1995. The grounds had already been established for my decision to privatise it.

Four directors, backed by 3i Group PLC, became the first private owners through a management buyout. Established on 1 April 1997, the agency employed 1,200 staff and had a turnover approaching £50 million. A significant proportion of the reduction in staff numbers that followed came through the transfer of bodies such as the veterinary service and the major science service laboratories into independent bodies. The latter was itself subsequently privatised.

The business was bought by RSK Group on 5 December 2016, when the company employed 320 and had a turnover of £20 million. The latest figures show staff subsequently increased to 450 with a turnover of £36 million in the year to July 2024. It would be wrong to compare these two sets of figures in any way other than as an indicator of change. There were significant disposals and the removal of certain pension costs. The new owners regard the acquisition as one of their most successful and today, it continues to provide services for the Department for Environment, Food and Rural Affairs and its agencies and for many private sector clients as well.

LABORATORY OF THE GOVERNMENT CHEMIST

Laboratory of the Government Chemist was one of the Department for Trade and Industry's labs at Teddington that I placed on the road to privatisation in 1996. It employed 270 people when it was constrained by being in the public realm but now, renamed LGC, it employs over 4,300 people as a result of organic growth and acquisitions while retaining its unique function of the 'government chemist'.

I recall a later meeting with the then Home Secretary, Michael Howard, to discuss merging LGC with the Home Office's Forensic Science Service. The match was perfect, with much money to be saved, better careers for the scientists, more varied work and better facilities at Teddington instead of in Westminster. Yet I was quite unable to persuade him.

HER MAJESTY'S STATIONERY OFFICE

In 1996, I arranged the sale of the publishing operation of Her Majesty's Stationery Office. Renamed The Stationery Office (TSO), it remains the official publisher and distributor for legislation, command and House papers, select committee reports, Hansard and the UK government's three official journals of record, the London, Edinburgh and Belfast Gazettes. TSO went on to provide full digital access for all UK legislation going back to 1267. It has also published online all gazettes since 1662.

THE CIVIL SERVICE COLLEGE – THE ONE THAT GOT AWAY

My admiration for our civil servants is based entirely on my experiences during my seventeen years as a minister and a further seven years involved with the Cameron government, and I believe that my estimation is widely shared across the world.

I thought there was an opportunity to change the narrow remit of the existing Civil Service College by offering places to other countries to train their civil servants alongside ours. It is not rocket science. Our top universities are world class and attract large numbers of highly talented and motivated foreign students, bringing in tens of billions of overseas earnings for this country. All of our defence colleges have accepted and welcomed foreign students for many years, so that we can educate them to our standards of best practice. The 'soft power' of such attachments cannot be calculated but is nonetheless considerable. Several Commonwealth heads of state in the past were educated at Sandhurst; they were all much more pro-British than many others.

The benefits are obvious, not least the contribution this would make to young and inexperienced countries in providing them with people trained to the highest standards of loyalty and integrity as they exercise their growing power. Other advantages include the long-term positive influence that would flow to this country from students grateful for their experience here. More could be achieved by attracting students from the private sector as part of a policy to encourage more exchange between the two sectors.

When I became Deputy Prime Minister, I intended to make the necessary changes. Sir Robin Butler, then Cabinet Secretary, was implacably opposed to my privatisation proposal. I queried this with John Major and his advice was clear: 'If the Deputy Prime Minister comes to me with a proposal to which the Cabinet Secretary is opposed, I shall find for the Deputy Prime Minister.' Yet to proceed would have involved a serious rebuff to Butler, whose views were well known. Did I really want to start my new job against such a background? I decided not, but the opportunity remains.

The most powerful argument for regeneration through privatisation is that it helps overcome the constraints of the public sector, where you work exclusively for the government. The private sector, meanwhile, offers a vast array of opportunities. Setting these organisations free was the key to the privatisation argument and overall, in its different guises, it has been very successful. First of all, it has led to a wide dissemination of wealth throughout society. Second, the motivation of the private sector drives the expansion of the undertaking to the benefit of the economy at large. Overall, it creates a society where power is widely distributed as opposed to exclusively centred upon the state.

CHAPTER 8

THE IMPORTANCE OF INDUSTRIAL STRATEGY

Many moons ago, in 1947, as part of the recovery process from its election loss two years earlier, the Conservative Party published a policy document entitled 'Industrial Policy'. The foreword outlined the enormous national debt the country had accumulated during the war and set out 'what the Conservative Party plans to do on the industrial front to help you and the country back to good times'. It is worth looking at the document at length:

> We Conservatives want to release industry and those who work in industry from unnecessary controls so that energy and fresh ideas may be given their head. But we know that, as things are, there must be some central planning of the nation's work. The world is topsy-turvy. Raw materials are scarce. Stormy weather must be foreseen. There must be a hand on the helm and that hand must be the Government's.
>
> But we do not believe that it should be done as the socialists try to do it. They decide everything in Whitehall and their orders are then piped down to be obeyed in Glasgow, Manchester,

> Birmingham, Cardiff and everywhere else – even to Muddle-combe-in-the-Marsh... This means it will be done by men who know their job and without the endless interference of Government officials and their forms.
>
> One Cabinet Minister would be in charge of government policy instead of a bunch as now. He would be a Chairman of a Committee which would have on it employers and Trade Union leaders ... All the detailed work would be done by the industry's own employers and Trade Unions ... In this way we can have real partnership, a team instead of two sides, and all working for the benefit of all.

You can almost hear the dialogue of the men and women who drafted such a document. They had served together in the harshest of circumstances, where every sinew of the state was put into the national effort in a huge fight for survival. Working together through interdependence and in partnership – that was the message and it worked. The war effort was proof of industrial strategy at its best, but in the decades since, the debate has continued as to why and what an industrial strategy should be.

Anybody with even a GCSE in history will recognise that the partnership hoped for in that document remained out of reach for the rest of the twentieth century and that the activist role alluded to became progressively less fashionable on both sides of the political spectrum.

Anyone who keeps half an eye on the popular press will also know that UK manufacturing has suffered as a result. Nicholas Comfort, in his history of British manufacturing, *Surrender*, describes the plight of British industry since 1952. The book sets out in chilling detail the demise of British aeroplane makers, nuclear engineering industry, car manufacturers, ship builders, television set producers, truck and bus manufacturers and even fireworks manufacturers. Comfort calls it 'the greatest mass extinction since the dinosaurs'.

One big reason industries fail to develop on their own is that innovative new products are subject to great uncertainty and what economists call 'information spillovers'. Comfort tells the story of the British-made de Havilland Comet, the world's first commercial jet airliner. The Comet looked as though it would be highly profitable, orders began piling up and Britain seemed set to be the world leader in jet aircraft production. However, a year after coming into commercial service, two crashes from high altitude forced de Havilland to stop production. Tests eventually identified the cause of the fault as a rivet, which slowly weakened over time as the cabin pressurised and depressurised, eventually undermining the integrity of the whole fuselage. By the time the redesigned Comet returned to service, Boeing had brought their 707 model into service, having learned from the mistakes of the Comet, and captured the market in long-haul passenger flights.

This is a prime example of an information spillover. The pioneer bears many of the risks connected with the project, both in terms of the technical feasibility and economic viability of the product, and competitors can learn from their experience and avoid their mistakes. At the point that production of the Comet ceased, the aircraft had proved itself to be economically and almost technically feasible, but de Havilland was to reap little reward from its pioneering efforts, while others built on them. Who knows how many other firms have been put off by the same dynamic?

From June 1970, first as Minister for Aerospace and Shipping, then later as Secretary of State for Defence and, a decade or so after that, as President of the Board of Trade, I was confronted time and again with decisions critical to our country's capacity to defend itself and support its industrial base. It is now commonplace for junior ministers to be given delegated status and responsibility, although under the constitution, the Secretary of State remains accountable. I was fortunate in that Peter Walker, my first Secretary of State, was an exceptional departmental manager with an instinct to delegate to and to trust his subordinates.

Perhaps the most famous industrial policy intervention of the last century was Ted Heath's decision to nationalise Rolls-Royce, the bankrupt engineering giant, in 1971. From day one, I was responsible for the financial wreckage that was the Rolls-Royce company at that time, as well as for the Anglo-French Concorde programme.

Rolls-Royce was, and still is, the most advanced aero-engine manufacturer in Europe. Its engines, both fossil-fuel and nuclear powered, are in service across a very wide range of civil and military aircraft and warships. At the time, a planned new generation of jet airliners needed an engine to power them. General Electric, one of Rolls-Royce's principal American competitors, had developed an engine, the CF6, to drive a defence project, which was paid for by the Pentagon's defence budget.

Britain had no equivalent project. There was a contract with Lockheed to power its new airliner, Tristar, whereby Rolls-Royce had to finance an alternative to the commercially adapted CF6 from its own resources. The costs rose and the date of its entry into service was delayed with the effect that it broke the company.

William Lazonick and Andrea Prencipe's working paper recounts how Rolls-Royce's efforts to develop this new generation of powerful three-shaft engines took them to the brink of disaster. The company made many great technological strides in developing the RB211 engine, but problems with creating the material for the fan blades dogged the project and this, combined with contractual arrangements that provided little leeway for development setbacks, drove the company into bankruptcy in 1971.

The Conservative government nationalised the company, saving it from almost certain overseas purchase or liquidation and break-up. Rolls-Royce received significant injections of public cash to sustain it through the early 1980s, during which time demand for civil aerospace products was particularly weak. By 1986, the problems with the RB211 had been overcome and an upturn in the market meant £3.1 billion of orders piled up. The company was privatised the next year, with the sale of government shares raising £1.36 billion. In their conclusion, Lazonick and Prencipe state, 'Rolls-Royce is a company that, because of sustained investment in its productive resources, has a technological capability that took decades to develop and that no other company in the world can replicate.' Today Rolls-Royce is the second-largest maker of aeroplane engines in the world and employs around 20,000 people in the UK.

The rescue ensured the survival of this essential building block of our defence capability and of our technological industrial base. It never occurred to me at the time that there was any other credible alternative. The government, in returning the company to private ownership, retained a blocking 'golden share' arrangement to prevent any hostile takeover. Later, I refused to remove this and another arrangement of the same kind within British Aerospace when I was President of the Board of Trade in 1992.

During the 1970s, I also had to come to grips with the Concorde supersonic airliner programme. Geoffrey Rippon and Julian Amery, the ministers originally responsible, had rightly anticipated that any subsequent government would lose its nerve as the costs of the programme increased remorselessly and as delays arose. There were also two further problems. Concorde was conceived for the lucrative transatlantic trade with its 3,000-mile range. To fly from the west to the Middle East and Asia, there had to be refuelling stops, at a time when new long-range, wide-bodied aircraft were on the drawing board. As part of my attempt to reassure the public concern about the rising costs, I asked officials to prepare a speech outlining the effect that such an advanced technological programme would have throughout the supply chain of British industry. The problem, I was told, is that there was very little new technology in Concorde. It is existing technology pushed to its limit. There is no stretch.

My job as Minister for Aerospace had two aspects and they were sometimes difficult to reconcile. My first responsibility was to Parliament and the taxpayer, but I was also expected to be a salesman and try to sell Concorde. If the nationalised British and French airlines would not buy it, who would? The conflicting advice from the sales team at British Aerospace and my officials could not have been more difficult for me to reconcile; it was the difference between eighty projected sales and virtually none. In mid-1973, I put a paper to Cabinet outlining the difficulties and suggested we should propose to the French that we invite Boeing to join the delayed international project. But Ted Heath and Anthony Barber, Chancellor of the Exchequer, were undoubtedly right that, if only because the French had seen too many British attempts to cancel the project, they would never consider such a proposal.

It was essential that the sales position with our domestic airline be clarified. British Airways were not prepared to buy any Concordes with their own resources but agreed to take seven in return for public dividend capital remunerated from any future profits. This deal, negotiated with Sir Kenneth Keith, who was on the Board of British Airways, was the best I could get. I was further humiliated when he insisted that John Davies sign the contract in my place, as the Secretary of State. I did secure an intention from the Shah of Iran to purchase two planes, but he was deposed before any contract could be signed.

Rolls-Royce and Concorde both confronted me with many of the issues facing any government in its research, defence and procurement policies and its relationships with the industrial base. What does private sector competition mean when much of the cost of developing products has been borne by the public sector? How long should government research money be used to develop products when new technology is already threatening their viability? But for me, they were both inherited problems and not of my making; they were in my in-tray on the day I arrived.

Looking back, space policy also stands out as an example of a policy vacuum. There was no inherited project, responsibility was scattered across Whitehall with no coordinating mechanism and within my department, it occupied a dark corner where little ministerial light ever shone. In 1973, I scanned through a submission requesting that I authorise £6 million to finance an initiative with a British company. I asked for two figures in response – the total European space spend and its American equivalent. In the money of that time, Europe was spending £200 million and the Americans £1.2 billion per annum – six times as much. I pointed out the toy town nature of the submission and said that if we wanted to play a full part in a properly resourced European response to the US commitment to exploring space, we would need to take the opportunity much more seriously than we had hitherto.

I set out to explore the option of a much more ambitious pan-European programme. To do this, I needed three answers. Would the rest of Whitehall, particularly the Department of Education and the Ministry of Defence, take part? What would British industry wish to emerge from any such arrangement? And what would the rest of Europe find attractive?

The answer from Whitehall was predictable: you do what you like with your money but count us out. Margaret Thatcher's Department for Education was an unlikely ally. The Ministry of Defence warned of the threat to the special relationship and the threat to transatlantic intelligence. (No one could have known that years later, Geoffrey Pattie, when he was Minister of State for Industry and Information Technology, would write to me as Secretary of State for Defence seeking our involvement in a National Space Agency. I found that the Ministry of Defence had no serious objections and agreed.) The response from British industry, particularly from Marconi, was enthusiastic. It was at the top of their agenda to secure the lead in satellite technology. France wanted us back in its Launcher programme and Germany wanted our participation in the American-led, post-Apollo programme to launch a space station with the means to service it.

In May 1975, the European Space Agency was born. We agreed to both the French and German conditions and with our acknowledged expertise in satellite technology, we took the lead. Marconi was already in partnership with the French company Thomson-CSF (now Thales) in joint ventures in satellite and sonar businesses, which may account for the relaxed view of the French towards our leadership.

• • •

The first essential of any industrial strategy is to get the economics right. Low inflation, low interest rates, tax incentives and benign regulation are all extremely significant when it comes to pursuing growth. Their existence creates confidence and the consequent commitment of the private sector to invest. Globalisation is accelerating the pressure to conform to this economic pattern, although there is a note of caution. A benign climate in a buoyant market can ease the pressure on indifferent management to raise their game.

Second, modern economies require first-class infrastructure. Airports, ports, roads and rail power all underpin our industrial capability. Competitor economies have recognised this and we are pressed to keep up with their investment, let alone get ahead in this race. HS2 has illustrated the problem we have in undertaking major strategic projects, while the inability to unblock the planning regime indicates the political challenge any significant change faces.

Third, the provision of a skilled, educated and motivated workforce is ever more important in today's world. For more than a century, report after report, including those from the government inspectorate itself, has warned of the relative slippage in our educational standards. We have world-beating standards at the top end of our educational establishment but for those of average ability and – even more importantly – those at the very bottom, we are still schooling too many children for a life on welfare. One such report referred to a culture of tolerance by local authorities in the north of England to low standards.

Diagnosis is the easy bit. An industrial strategy requires an awareness of all the factors that add up to a nation's competitiveness. We have to know what our competitors are doing so that we can help our companies to win. It is a grinding process of detail, in which our progress in the race against the competition is measured annually in tiny percentages, but in the longer term, the gaps become too wide to close.

When we compare our policies with those of our competitors, we find that, across the board, many of them work to raise standards more comprehensively than we do. They have a more constructive relationship between government and private sector and do not tolerate the acceptance of low standards.

In the UK, the components of an industrial strategy are imposed top-down from Whitehall departments that are uncoordinated and ill-equipped internally for industrial sponsorship. Industrial strategy, from its conception, depends on the active participation of the private sector, the quangos and the academic world. The state needs to be market-oriented, internationally competitive and accept there are many ways that the public sector can support our companies.

In this country, neither of the parties are well prepared for such a dialogue. Cabinet ministers barely have time to grasp the portfolio they have been given before they are moved on. All too frequently, they have doctrinal objections to the sense of cooperation that progress demands. The collective memory of the civil service is also not strengthened by the relatively short-term nature of their postings.

I must make two qualifications here. Many British companies are world class; their products are excellent and their management have the will and resource to commit the research and development to keep them that way. However, when I was running the Department for Trade and Industry, I was advised that this accolade applied to only 40 per cent of our companies but to 60 per cent of German ones. In consequence this means that our average performance – the one against which we are judged – will lag behind and increase the urgency to address the problem of our underperformers. There is no short-term fix for this situation. Governments naturally look for the new initiatives, the specific stimulus or the fashionable growth sector.

To look at it another way, there were fourteen Ministers for

Housing in the fourteen years after the Tories returned to government in 2010. I don't make this as a party-political point; a similar pattern existed under previous Labour governments. You could not be blamed for believing that the body politic holds the value of its relationship with industry in low regard. I have even heard serious politicians argue that the business department should be closed down.

One of the more difficult questions in any dialogue with the private sector is how to come to terms with the role and responsibilities of shareholders in publicly quoted companies. Family businesses usually combine the virtues of a creative tension between management and shareholders and do so in a long-term relationship. The huge scale of modern corporate activity has long resulted in the growth of the quoted company, but it seems that in this country, uniquely, the relationship between management and owner appears hardly to exist. The accepted habits of the quarterly bonus and the huge payoffs that follow a takeover are seen as the western model of capitalism, but this comparison is too simple. Most significant American companies are too big to be taken over, and the government there has specific legislative arrangements to scrutinise such activities.

We are therefore uniquely exposed to the problems of short-termism. Every instinct I have tells me that this culture smacks too much of the absentee landlords of eighteenth-century Europe. Such a concept becomes more relevant the more one looks at the source of the funds that operate in the City and the nationality of the men and women who work there. Everything is for sale if the price is right. Few other countries accept so narrow an interpretation of shareholders' responsibility.

I am proud to have privatised more state assets than any other minister because I know that there is no stimulus to compare with that of the market. However, each case must be carefully considered and not all companies will be capable of being made subject to tight enough regulation, particularly where one is dealing with effectively monopolistic situations.

Each industry is sponsored by a Whitehall department. This sponsorship should mean just that. Industry by industry, department by department, there should be a knowledge of the strengths and weaknesses of our companies, their competitive standing in the world market and what other countries are doing to support their equivalent industries. No other such comprehensive knowledge base exists. An industrial strategy therefore requires an understanding that enterprise is not a monopoly of the private sector. Officials have the ability to influence economic performance. At its simplest, they can speed the decision-making process. The research budgets of NASA and the Department of Defence inject technological expertise into the American economy. Chinese officials have planned and controlled a centralised process that drove a backward agrarian economy into the space age in a third of a century. French officials helped their industrial base assume the dominant European role in nuclear power, space launchers and civil aviation. The civil service needs longer-term postings and a continuing flow into and out of the private sector to develop the necessary expertise to be able to do this in our country.

The ability of British industries to cope with such a dialogue is also defective. Trade associations have to judge any statement against the likely reaction of their voluntary membership, which makes it very difficult for them to admit to any weaknesses or agree to any changes that reflect uncomfortably on their members. Meanwhile, our competitors elsewhere in Europe have to join their representative Chambers of Commerce, which are thus much richer, provide much more effective support (particularly in exports) and are strong enough to withstand criticism from their least effective members.

Any debate about regulation can only be conducted within a dialogue about detail. There have been many deregulation initiatives over my decades in politics, but I can't think of a single one – including mine – that has achieved any significant success. There are many reasons for this. Modern governments represent sophisticated, self-interested and relatively prosperous electorates, who value many of the services guaranteed by regulation. Ministers charged with getting off this or that person's back rapidly count the votes of those whose backs are to be got off.

Such regulations can create whole new opportunities within industries. I can remember the introduction of quality control of cars and lorries in the 1980s. The regular testing of vehicles that followed not only raised safety standards and drove the old bangers off the roads, it also created countless jobs for people who had to carry out this work. It is certain that when the government brings in legislation as a result of the Grenfell Tower inquiry, the resulting safety regulations in the building industry will have a similar consequence.

Regulation of the quality of products remains an area of controversy. The German government-led DIN system frequently raises standards to force up the quality of products, with the worst performers catching up or closing down. We, however, tend to set standards acceptable to the least effective companies.

It is no accident that two of our most successful exporting industries, pharmaceuticals and defence, are in industries where quality is tightly controlled by government. I faced controversy surrounding such regulation when I returned to the Department for Trade and Industry (DTI) in 1992. By the time I left the Ministry of Defence in 1986, the concept of an industrial strategy was about as unfashionable as it was possible to be. I was, however, more certain than ever that a smart industrial strategy was essential for our economy. My accumulated experience showed me that other countries have strategies to advance and coordinate their wealth-creating processes for the long term by building interrelationships between the public and private sector.

It was with this set of conclusions that I re-entered the DTI in 1992. The first question I asked was, 'What is our industrial strategy?' This brought the reply that these words were banned in the office. During my career in government, I had been responsible for the roads programme, space policy, airlines, the aircraft and shipping industries, the ports infrastructure, government and university research programmes directly assisting British companies, the defence procurement budget, housing and construction, the water industry and the procurement programmes of local government. Was it seriously suggested that in the myriad decisions I took, I never thought about British self-interest, the consequences for our companies or our wealth-creating process?

I set about remoulding the DTI towards taking a more positive approach. The centrepiece was a new Competitiveness Unit, charged with publishing white papers that provided a serious, deep analysis of the UK's competitive strengths and weaknesses. To be of any value, the unit would not only have to admire success but also acknowledge weakness. Failure to do so undermines credibility and disguises the challenges that must be faced.

At that time, our strengths included political stability, legal clarity and our position at the heart of Europe. Among our most critical weaknesses were those centred on investment in the most important element of our infrastructure – our people, whose skills and training, education and motivation were in need of urgent attention. Politics being what it is, Gordon Brown immediately used these weaknesses as examples of the failure of government by their own admission.

I have often praised the officials who worked for and advised me in government. Bob Dobbie was outstanding as head of the Competitiveness Unit, while Mark Gibson was not only of particular help but went on to become my private secretary while I was Deputy Prime Minister. He is now a non-executive director of Haymarket. It was noticeable that among the brightest of civil servants were those who were in charge of nationalised industries, industries in receipt of public money or for which they had both accountability and regulatory responsibilities.

Together, we created sector sponsorship divisions to reflect the successful industries of our country. No one had thought that there might be ways to help the successful and the strong. We created the Business Link service to bring together the powers and opportunities that central government's services were making available to the private sector. The idea was to co-locate these with the Chambers of Commerce in order to bolster the chambers and redress the balance that made the British chambers resemble very pale shadows of their continental equivalents. Britain was good at creating small businesses but not so good at enabling them to become larger enterprises.

Many rival organisations – the Confederation of British Industry, the Institute of Directors, Make UK and the Federation of Small Businesses – exist to lobby for more specific cases and tend to have a more partisan approach than that of the Chambers. All these organisations have their own agenda and depend on their members continuing to pay their fees because they are convinced that their interests are being served. They are not set up to conduct a realistic appraisal of the performance of their members, and any attempt to change that would be deeply controversial and something that ministers and officials would do well to avoid.

So, I created Business Link as a one-stop shop where small businesses could discuss their problems and ambitions. They were intended to provide somewhere collective experience could be shared, contacts could be made and advice and encouragement given.

The subsequent Labour government was focused on creating Regional Development Agencies (RDAs) and in consequence, the Business Link programme was increasingly left to its own devices over the years. That changed in 2010 when Eric Pickles became Secretary of State for Communities and Local Government. He had been leader of Bradford council and, like so many from that background, disliked the large budgets and powers of RDAs. He set about getting rid of them. It is unclear whether Business Link went as part of that programme or as a separate decision. With the scrapping of regional offices of government, he had got rid of two of my major innovations. I was appalled by the decision.

Pickles replaced the RDAs with the Local Enterprise Partnerships, which in practice were little more than fig leaves to justify the decision. Later, with the help of grant aid from the Regional Growth Fund, I financed Lancaster University to design an effective replacement for the Business Link concept. Unfortunately, this ultimately suffered the same fate and they were eventually closed after the Covid pandemic. I argued with the ministers involved in these decisions but to no avail. The whole saga illustrates the ever-present suspicion within the Conservative Party of any real attempt to support our small-company sector.

Back in 1992, John Major used his party conference speech to confront the widespread problem of regulation. 'Go to it, Tarzan,' he urged me. 'Swing in there.'

I took up the challenge. There is more nonsense talked about regulation and its custodian, the civil servant, than is widely recognised. My approach was comprehensive. In each department, a minister was appointed to survey its regulatory framework. I published some 3,000 regulations, so that everyone, including the media, knew what we were talking about. Only *The Guardian* showed any interest in this treasure trove of information, which should have provided the factual basis for an informed debate about regulation. It is always much easier to hurl generalised abuse at bureaucrats than to plough through the detailed reality, which is a hard grind.

I set up committees of academics, officials and, crucially, captains of industry to survey this accumulation of regulations. Significantly, one of these was chaired by John Sainsbury, one of the most outspoken critics of the regulatory jungle. Our relationship never recovered from my conclusions about how little the deregulatory exercise had achieved. I wrote to every Trade Association and invited them to send me any regulation that caused offence, together with a proposed redraft. This was a thorough and comprehensive response to John's challenge. But the result was minimal. Not one Trade Association responded to my offer. At the end of it all, very few regulations were dropped or changed.

People too often criticise the minutiae and detail associated with the regulatory process. They have never sat in a minister's chair or behind an official's desk. Those of us who have know all too well that there is an army of eagle-eyed lawyers who, for whatever reason, will seek to find a way to avoid the purpose of any regulation we enact.

The vast majority of citizens respect the law, but a tiny minority will seek to profit from exploiting loopholes. The judicial review system permits the scrutiny of the slightest imperfection in drafting, and the press show no mercy to those who designed defective regulation. Ministers and civil servants are wise to find the loopholes first, before the police or the courts discover them.

• • •

The rest of the developed world and much of the developing world, including those often thought to be the least interventionist, design and carry out industrial policy. The question, therefore, should not be whether we engage in such a policy but rather when and how we do so. We have seen several examples of both terrible failure and awesome success in our efforts, so surely it is now time to move on and begin asking what it is that makes a specific intervention more or less likely to succeed?

Here are ten guiding principles that should drive sound industrial policy.

1. Industrial policy should be tailored to the specific industry and circumstances concerned and not simply be the application of clumsy, one-size-fits-all solutions. Nor should it try to correct over-simplistic 'lessons learned' from previous experiences. Industrial policy has to be, by its very nature, highly specific, designed for a particular enterprise, for a particular market and for a particular time. Anything more detailed would be likely to be counterproductive.

2. Industrial policy should focus on developing new capabilities in areas that are subject to information spillovers, coordination failures and other unforeseen uncertainties. It should *not* be about featherbedding established concerns. For too long it has operated on a carte blanche basis in which the nature and extent of government involvement has been determined by the whims of the minister involved. Government must recognise that its capabilities are limited to providing essential public finance, using its central authority to coordinate activities that would otherwise not occur and using its resources to help nurture new economic capabilities at times when the market itself might fail to do so. Government intervention in specific industries must rest on the logic described above. Intervening in the absence of such conditions should require additional and explicit justification.
3. Industrial policy must be approached with patience and caution and never under the illusion that quick fixes and easy solutions are available. Although the government does have the power to bring about diversification and development into new areas, particularly where its research budgets can lead technological development, the extent to which it can do this is limited. Government is capable of oiling the wheels of economic development, not generating it, and influencing the way in which it is developing at any given time, not determining it. Nurturing new economic capacities will sometimes require sustained engagement and a willingness to explore options, while acknowledging that not all of these new capacities will succeed.
4. Industrial policy must have predetermined and agreed success and failure criteria, with 'sunset clauses' in place to prevent mission creep and permanent subsidy. There must be a publicly announced and measurable aim, so that it is possible to judge

whether that aim has been achieved or not. This is essential to guard against a situation where the option that makes economic sense is ruled out by the costs of taking that decision. A nationalised company, for example, might be allowed to remain under state ownership, receiving continuous and expensive subsidy, because the government does not believe that there is any realistic prospect of reviving the firm and thus recovering the investment of public funds.

5. Industrial policy should be focused on increasing productive capabilities and should not be about protecting jobs. Whenever that becomes the motivation for intervention, the likelihood increases that it will be deployed inappropriately and will become a permanent subsidy.
6. Industrial policy must be based on helping the private sector overcome limited information, not on working on the assumption that 'the state knows best'. Government must recognise that it is not capable of running companies, nor is that their business. Its role in industrial policy should be based on the proposition that all economic agencies have limited information, so only through collaboration and the combination of complementary information can the best decisions be made.
7. Industrial policy should be about developing broad areas of capacity where there is a reason to believe that we will be competitive, rather than about developing an industry based around a specific product. Firms often miscalculate the cost of introducing a new product. Government has even less ability to do so. For this reason, it would be absurd for them to direct the economy to begin producing a new generation of, for example, TV screens. Instead, they should constantly be looking for broad and stable market trends. If a successful cluster has developed

around mobile phone apps, for example, and the market for the product looks set to expand, then government might ask whether or not our university system is creating enough people with the specific skills required and what incentives it could offer to ensure this.

8. Industrial policy must be administered by a government which is highly knowledgeable of and closely linked to the private sector. Market opportunities are often short-lived, so collaborative responses between the public and private sectors need to be able to get off the ground quickly if they are to be worthwhile. Furthermore, market opportunities may not be visible to either party unless they combine their information. For these reasons, constant communication between the public and private sectors is essential.
9. Industrial policy must be seen as a complement to globalisation, not an attempt to hold back the inevitable effects it has on an open economy. It can help reduce some of the frictions in economic restructuring and, in doing so, accelerate the pace at which it happens. In an open economy, however, no one can hold back the tide of structural decline in particular industries. If an industry is in terminal decline, then a policy must be created and introduced to regenerate the area concerned by facilitating the creation or expansion of new enterprises to replace the old.
10. Industrial policy must be evaluated in the round, not on the basis of a minority of high-profile disasters. Some industrial policy will fail. Government has limited information, so industrial policy is always a gamble. If the previous nine principles are observed, government should be gambling intelligently, systematically reducing the risks of big losses and maximising the chances of gain. It is inevitable, however, that some of the gambles will result in a loss for the taxpayer. Industrial policy

will still be worthwhile, however, as long as the gains outweigh the losses.

Not all of these proposals will be wholly welcomed. The media tends to concentrate more on criticising losses than on welcoming gains – so the public gets a biased view of how well any particular policy is doing.

• • •

I greatly welcomed Greg Clark's appointment as Secretary of State for Business in 2016. Here was a Secretary of State, trained in the private sector and experienced in the City, who actually believed that the words 'industrial strategy' had a relevance and an urgency. The moment he arrived, he set to work on devising a proper industrial strategy for the government – embracing the best of the past but with a clear eye to the challenges of the future. I was delighted to be associated with the work that he was doing.

My sacking by Theresa May over Brexit in March 2017 left me with a dilemma. Greg had not finished his paper – and there was plenty of input I had hoped to make. So, I decided to produce my own document entitled 'Industrial Strategy', which I did in November 2017. Bringing together a lifetime of work in this area, I contrasted the UK's position with that of Germany and set out some clear solutions based on what Greg was seeking to do in government.

I addressed first the problems in the UK. Here, the role of the Department for Business – even its very existence – has been constantly questioned. This is unlike Germany, which is a federation where the states have much more influence. Central government here is hugely powerful and functionally monopolistic. Ministers think of housing, education, roads or transport individually and separately. They don't think of the interests of Birmingham, Manchester, Liverpool or the other economic power houses of our economy collectively. There are serious deficiencies in our industrial policy.

In my paper, I argued that, over my time in public office, I had learned that there has to be a partnership between the public and private sectors upon which modern commerce and industry can depend. I pointed out that 'every government of which I have had experience has an industrial strategy', whether it was a mere sentiment or a serious policy direction. I suggested that our national ambition was 'not to improve the world-beating quality of many of our companies but to use that excellence as a stimulus to raise the standards of those that fall a good way behind'. Although I remained suspicions of the various forms, bureaucrats, regulations and the numerous restraints woven by the public sector, I insisted that the real enemy to a proper industrial strategy was the inadequacy of successive governments to acknowledge the failings of their own centralised structure in galvanising the potential of the whole economy and the enthusiasm of all the people who contribute to it.

The report noted that knowledge of business – what I termed 'sponsorship' – is deficient and scattered across Whitehall. A significant contribution towards a serious industrial strategy would require a clear grasp by departments of how they can best help their sponsored industries to win and how they compare with international practice. In Germany, thanks to their federal constitution, regional governments and local authorities are closer to industry and very knowledgeable about it. The UK's approach to policy can often consist of wholesale dismemberment of established organisations that are considered unsuccessful, rather than making changes to overcome their weaknesses while building on their strengths.

Our media also tends to focus not on the industries themselves but on the financial markets and share prices. The BBC's *Today* programme has a regular slot on markets every morning. The number of serious industrial correspondents in our national newspapers can be counted on the fingers of one hand. The City is driven by short-term business performance and the quarterly results of fund managers. There is no long-term attitude to ownership. Shareholders are more likely to sell than tackle the more demanding task of improving weak management performance.

'Industrial Strategy' also highlighted the major problems of our education system that I alluded to earlier, which has, to put it mildly, been the subject of endless organisational changes based on patchy evidence. The quality of its output has not improved relative to our competitors. We still have about 40 per cent of our children failing to achieve five good GCSEs, including in English and Maths. This would suggest that in all these reorganisations, we have not concentrated enough on what really matters, which is the quality of the teaching. As former Conservative Cabinet minister Michael Gove so rightly said, 'If we want to have an education system that ranks with the best in the world, then we need to attract the best people to teach and we need to give them outstanding training.'

The success of the education system also depends on the aspirations of young people and their parents. These are high for some, particularly in Asian communities, but for too many they are too low. This too must change. Enthusiasm for apprenticeships has varied in government and has never been great in our business sector, unlike in our competitor nations. Fortunately, they are now valued again by government and by some excellent employers who, like Rolls-Royce and BAE Systems, have always recognised the worth of training through formal apprenticeships.

But even in 2017, I believed that the outlook is not all gloom. It is ironic that in a country like ours, inclined to deride the concept of an industrial strategy, two of our most successful industries are those closest to government. As I stated earlier, we have an outstanding pharmaceutical industry, which has much to do with the fact that the NHS is supported across the whole political spectrum, so funding has been consistently protected and high standards maintained. We have a strong defence and aerospace sector too, due to defence funding still being relatively high compared to other countries and governments of all political persuasions being willing to support companies such as Rolls-Royce and Airbus for the long term with loans and grants for research funding. Our defence sector has also received huge government help in winning contracts overseas, certainly more than the rest of UK industry.

It is no accident either that for both these sectors, there are civil servants in the Department of Health, the Department of Business and the Ministry of Defence who have a deep knowledge of how these companies operate. We have also been fortunate that some foreign owners of UK-based businesses have taken the long-term view and invested consistently and well. Inward investors like Toyota and Nissan have been good for the UK, introducing better management, hugely improved quality and achieving world-class productivity. It is interesting that Tata, the Indian-based steel giants who now own Jaguar Land Rover, are now engaged in longer-term planning.

All governments have to make choices in a whole range of policy areas, from financial funding to procurement to regulation. The key is to think in terms of backing winners, not bailing out losers. For me, industrial strategy is not about favouring either the manufacturing *or* the services sector. A significant proportion of the added value of manufacturing comes from research, development and design, as well as from the manufacturing process. Manufacturing and services are now inextricably interlinked and both need to improve. Nor is it about concentrating on high intellectual jobs or selected 'fashionable' industrial sectors; we have to provide too many jobs – often low-skilled ones – for that.

For a successful industrial strategy, we need to boost our national infrastructure – airports, ports, roads, rail power and telecoms – that underpins our national economy. Failure to invest in infrastructure can be disguised in the short run but is disastrous in the long. Exactly the same applies to investment in research and development.

However, a word of caution here. We must compare ourselves to our competitors in infrastructure investment, not simply give ourselves a pat on the back for moving forwards. I am truly delighted that Crossrail has been built, but it has taken decades of 'on-off' to get there. The picture is much the same for our airports. Again, look elsewhere in Europe to see how our competitors are making strategic investments in airports.

Crucially, the British state needs more officials who have a detailed knowledge of business, sector by sector. We need those who understand that there are many ways they can and should support businesses. We need businesspeople, particularly in the trade associations, who accept that government can play a supportive role, are critical of their own performance and do more than simply lobby.

For the civil service, I offer two specific suggestions. First, longer postings. This would give the official time to accumulate the knowledge and experience to improve their performance and delivery. Second, more secondment of employees between the public and the private sectors, in order to create a greater familiarisation with the different cultures and disciplines involved in each. This process has improved but needs to go further, particularly concentrating on cross-fertilisation early in people's careers. This would help both parties become more aware of how the other system functions and of its strengths and weaknesses. It might also help both of them to think about the UK's long-term industrial capability when making decisions, rather than just the short-term economic factors.

We also need a supportive financial sector. Our booming financial services sector deserves to be fully supported by government. In exchange, it also needs to be more supportive of other wealth creators throughout the economy. I would like to see a return to relationship banking, where a named manager takes responsibility for decisions on individual companies, on the basis of a sound, long-term understanding of the business and the people involved. This may be expensive but would be hugely beneficial in the medium and long term.

We have a tax system that encourages individual and corporate endeavour while being able to fund well-delivered public services as well. Levels of tax need to be internationally competitive in this globalised world, but just as important is the efficiency of the tax system, including the full collection of tax that is due.

Directly elected mayors in our big English cities will enable these economic powerhouses to help and support their local enterprises, as is commonplace in other developed nations.

Finally, continuity and consistency matter as much as change. The costs of change are often underestimated; past government reorganisations have achieved little or no benefit but have brought massive disruption and frustration to customers and civil servants alike. (The current government has, thankfully, so far avoided the cosmetic rearrangement of the deckchairs in Whitehall.) Governments naturally look for the new initiative, the specific stimulus or the fashionable growth sector to support, forgetting that the companies have to deal with every intervention, not just the last one. But businesses need government to be consistent so they can plan for the long term. That is why they have strategies themselves.

In the conclusion to 'Industrial Strategy', I argued that our economic future relied on moving away from legislative changes, new subsidies or headline-grabbing initiatives:

> It is about changing attitudes, involving people, raising standards. It is about spreading the excellence so conspicuous in much of our economy into places where performance is very different. It is at least as much about persuading companies that don't export as it is about persuading those that do to ship more. It is about breaking the ever too present assumption that concentrating decision making in Whitehall can ever be so effective as trusting and sharing power with our citizens who are the heartbeat in our economic centres across the United Kingdom.
>
> It is about lauding the quality of our great universities and outstanding comprehensive and grammar schools while adopting a policy of zero tolerance to schools that are failing a generation of young people. An industrial strategy recognises that as employers, employees, purchasers, consumers, savers and spenders, politicians and councillors, officials and volunteers, we are all in this together with a part to play and a future to win.

I concluded the paper by echoing the sentiment I expressed when I returned to the business department in the early 1990s. We need to intervene to help Britain's companies win – before lunch, before tea, before dinner and then get up and intervene before breakfast all over again. We had better get up early because our competitors will have been up before dawn.

CHAPTER 9

WESTLAND REVISITED

During my time at the Department for the Environment, there was little opportunity for Margaret Thatcher's Euroscepticism and my views to clash. That situation was soon to change – dramatically.

In 1983, she appointed me Secretary of State for Defence; she wanted me to take a more robust attitude towards the supporters of the Campaign for Nuclear Disarmament (CND), who were opposed to both Britain's nuclear deterrent and the deployment of US nuclear-armed cruise missiles at British bases. The government also faced the problem of the women's peace camp at the Greenham Common base, seeking to interfere with the deployment of cruise missiles there. The protests were vociferous, a nuisance and caused considerable disruption and damage. I think Thatcher hoped that, if she put me in to bat at this stage, we might score some easy political runs. Michael Foot was at his weakest over the issue of defence, and many in his party were active CND supporters. I don't think that Europe was even at the back of her mind when she made the appointment.

Shortly after taking up the reins at defence, I presented my first annual review of the department's policies and expenditure to Cabinet. It was a voluminous document, mostly for the record rather than inviting widespread debate.

When I had finished, she asked, 'What is all this reference to pan-European cooperation?' My officials had anticipated the question.

'I think you will find it is a quotation from our manifesto, Prime Minister,' I replied.

Within days of arriving at the Ministry of Defence, the question of a replacement for the RAF Tornado combat plane arose. The plane had been developed through a consortium of British Aerospace, Germany's MBB and Italy's Aeroitalia. As well as the three original creators, Saudi Arabia became a crucially important customer for the Tornadoes after an agreement with the UK in 1985.

Officials told me that the French had brokered a partnership with Germany, Italy and Spain to develop the next generation of military fighter aircraft. I was appalled at the dilemma that British Aerospace and Rolls-Royce were left in, with no credible partners and a gaping hole in their cost structure to replace the ageing Tornados. I set off across Europe, ignoring the warning that the die was cast. As a result, the Eurofighter project came to fruition in 1985, a collaborative venture between Germany, Italy, Spain and the UK to build the next generation of aircraft called the Eurofighter Typhoon.

I have only one regret about this project and that is my private conversation with the Defence Minister of France, Charles Hernu, when he realised that France now faced the risk of exclusion from the deal I was close to concluding with Germany, Italy and Spain.

He asked me, 'If you have the engine, could France have the avionics?' I replied, 'I can't do that. I have British Aerospace and Rolls-Royce to consider.'

It was probably the only answer and the right answer. But doubts lingered. What if I had put that question to the two British companies? Could they have found some face-saving compromises that would have allowed Britain and France to claim another Concorde? Would British Aerospace and Rolls-Royce ever have tried to make such a compromise work, knowing that I had already signed up the other three partners? The answer came in the memoirs of Admiral Sir Ray Lygo, of British Aerospace, who recalled in detail the efforts he had made, together with Manfred Wörner, the German Defence Minister, to find such a compromise but without success.

The Eurofighter was the biggest industrial deal in British history. The conclusion of the deal left me with a strong personal relationship with defence ministers of important European countries and their professional staff. It was this experience and these relationships – coupled with my defence responsibilities for Westland Ltd, a British manufacturer of helicopters who were in financial trouble – that prompted me to ask Leon Brittan, Secretary of State for Trade and Industry, if I could help with his responsibilities towards the company and to see whether there was a European solution on offer. He welcomed the offer.

Before going into more detail about the dispute within the Cabinet, which eventually led to my resignation from Thatcher's government, I should record an earlier incident that became something of a stage setter for the later confrontation. I wrote extensively about this in *Life in the Jungle*, but a brief explanation is needed to set the scene for what was to happen.

In 1984, Norman Tebbit was the Secretary of State for Trade and Industry and as such had responsibility for the shipbuilding industry, which Labour had nationalised in 1977. As Secretary of State for Defence, the procurement and tendering process for defence equipment was entirely the responsibility of my department. The Royal Navy had a requirement for two new Type 22 frigates and the competition to tender was between two shipyards – Cammell Laird on Merseyside and Swan Hunter on Tyneside.

Both shipyards were in financial difficulty, and whichever won the tender, the other would have great difficulty in surviving. Cammell Laird produced the cheaper tender for the two ships and in normal circumstances would have been given the contract. However, strike action at their yard prompted a Cabinet committee to look at the matter again and they decided to rerun the competition. Norman, without consulting anyone, instructed the chairman of British Shipbuilders that Cammell should bid for only one ship, while Swan would proceed as before and bid for both. This left Cammell with virtually no chance of success, as they would be unable to spread their overheads over the two ships.

When I found out about this, I telephoned Cammell Laird to ask them what was going on and was told by the managing director that the instructions had come from head office (i.e. British Shipbuilders) that they were only to bid for one frigate. They were dismayed at the probable consequences.

When the matter came back to Cabinet, I formally complained that my tendering procedures had been interfered with and that Norman had deliberately fixed matters so that Swan would win the competition. After some discussion, the Prime Minister concluded that Swan Hunter had won the bid. I immediately said that I would not accept such a decision; another minister had interfered with my procurement process in order to ensure that one company would win, the consequence of which would be the demise of the company that had originally won the competition.

Before I had time to walk across Whitehall from No. 10 and back to my department, Sir Robert Armstrong, the Cabinet Secretary, had been on the telephone to Sir Clive Whitmore, my Permanent

Secretary. He told him that there had been a major disagreement and the Prime Minister had instructed him that a solution should be produced which was acceptable to me, so that the issue could be resolved. Thatcher had realised that what she had done was wrong and, if it was not corrected, it would have difficult consequences for her. I had challenged her authority and such an affront was not to be forgotten, as we shall see.

• • •

Westland Helicopters Ltd had been building aircraft since 1935 at facilities in Yeovil in the West Country. After the Second World War, the company decided to concentrate on building helicopters and were successful in supplying our services with a range of helicopters in different roles. They included helicopters built under licence from Sikorsky, an American aircraft company, such as the Wessex and later the Sea King. The company also participated in a joint helicopter programme with the French company Aérospatiale, manufacturing three new helicopters under this agreement including the Puma and the Lynx.

In the early 1980s, the company was working on a joint venture with an Italian company, Augusta, to develop a successor to the Sea King. While the company continued to produce helicopters for both military and civil markets, the Ministry of Defence was by far their largest customer. But by the 1980s, given the huge advances in technology and the necessity to remain competitive, there had been many mergers and takeovers within the defence industries and much economy of scale had been achieved. Westland remained comparatively small and was struggling to remain competitive. Sir John Cuckney was appointed chairman of the ailing company in

1985, having made a reputation as a 'company doctor' after a career in MI5. He was later raised to the peerage by Thatcher.

Much of the story has been told before, but here is a brief summary. Westland was in financial difficulties and, as the sponsoring ministry, the Department for Trade and Industry was responsible for managing the consequences. As Secretary of State for Defence, I had an important interest in the company's survival, as it was a major supplier of defence equipment.

The position of Leon Brittan, Secretary of State for Trade and Industry, was quite clear and was spelt out to Sir John Cuckney, chairman of Westland. Sikorsky, an American company that had a long association with Westland, was interested. They wanted a market for their Black Hawk helicopter and they saw the potential for it to be manufactured under licence by Westland, for both the UK Ministry of Defence and export markets not open to them as an American company. But my department had no operational requirement for this type of helicopter. Sikorsky, however, hoped that the politics of any rescue would lead to a change of position by the ministry.

Many years later, I have now been able to read the official papers of the Department for Trade and Industry from that time, which are in the National Archive. Leon Brittan's position was faithfully reported by his Permanent Secretary, Sir Brian Hayes. He wrote, 'Although unlikely, a European minority stake in Westland would be in the political and commercial interests of the government and such an option should be explored. I would need to be convinced that Sikorsky was the best or, indeed, the only option.'

There was never the slightest doubt about Sikorsky's motivation; they spelt it out from the very beginning of the negotiations and it was a perfectly honourable commercial initiative.

The 'blue booby party', as we named ourselves, on our tour of the Galapagos Islands. Our party included Douglas Hurd, Penny Hastings, Gillian Clarke, Gillian Isaacs, Judy Hurd, me, Jeremy Isaacs, Max Hastings, our guide Petra Kapohl, Ken Clarke and Anne, my wife. Caroline Waldegrave took the photograph.

A blue-footed booby. This is one of the most famous birds to be seen in the Galapagos Islands – about half of all breeding pairs nest there.

Fishing on the Lower Varzuga, one of Russia's great salmon rivers. Our party included Max Hastings, Christopher Bland, my son Rupert and me.

The Varzuga and Kitza are huge rivers and teeming with fish. I came bottom of the class, catching only sixteen salmon of the 224 our group caught in total. They were all put back in the river.

My introduction into the House of Lords in 2001, which was sponsored by Lord Weinstock and Lord Carrington.

I was pleased to open the China Club in Hong Kong in 1991, a private members' club founded by David Tang. Source: China Club

Haymarket Asia's twenty-fifth anniversary celebrations in 2023, featuring managing director Atifa Silk and her colleagues. Today, Haymarket Asia is almost entirely staffed by local citizens and we are spearheading an expansion across Asia, the scale of which is very exciting.
© Haymarket Asia

Lenin in the sculpture garden at Thenford, our house. This massive bust of the man who led Russia from 1917 to 1924 was rescued from Latvia after the collapse of the Soviet Union in 1991 and made its way back to the UK, where we purchased it at an auction.
© Nicholas Posner

The visitor facility courtyard at Thenford before we developed it. We never envisaged when we first started working on the garden that we would end up opening it to the public nearly forty years later.

What the visitor facility courtyard looks like now. We hope our visitors enjoy the garden and arboretum as much as we do. They are most appreciative and many bring specialist knowledge with them.

Thomas Kufen, Lord Mayor of Essen, planting *Acer rubrum* 'Redpointe' at Thenford. The mayor donated and planted the tree in recognition of Haymarket's relationship with Germany's horticultural exhibition, IPM Essen. © Haymarket Media Group

What the walled garden looked like before. The formal structure of the walled garden had long gone by the time of our arrival at Thenford in 1976. Instead, the area was used for raising lambs.

An aerial view of the walled garden, taken by Rupert after the implementation of George Carter's redesign in 2001.

Anne and me in my essential conveyance, being greeted by our dogs Fred and Fergus.
© Nicholas Posner

In my office at Thenford – the nerve centre. © Nicholas Posner

With Dame Shirley Bassey at Haymarket's fiftieth anniversary celebrations in 2007.

Filling the Grosvenor House ballroom at the anniversary celebrations. When I started Haymarket, I had worked as an articled clerk for eighteen months, but I instinctively knew it was not for me. I sought the financial independence that the creation of a successful business ensures.

The board of Westland, chaired by Sir John Cuckney, continued their dialogue with United Technologies Corporation, the ultimate owners of Sikorsky, while the European companies MBB (Germany), Aérospatiale (France) and Augusta (Italy) prepared an alternative proposal coordinated by David Horne from Lloyds Merchant Bank. Rapidly, this merged into a British-led consortium with British Aerospace and GEC. It was at this juncture that the politics became especially difficult and ultimately led to my resignation.

Cuckney was pressing No. 10 for clarification of the government's position – specifically over the recommendation of the National Armaments Directors of the UK, France, Germany and Italy that certain helicopter requirements should in future be met solely by aircraft designed and built in Europe.

Thatcher called together a group of the ministers closely involved. She wanted to close down the European initiative and leave Westland free to make their own decision. At that meeting, held on 6 December 1985, a majority of those present decided, contrary to the Prime Minister's wishes, that more time should be allowed for the European offer to reach a form in which a proper comparison could be made with the American-led option.

Thatcher was far from pleased and concluded that it would be necessary to call a meeting of the Cabinet's Economic Affairs Committee to revisit this decision, which was then held on 9 December. She issued a highly unusual invitation to Cuckney to attend, in order to put his case in front of colleagues.

Once again, the majority concluded that they were not yet prepared to support the American proposal to the exclusion of the bid led by British Aerospace. Thatcher, meanwhile, was under pressure from Sir John to reach a conclusion to the central question of Britain's commitment to European procurement, because Westland's annual general meeting was imminent and this fundamental question of policy needed to be clarified.

Frustrated by the second refusal of the majority of her colleagues to write off the British-European option, Thatcher concluded this meeting with the words, 'Very well, we will meet on Friday [13 December] after the stock exchange has closed to determine this matter.'

By now I had a sense of déjà vu about all this. I could see that we were heading into similar territory as we had with the dispute over the frigates. Earlier, and informally, I had warned Charles Powell, the Prime Minister's principal foreign policy adviser, that I was as determined that the proper procedures be followed here as I had been with the Cammell Laird incident some time before.

The Cabinet Office then set about calling a meeting for the Friday afternoon, as the Prime Minister had instructed, but a short time later, officials in No. 10 started raising obstacles and indicating that such a meeting was no longer necessary.

Having lost the argument over Westland's future in two specially convened groups of relevant ministers, it is easy to understand the apprehension within No. 10 at the prospect of a rerun. But Thatcher had promised a conclusive third meeting to decide the government's position. This was verified by Sir Clive Whitmore, my Permanent Secretary at the Ministry of Defence, who examined the notes taken by officials during the meeting itself. Officials had set up a third special meeting, but No. 10 intervened to cancel it – thus ensuring that the case for the British-led European consortium was never properly judged against the rival American bid. No further formal discussions were held on the merits of the UK government, as Westland's main customer, seeking an outcome in line with its policy on European defence collaboration. Thatcher was simply not prepared to lose the argument for the third time.

At the same time, Sir Robert Armstrong, the Cabinet Secretary, was playing a much more prominent part in trying to steer the ship of state back on course. I had cause to challenge him personally because in the official minutes (which Armstrong was responsible for writing) of the regular Cabinet meeting on 12 December, there was no mention of the fact that Westland had been discussed at all, never mind that I had protested that I had not been allowed to state my case. Armstrong wrote me a three-page letter explaining that he had omitted certain parts which he considered too sensitive to be issued as a general Cabinet minute, and due to a 'misunderstanding', the whole section about Westland had been deleted and he was not aware of this until a week later.

Perhaps it is pertinent to point out here that Sir Robert Armstrong was, by common consent, considered one of the outstanding civil servants of his generation, with a 'Rolls-Royce' intellect and a formidable reputation for efficiency and accuracy. So, a 'misunderstanding', of which he was unaware for a week, about one of the most sensitive issues of the day was an extraordinary lapse from his very high standards of efficiency – if Armstrong's explanation to me is to be believed. Armstrong also wrote to Leon Brittan's private secretary, advising him to persuade Leon not to make public the details of a meeting he had held with Sir Ray Lygo because it would not be helpful.

Thus, it becomes clear that the evidence points towards Sir Robert, either by choice or under instruction, protecting the interests of the Prime Minister rather than recording the conclusions of the Cabinet as a whole.

Looking through the official archives, another most unusual and mysterious occurrence is revealed. A search for the Cabinet minutes of 12 December produces the comment 'item destroyed'. Not 'further withheld for reasons of sensitivity' or even 'lost' – just destroyed. But they can be found in full in the archives of the Margaret Thatcher Foundation, complete with the Westland item.

Charles Moore's second volume of Thatcher's official biography was published in October 2015. It is worth noting what William Whitelaw, then the de facto Deputy Prime Minister, is quoted as saying in an interview with the BBC. I quote his exact words, commenting on my position:

> It would have been better if there had been more discussion – well, put it this way, he could have felt that he'd been able to put his case more strongly to Cabinet. He always felt he'd been denied that. And I think it was perhaps … looking back on it … a pity that he always appeared to feel that and I think to some extent he had been denied it.

In Moore's account of the Westland affair, he recorded that officials had begun to ring round to make provisional arrangements for setting up a subsequent discussion at the promised meeting on 13 December. Others had been carrying out Thatcher's will and making sure the meeting did not happen.

Moore goes on: 'She would have done better to make sure that Heseltine could have his meeting – and make sure that he would not prevail in it.' I agree with his judgement. My position would have been totally defensible and I would have done what was asked of me. I would have explained that my colleagues had considered all the options and taken a different view.

No. 10's position was that at the earlier meetings, there had been a clear majority in favour of Sikorsky, which was simply not true. If it had been true, what conceivable risk would have been involved in expecting the Cabinet's Economic Affairs Committee or the Cabinet itself to consider the issue again? Equally, if the clear majority had existed, surely the Prime Minister, having got what she wanted, would have concluded the meeting and avoided any question of putting the issue to the Cabinet?

The dilemma for No. 10 was plain. There had been a clear majority in favour of considering the European option, the details of which were, by this time, firmer and clearer. Incidentally, they included the development of the EH101 helicopter, later a joint naval project with the Italians, which was to provide a substantial part of Westland's workload after the eventual Sikorsky takeover. In my opinion, Thatcher would have been able to secure a majority for her pro-American position if Willie Whitelaw had been set to work. But it is pointless to speculate how events might then have developed, as Cuckney was asking for confirmation that there was no blockage on a potential Black Hawk order, which was the whole point of the Sikorsky bid – and there was no chance the Black Hawk helicopter would have been purchased by the MoD.

In no way would I have been prepared to lie and pretend there was a chance of such an order, given the clear advice I had received from my department. My successor at the Ministry of Defence, George Younger, also refused. In addition, there remained the serious possibility that British Aerospace would continue with its efforts to take over Westland. Ultimately, that happened, and British Aerospace only lost because some of Thatcher's supporters assembled a 'concert party' and acquired enough Westland shares to frustrate their efforts.

As the controversy developed, I had been asked by the European consortium about the British share of European projects in the event of an American takeover, against the background of the government's clear commitment to buy European defence equipment. Cuckney wrote to the Prime Minister asking if Westland would still be considered a European company if 30 per cent of its shares were owned by a NATO company outside Europe.

A draft response was circulated by No. 10, to which I responded that it contained material inaccuracies and should be referred to the law officers. Sir Patrick Mayhew, the Solicitor General, insisted on significant changes to reflect the risk that a number of projects might be lost by Westland if the Sikorsky bid was accepted. I wrote to Lloyds Bank summarising all the relevant information about the negotiations. Cuckney did not get the reassurance he had sought.

This so incensed Thatcher that Charles Powell was instructed to approach Mayhew to persuade him to write another letter to me, giving his opinion that what I had said was untrue. (Charles Moore describes this in his biography of Thatcher.) Powell, in his own words, had got in touch with Mayhew and 'told him what was expected of him'. The letter I received from Mayhew certainly included words to the effect that what I had said contained material inaccuracies, but his judgement was qualified by the words 'on the basis of facts known to me'.

Shortly afterwards, this letter was leaked to Chris Moncrieff, political editor of the Press Association, but crucially, those key qualifying words had been omitted. Moncrieff later described this as 'a major act of deception'. Leon Brittan recalled that Thatcher and her entourage were extremely keen for the letter to be in the public domain, enabling *The Sun* to blazon the words 'You Liar', directed at me, across its front page. In truth, the letter as originally drafted presented no problem to me. I wrote back at once with the up-to-date information that Mayhew had not had at his disposal. Both the Solicitor General and the Attorney General, however, were furious.

Sir Michael Havers, the Attorney General, who had been on sick leave, returned and threatened to bring the police into No. 10 if there was no inquiry into the leaking of the letter.

Moore's book is indicative of the lengths to which those close to Thatcher were prepared to go to thwart me. A particularly distasteful aspect of the whole tale arises at this point. Mayhew was a man of outstanding integrity, and Moore was told that Mayhew and I were old friends going back to our Oxford days and that Mayhew's letter was more a favour to a friend than a considered document that was strictly necessary from a legal point of view. This slanderous suggestion does not reflect the facts. Mayhew was president of the Oxford Union in the Michaelmas term of 1952; I was a year behind him and from a different college. As president, he invited me to speak from the union's dispatch box for the first time. He had to do this as a matter of routine for some twenty undergraduates in his term. That does not constitute friendship 'from Oxford days'. Certainly, I liked and respected him and regarded him as a good colleague, but by no stretch of the imagination can this be interpreted as a relationship that would motivate a government law officer to bestow some favour on me.

What is clear is that there were no lengths to which Charles Powell was not prepared to go on behalf of his boss to personalise the Westland debate and to use the machinery of government to represent only part of the law officers' position. But even this ultra-loyal civil servant admitted later in an interview that Thatcher had been complicit in the conspiracy to suppress the truth. As Charles Moore wrote in his biography, 'What she really feared in this case was accuracy itself. As Charles Powell himself put it, "Her hands were not entirely clean."'

By this time, as we now know from the archives, the staff in

No. 10 were becoming seriously concerned that they were losing control, as was the Prime Minister herself. She rightly anticipated that the matter would come up again when the Cabinet met for the first time after Christmas on 9 January 1986. Using the archival material, we can read the notes with which she prepared for the meeting. She gathered her thoughts on paper and, in her own hand, summed up the situation as she saw it over four pages of script. Her conclusions were that she needed to act firmly and fast to correct a situation that was making the government look incompetent to say the least. She had hoped to end the dispute there and then, but I refused to walk into a rather crude trap that the Prime Minister had prepared for that fateful meeting.

The trap was simple. No member of the Cabinet would be allowed to answer any future questions without prior reference to the Cabinet Secretary. Any politics undergraduate would have seen straight away the consequence of such a conclusion. I immediately asked if this meant that if I was asked identical questions to those I had already answered in recent weeks, I would have first to consult Sir Robert Armstrong. The answer was 'Yes'.

No Cabinet member and certainly no Defence Secretary worth their salt would have accepted such an insulting and degrading sanction. I rose in my place, gathered my papers and, having said that I could no longer serve in this Cabinet, I left.

If I had not resigned then and there, Bernard Ingham, chief press secretary at No. 10, would have had a field day with his friends in Fleet Street. I had learned the hard way the lengths to which Ingham was prepared to go to defend Thatcher. I would have been humiliated in front of my colleagues as he went to work putting out stories that portrayed me as a broken reed. My overseas ministerial colleagues would never have taken me seriously again and two of

Britain's leading companies would have felt betrayed by their own government.

Years later, a further example emerged of the government machine's determination to hide from the public a true, contemporary account of what took place at that Cabinet meeting. A freedom of information application was made to see the minutes of that meeting. It took almost five years of delay and prevarication before the application was initially denied. This decision was reversed when the applicant appealed to a judicial tribunal. Having found against the government's refusal to publish these minutes almost twenty years later, the judge added this stinging rebuke on the way in which the government had behaved:

> We expressed ... our alarm at the inordinate delay ... in processing this complaint. It exceeds anything that we have previously seen. It is particularly reprehensible since the investigation was not factually complex, even though the issues raised were of great importance.
>
> This lack of progress makes a mockery of the right to information. We do not know what use [the applicant] proposed to make of these minutes ... Whatever it was, it was thwarted utterly by inexcusable maladministration. If we value serious investigative journalism, it is imperative that information, if it should be disclosed, be made available, whilst of some practical value.

At the top of her notes, the Prime Minister had scrawled '11/7 [presumably the time I left the meeting – 11.07 a.m.] End of Discussion. MH resigns.' She had got her way, but the damage to her reputation and to those close to her was great – as we shall see.

Government papers, now released, highlight the panic in No. 10

and how everyone from the Cabinet Secretary downwards was determined to ensure that the select committees, who were preparing to investigate the whole affair, should not get anywhere near the Prime Minister herself, nor any of the civil servants involved.

The tactic adopted was that Sir Robert would appear himself, on behalf of No. 10 staff, and Sir Brian Hayes, the Permanent Secretary at the Department for Trade and Industry, would appear on behalf of his staff. Both senior officials would answer questions not as the officials remembered the answers but as they believed to have been the ministerial view at the time. According to official guidance now issued by the Cabinet Office, any officials giving parliamentary evidence must stick to the facts and alert their respective ministers as to what they intend to say.

The dangers posed by the existence of the select committees, hungry to interview the people most involved, were self-evident, as Moore was to conclude: 'If the committee had known and published what had really happened, however, and been allowed to question the officials involved, it is hard to see how Mrs Thatcher would have been able to remain in office.' Years later, Boris Johnson was forced from office, having been found to have lied to the House of Commons. Moore's conclusion is undoubtedly correct.

I was gratified to read of the distaste shown by colleagues who had been questioned by Moore for his authoritative official biography of Thatcher in this latter-day account of events. I also appreciated the personal message written in the copy he sent to me: 'You won't hate all of this.' Moore included references to Sir John Nott's book and its disclosure of names as part of what is described in Moore's book as a great deal of intervention by mystery buyers and other City jiggery-pokery, which was the essential factor in persuading the Westland shareholders finally to accept the Sikorsky bid, sparing

Thatcher further embarrassment. I tell this story in more detail below.

A sad and regrettable consequence of the tensions that the Westland affair caused was the resignation of Leon Brittan as Secretary of State for Trade and Industry. He had been instructed by No. 10 to leak the selective and misleading extracts from Paddy Mayhew's letter. In turn, Leon had instructed his chief information officer, Colette Bowe, to release the adulterated letter. She initially demurred and appealed to her professional boss, Bernard Ingham; the order to publish was repeated even more forcefully. I had been fortunate in having Colette as one of my team in Liverpool in 1981. I knew her to be an admirable and industrious civil servant and she would never have done such a thing of her own volition. Thankfully, she continued to enjoy a distinguished career in public service.

In the event, my resignation did not change British Aerospace or GEC's determination to pursue a European partnership. On Friday 10 January (the day after I resigned), I attended a meeting with Sir Ray Lygo, managing director of British Aerospace, and two members of the board of Flemings, the merchant bankers. At the meeting, we learned that they were proposing to vote their 9 per cent holding in support of the European bid, which could have proved critical in the final result. I do not know how – or, more importantly, by whom – this information was conveyed to No. 10 or Sikorsky, but the consequence was immediate. Over the weekend, a group of Thatcher's supporters were mobilised to form a concert party.

This is the definition of a concert party: 'Persons acting in concert comprise persons who, pursuant to an agreement or understanding (whether formal or informal), cooperate to obtain or consolidate control of a company or to frustrate the successful outcome of an offer for a company.'

That is illegal.

On Sunday 12 January, James Hanson, whom Margaret Thatcher made a life peer in 1983, agreed to buy the shares that Flemings held, adding them to his company's existing holdings. A number of other purchases took place, which remained below the five per cent threshold above which the beneficial holder had to be disclosed. It later emerged that TNT, Rupert Murdoch's associated company, had made one of these purchases. These activities were the subject of growing anxiety in the Council of the Stock Exchange and the curiosity of both the defence and the trade and industry House of Commons select committees, both of which had Conservative majorities and chairmen. The stock exchange reported their anxieties to the Department of Trade and Industry, on the basis that this was the appropriate organisation to explore the facts. Paul Channon, who replaced Leon Brittan as Secretary of State in the department, refused to accept his Permanent Secretary's advice to proceed with an inquiry.

Less hesitant, however, were the reports of the two backbench select committees. The defence committee quoted the Stock Exchange Special Committee's observation that the stock market's credulity was sufficiently strained to be sceptical as to the absence of a concert party and concluded that it was unacceptable that the future of a public company, which was important to the defence interest of the UK, should be decided on the votes of anonymous shareholders.

One section from the report was particularly damning:

> The method of disclosure that was adopted, the unattributable communication of tendentious extracts from the letter, was disreputable. Both the Prime Minister and Mr Brittan agreed that the method of disclosure was wrong and regretted that it had been done in that way. We have noted that Mr Brittan did not express

> a view about the method of disclosure that was to be adopted … The disclosure of the Solicitor-General's letter without his permission was an improper act. Whatever authority the five officials may have thought they had – whether explicit in the case of the officials at the DTI, or implicit in the case of the officials at No. 10 – they were wrong to disclose it or to connive at its disclosure. Yet we understand from Sir Robert Armstrong's evidence that no disciplinary action is to be taken against any of the officials concerned. We find this extraordinary.

Let us not forget that this was the report, agreed unanimously, of a committee with a government majority and a Tory chairman who had been one of Thatcher's Cabinet ministers and her former Chief Whip.

The conclusions of the trade and industry committee, with the same Conservative majority, were just as robust: 'We therefore entertain substantial suspicions, which, however, fall short of proof, that a concert party operated to purchase Westland's shares for locations outside the United Kingdom jurisdiction.'

Having read John Nott's and Charles Moore's account of these events, I make no apology for the part I played. It was a Conservative manifesto pledge that we would purchase European defence equipment. Sikorsky, from the outset, made it clear that they wanted to persuade my ministry to buy their Black Hawk helicopter, for which I was advised there was no requirement. I was asked by Leon Brittan to help provide a European alternative to the American proposal. All of this information was either in the public domain or had to be made available to any purchaser considering an acquisition of Westland.

I remain appalled by the behaviour of those advising Thatcher.

They had persuaded themselves that this was some scurrilous plot to replace her, despite there being not a shred of evidence to support such an idea – for the simplest of reasons that no such plot existed. Outside of the organised meetings, I made no attempt to mobilise support in the Cabinet for my position. I even tried to contact Willie Whitelaw and Lord Hailsham in the hope that they could help resolve the growing controversy. They both proved unavailable.

I had not been involved in any way with the 'wet' group of ministers that had caused her such trouble in her first term as Prime Minister. Mere months before Westland became an issue, I had made what Michael Portillo, a prominent Thatcherite, described as one of the best speeches he had ever heard in the House of Commons, in which I defended her record over the sinking of the Argentinian battleship *General Belgrano* during the Falklands War. I was at lunch with Mrs Thatcher in No. 10 when the news broke that Clive Ponting had been acquitted over charges that he had broken the Official Secrets Act by leaking documents about the *Belgrano*. I was the first to speak when we received the news and immediately offered to go to the House and defend the Prime Minister's position – hardly the act of someone looking for the opportunity to damage her.

A serious criticism of my ultimate challenge for the leadership years later was that I had never spent enough time in the Commons tea room chatting up colleagues. Norman Fowler, later Lord Speaker in the House of Lords, recorded in his autobiography *The Best of Enemies* his immediate response after the Cabinet meeting at which I resigned. He asked Peter Walker, who would have been the first target if I had lobbied anyone, whether I'd said anything to him before the meeting and Walker said, 'No.' Fowler concluded, 'Michael walks by himself. He seeks no allies, discusses no tactics.'

I welcome this note from a diary of the time. It is hardly the stuff of someone conspiring the downfall of a Prime Minister.

Norman goes on to record his view of the proposal that caused my resignation: '"Heseltine silenced." That means that had he agreed to the Prime Minister's proposal, the press would have reported it as a victory for her and a crushing defeat for him.' He did not speculate as to how the press would have learned of the Cabinet decision. I was not the only one to see a trap before me.

I remember forecasting in my original account of the affair, written in 2000, that over the years, and from whatever source, information would eventually emerge that would cast further light on these Westland events. However, I could never have imagined what that source might be even in my wildest dreams.

The revelation came in 2002, when my predecessor as Defence Secretary, Sir John Nott, wrote his autobiography *Here Today, Gone Tomorrow: Recollections of an Errant Politician*. John had left the government after the Falklands War and retired from Parliament in 1983. He then became chairman of Lazard's, the bank that acted for Sikorsky's owners, United Technologies Corporation (UTC).

In the index of John's book is the entry 'Goldsmith, Jimmy, 338', which should indicate where he is mentioned in the text. Oddly, the book as published contains no reference to Goldsmith on that page. His name is mentioned on the page before but in a different context. But it so happens that I have retrieved an advance copy of the book, which was distributed to the press. The offending page has been ripped out and it goes straight from p.336 to p.339.

An article by George Jones, the distinguished political editor of the *Daily Telegraph*, appeared on the front page of the *Telegraph* on 15 March 2002. In it, George stated, 'The Westland affair – which led to Michael Heseltine storming out of Lady Thatcher's Cabinet – reared its head again last night, causing a page to be ripped from Sir John Nott's autobiography four days before publication.'

Jones went on to say that the offending passage that had been taken out of the book described the role played by three of Thatcher's richest supporters – Lord Hanson, Sir James Goldsmith and Gianni Agnelli, head of the Fiat empire – in acting to ensure that Westland was rescued by an American consortium rather than the European group I favoured. The passage in question also discussed the role of 'mystery millionaires' rumoured to have bought a holding in Westland under the cover provided by Swiss banks. Jones reported that Hanson immediately rang Nott and threatened to sue if the passage appeared in the book. Nott then issued a statement explaining that he had not intended to implicate anyone in a secret conspiracy. A page was hurriedly removed, rewritten and replaced in time for the book's launch.

George Jones went on: 'The drastic action over the book … follows a behind-the-scenes row about Sir John's recollection of one of the most serious crises of Lady Thatcher's time in office, which came close to splitting the Tory Party.'

Lord Hanson issued a statement that his company had bought shares in the troubled Westland because of their interest in the helicopter business through Air Hanson Ltd, a stake which was sold to the eventual buyer of Westland, GKN, at a profit for Hanson shareholders. 'Such share purchase decisions,' the statement added, 'were always made for purely commercial reasons and never for political reasons.'

The bank acting for Westland therefore knew the names of most of those believed to have acted in concert. No one else knew at the time, and if John Nott had not himself disclosed what he knew – not just his knowledge that there had indeed been a concert party but the critical missing name – the mystery could have lasted to this day.

A look at Nott's papers in the archives confirms that in his correspondence with Hanson, he had made clear his support for the American bid over the European. The reason, wrote Hanson, that he had threatened action against Nott was because he had bought the shares openly in the name of his company and not through any anonymous intermediary. But of course, that says nothing about why he did so at that particular moment in time in the first place, although his partner Gordon White did give us a clue. When White was asked the same question, he gave a more qualified answer to the effect that the motivation for Hanson's intervention was part political. It may be relevant to note here that White was also raised to the peerage by Thatcher in her resignation honours four years later.

James Hanson, Gianni Agnelli and, finally, James Goldsmith had each apparently discovered a sudden and urgent need to increase their holding or acquire shares in the same small helicopter company at the same time. Or, to put it another way, they had entered together into a criminal conspiracy, which is a more robust way of describing the concert party.

Sir Nicholas Goodison, chairman of the London Stock Exchange, was so concerned that on 4 February 1986, he invited Peter Wills, his former deputy chairman, to chair an investigation into whether rules had been infringed. I appeared before him on 11 February. During that meeting, a draft press release that the stock exchange proposed to send out was produced. Among other things, it said, '20.33 per cent of the total issued share capital of Westland is now in the hands of nominee owners, registered overseas.' When Wills asked me to comment, I said to him, 'I don't know who they are. You don't. It's a scandal.'

John's book mentions another appointment that, to my knowledge, was not known at the time. Gordon Reece was as close to Thatcher as any of her advisers. His relationship with her was sufficiently close that he is credited with changing her sense of dress, her hairstyle, her vowels and voice. He was also appointed to advise the Westland board on its conduct of the takeover battle. John Nott's words have their own significance:

> We were also fortunate that Cuckney had taken on Gordon Reece as his PR adviser. Gordon had helped Margaret in her early days as leader, knew her well and was generally a source of strength. And so he was bringing to the party not just his relationship with the Prime Minister but an invaluable relationship with her admirers and supporters.

An interesting twist to this tale is that, after the Westland affair was over, Nott appointed Gordon Reece as his own PR adviser at Lazard.

Looking back at these events, there is one in particular that stands out to reinforce the clear conclusion that the position of the Prime Minister and the officials around her was indefensible. The matter was bound to come to the floor of the House, which it did on 25 January 1986, some weeks after my resignation.

There was obvious concern about what I would say. John Wakeham, the Chief Whip, approached me and we reached an agreement. Thatcher would not attack me and would include a form of words accepting personal responsibility for things that had gone wrong. In that event, she would have no trouble with me. As a result of that deal, my speech was able to be coached in terms attractive to me, as I was anxious to remain in the fold of the Tory Party.

In the event, I was able to combine the words I had agreed with an attack on the Labour Party. Neil Kinnock lost the plot in an outpouring of verbiage. My speech was well received on the backbenches, and my purpose from that point was survival until the next leader of the party brought me back. Of course, issues remained. Much was made by Thatcher's supporters of the threat that I was thought to be. Certainly, at that time, she was facing considerable criticism and my name, inevitably, featured on any list of potential successors. But that does not justify the lies about my behaviour and intentions. Would this sort of comment, which is the speculation every Prime Minister has to face, have been enough to persuade her prominent supporters to risk criminal prosecution by participating in a concert party to acquire Westland?

In my earlier autobiography, *Life in the Jungle*, I recorded an alternative occurrence that remains unexplained. As the controversy over the future of Westland developed, Thatcher received a telephone call from General Alexander Haig, who was the American Secretary of State at the time of the Falklands War. After he left government, he returned to UTC, Sikorsky's parent company, where he had previously held a senior position. He was also to claim that he had 'called in his markers' for the American bid. It appears that Thatcher might, therefore, have been persuaded not only by those around her, but senior figures from the American military establishment that Sikorsky was the route to take.

I am only glad that the truth about the Westland affair and how I was deceived has finally come to light – as I always knew it eventually would.

PART III

A RETURN TO GOVERNMENT

CHAPTER 10

CAMERON: A TIPTOE BACK

I first met David Cameron during the mid- to late 1980s. He was one of several young people that came along to our house as friends of our younger daughter, Alexandra. Friends of your children are not people you keep a particularly close eye on. They are part of a group; they come and go. But as part of their chat, I recall hearing the words 'Prime Minister', reflecting the view of his contemporaries of a possible and potential career destination. To identify the possible qualifications for a leader, even at that time, the words 'Eton' and 'Oxford' would be high on that list. He already had an assuredness and self-confidence so often associated with such a background.

It was not until I read his book decades later that I discovered that he was working in Conservative Central Office in the early 1990s when I stood against Margaret Thatcher for the leadership. He was right to state in his memoirs that the conflict within the party over her legacy was deep, very bitter and lasted right through the following years. Thatcher's legacy was potent throughout the years we spent in opposition. When we lost the 1997 election, the Conservative Party elected three leaders in succession from the right:

William Hague, Iain Duncan Smith and, finally, Michael Howard. Significantly, they all had strong Eurosceptic convictions.

It was not until the Conservative Party had suffered two more substantial election defeats in 2001 and 2005 that they once again became interested in finding a credible candidate who could lead us back to power. David, who had only been elected to Parliament for the first time four years earlier, stood in the Conservative Party leadership election, won and became Leader of the Opposition after Howard's defeat in 2005.

My first serious conversation with him took place when, on John Major's advice, he came to see me, as he was contemplating standing for the leadership. I explained that my loyalties remained with Ken Clarke, as long as his hat was in the ring and he remained a credible candidate. In the event that Ken decided to stand aside, I told him he could count on what support I could offer.

A few months after he became leader of the party, he asked me to join him on a trip to Liverpool – echoing my time walking the streets in 1981 following the riots in Toxteth. By 2005, the renaissance of Liverpool was clear and the city was transformed from the one I had visited decades before. The trip, which was captioned 'Regeneration Game' on the front page of the *Financial Times*, was obviously symbolic and was treated so by the press. The paper noted, 'The tyro Tory leader was keen to demonstrate that the party does not speak only to those living in affluent areas.' David stressed that cities were part of his vision to change the party, saying, 'For too long Conservatives have been seen as the party of the leafy suburbs. That's changing.' But, in a hint of the trouble that would lie ahead, some of the coverage of the Liverpool trip reflected an issue that we took very different views on: Europe. David's decision to take the Conservatives out of the European People's Party would start the journey towards Brexit. I happily told the BBC that I thought he was wrong to make the pledge. As I said on that trip, 'If you are not in the team, you are selling out British interests.' A party spokesperson dryly noted, discussing our different opinions, that I had 'long-held views on Europe.'

As Cameron was to discover, trying to do a deal with the right wing of the Conservative Party was to give him only temporary breathing space. Later, he was to find to his cost that Rudyard Kipling's famous line 'Once you have paid him the Dane-geld / You never get rid of the Dane' was to prove devastatingly true.

The trip to Liverpool was followed by an invitation to chair a policy group and explore ideas that would provide 'forgotten Britain' with a series of action plans for urban regeneration. This was one of several such groups, involving Ken Clarke and other figures from the party's past, working to propose ideas for the 2010 manifesto.

Working independently of the party, my task force had an illustrious membership that included Alistair Burt, MP for North East Bedfordshire; Dame Mavis McDonald, a trustee of the Joseph Rowntree Foundation; Lord Bruce-Lockhart of the Local Government Association; Susan Williams, leader of Trafford Council and later Chief Whip in the House of Lords; and Baroness Warsi, then the party's co-chair. We fed our ideas directly to the shadow Cabinet.

My report concluded that the regional tier of government should be devolved downwards to local authorities and that the larger urban ones should have a single elected figure of authority to shape their vision for the future. This recommendation was accepted and set out in the party manifesto of 2010, with the words, 'We have seen that a single municipal leader can inject dynamism and ambition into their communities. So, initially, we will give the citizens in each of England's twelve largest cities the chance of having an elected mayor.'

But there was one major issue: we didn't quite win! The 2010 general election produced a coalition government, with the Conservatives doing well by gaining ninety-six seats but missing out on an overall parliamentary majority by twenty or so. David reached out to the Liberal Democrats to form the coalition, who were dead against the concept of elected mayors from the start.

The inevitable compromises followed, and sadly we were unable to implement almost all the local authority reforms in which I had been involved since the 1960s. What progress could be made had to be made by agreement and, inevitably, that meant proceeding at the speed of the slowest ship in the convoy. There were enthusiasts for devolution within the Lib Dems, but this was not the view at the top of the party. Holding some of the reins of office for the first time, led by Nick Clegg as Deputy Prime Minister, I suppose it was no surprise that they were reluctant to start by devolving power away from themselves.

As a result, a small group of us devolution advocates used to meet in a bunker in 10 Downing Street. The group included Lord Adonis, who had been Secretary of State for Transport under Tony Blair, Gavin Barwell, then a rising young Conservative MP, Steve Hilton, the Prime Minister's director of strategy, and me. We did have some media support, particularly from the *Birmingham Post*, *Birmingham Mail* and the *Yorkshire Post*, but the attempts to win local referendums to introduce mayors were deeply disappointing. In 2012, twelve referendums were held for directly elected mayors in the biggest cities, but only two cities returned a positive result – Bristol said yes and Doncaster opted to retain its existing one. Cities including Birmingham, Leeds, Manchester, Newcastle, Nottingham, Sheffield and Wakefield all said no. Liverpool had bypassed the process by adopting its own mayor.

The mayoral concepts were rejected on the tiniest of turnouts. The opposition was largely orchestrated by local councillors, determined to preserve their existing powerbase, and MPs all too aware that such figures, given more executive authority, would undermine their own position. The campaign itself was half-hearted and lacked any substantial incentive to persuade local communities that there was anything in it for them. In the case of Bristol, the result was a shock caused by infighting within the Labour Party, which led to the election of an independent, George Ferguson – a man very well qualified for the job, who had devoted his adult life to building a sense of community purpose. The introduction of various remuneration systems for councillors has, more recently, increased their reluctance to accept any change of the system, where a natural instinct to hold on to what you have has strengthened the resistance of anyone about to see power slip from their grasp.

After Cameron became Prime Minister in 2010, I was invited to join him on another trip to Liverpool. Inevitably, I talked of my experiences nearly thirty years earlier and the changes that had followed. In consequence, he asked me to work with Terry Leahy, himself a Liverpudlian and former chief executive of Tesco, and revisit the report 'It Took a Riot', which I had written in 1981. I gave my report that title because what was said to me on the streets of Liverpool at the time was 'it took a riot to get you to come here' – and, of course, they were quite right.

One small example of the UK's dysfunction arose from that visit. Liverpool's port was enjoying a renaissance and its tonnage was at an all-time high. But little progress had been made in recreating the great liner trade for which Liverpool had once been famous but had now been overtaken by ports such as Felixstowe, Southampton and Newcastle. David expressed concern when I pointed out to him the frustrations and delays in building a new liner terminal necessary to facilitate the restoration of this trade and he instructed that it should be dealt with. In practice, it was fourteen months after that visit before the blockage was removed.

I did not realise at the time that I was walking on stepping stones leading me back towards the corridors of power. I was invited by Nick Clegg to assist the government in tackling one of its more acute political challenges. The public expenditure programmes of the outgoing Labour administration were unaffordable and had to be reduced, which meant significant cuts in public expenditure. It was evident that cutting overall public spending would have an especially harsh effect on those parts of the country where such funds were particularly important to the local economy.

In order to soften the consequences, the coalition government created a Regional Growth Fund of £3.2 billion to stimulate expenditure in those areas, and I was invited to chair an advisory committee to oversee this. Sir Ian Wrigglesworth, a former Labour MP who had joined the Social Democratic Party, which then merged with the Liberal Party to become the Lib Dems, was my deputy. He was also an entrepreneur in one of the northeastern ports. We enjoyed a most cordial relationship, rapidly finding a harmonious approach of working together.

It was a salutary experience for Conservatives to work closely with the Liberal Democrats. I was long familiar with the bitterness that existed between both parties. In the 1950s, I had been elected president of the Oxford Union with the active support of my friends Tony Howard and Jeremy Isaacs, both chairmen of the University Labour Club. We didn't share much in common politically, except one passionate hatred: the Liberals. The only candidates standing against me were from that party and our unholy alliance against them helped deliver me the presidency.

I had fought the old Liberal Party time and again on my journey into Parliament. I fought to become the member for Tavistock against the Liberals and again in Henley. In my experience, the divide between Liberal and Conservative policies is less over the issues on the ground. It is the personalities of the candidates, which are often associated with allegations, doubtless from both sides, of bad behaviour, disreputable campaigning and all the other human frailties within the political system that can so embitter dialogue. 'There are two Liberal candidates in this constituency,' I once joked. 'But I am going to win!'

In practice, it proved relatively simple to reach a consensus on most policy matters throughout the five years the coalition existed. The Lib Dems, however, were to pay a bitter and unfair price for taking part in the coalition.

David Cameron had that essential quality for electoral success: the ability to connect with people outside his own party. On his journey to the premiership, he had to challenge some controversial policies that had become dogma within the Conservative Party. Rather than trying to bypass them, his notable shift of emphasis from the right back towards the centre was more than mere political opportunism. It was based on an analysis of the sort of society he wanted to lead and for which he was prepared to fight. If that meant hugging hoodies or testing the prejudices of the party over same-sex marriage, then he was up for it.

He invited me to speak at the 2006 party conference and talk to his shadow Cabinet about running a government department. Later, he asked me to represent the British government at the funeral of Helmut Schmidt, the former West German Chancellor.

He may have pushed the bounds of his One Nation credo to the limits of plausibility, but it reflected a reality of which the

Conservatives needed reminding: we are the party that wins from the centre ground. Following the disastrous outcome of the 2024 general election, it is vital for the party to remember the character and determination of the person and the politics that brought us back into government in 2010.

His decision to resign as Prime Minister and leave the House of Commons after the Brexit referendum result was understandable but regrettable. The party is poorer for his loss, and the shambles that followed is too well documented to need repeating here. Suffice to say, there is no way the Conservatives will win again by lurching to the right, particularly if it is to try to win back those who voted for the fledgling Reform UK and its creator, Nigel Farage. For every vote potentially regained by pandering to them, many more are lost among traditional Conservatives supporters who are rightly appalled by their latent racism.

CHAPTER 11

REGIONAL GROWTH FUNDS AND LOCAL ENTERPRISE PARTNERSHIPS

After the 2010 election, which resulted in the Conservatives returning as the largest party but without an overall majority, I was asked to return to government for the first time in thirteen years to an area that was close to my heart: building up our local economies. The offer came in the form of chairing a new body set up in the wake of the financial crisis, the Regional Growth Fund. With an initial endowment of £1 billion, the opportunity to make a tangible difference to communities suffering from cuts in public expenditure was real. In the first Budget after the 2010 election, the coalition government announced the creation of Local Enterprise Partnerships to replace Labour's Regional Development Agencies, which were due to be closed down. These policies marked a continuation of the work I had done in the past, and I want to reflect on the important roles they played in developing local economies.

In the summer of 2010, soon after the election, I was given an office at the old Department for Trade and Industry – now rebranded as the Department for Business, Energy and Industrial Strategy

– in the very same building where I had served as President of the Board of Trade some twenty years before.

Sir Vince Cable was the Liberal Democrat Secretary of State in the department, with whom I enjoyed a cordial relationship. His real focus of attention appeared to be over his policy differences with George Osborne as Chancellor, rather than on policies that could properly be categorised as industrial strategy.

Early on, I appreciated how open he was to my views on industrial and devolution policy in the current climate. Vince invited me to a meeting that turned out to be formative. He had asked the department to brief him on industrial strategy, with senior officials and at least one junior minister present at the appointed hour. Cabinet ministers are always under great time pressure, however, and he was running some ten to fifteen minutes late. So I filled the vacuum by asking the individuals present to outline their responsibilities. Having listened to each of them, it was apparent that no one was in charge of industrial strategy; they all had individual roles but there was no coordination, a fact which I pointed out.

When Vince arrived and the briefing began, he listened patiently to the presentations of individual responsibilities and was about to leave. I had said nothing, feeling it was not my place as an observer to intrude. Just before he left, Vince turned to me and asked if I would like to contribute. I gave him my views on industrial strategy for a few minutes. He responded, 'I like that and can someone make a note of what Michael has said.' Immediately after the meeting, I joined the person responsible for doing what Vince had asked. It is one of the coincidences of life that the official was none other than Amanda Brooks, who had been my diary secretary when I was Deputy Prime Minister before she went on to be deputy high commissioner in Singapore. We sat in an outer office and I reconstructed the words that I had used in the meeting. Vince later generously paid public tribute to the formation of the government's industrial strategy from that very meeting.

The bidding to receive money from the Regional Growth Fund was open to a wide range of interested parties during its first four rounds, although this was narrowed to just those from the private sector for the final two rounds. One of the participants was the Local Enterprise Partnerships (LEPs), which had been established to justify the abolition of the Business Links advice service when the coalition came to power.

I did everything in my power to persuade Vince and Cabinet Office minister Francis Maude against closing Business Links but to no avail. As originally conceived during my tenure as President of the Board of Trade in the early 1990s, Business Links had no resources and were never intended to play an influential role or advise the government. Their purpose was to coordinate advice and provide support, particularly in exporting, for the small business sector, advice similar to that provided by the Chambers of Commerce in Europe.

Fortunately, I was able to persuade my colleagues on the Regional Growth Committee to grant assistance to Lancaster University, in order to examine how LEPs could be restructured to fill a bigger role in empowering local economies and provide the services that had previously been found in Business Links.

As mentioned, in the June 2010 Budget the coalition government announced the creation of Local Enterprise Partnerships. In essence, these were intended to create a framework within which stakeholders in each local economy could work together to frame a strategy for growth, based on local circumstances. They had featured in the Conservative's 2010 manifesto, but when the new ministers Eric Pickles and Grant Shapps arrived at the Ministry of Housing, Communities and Local Government, it became clear that little thought had gone into how to convert the promise into an effective structure. In the early discussions, officials offered to produce guidance to support local areas in the creation of these partnerships, but ministers resisted. Eric was clear that Whitehall doesn't know best and local areas should be left to develop the partnerships themselves.

This result was that LEPs ended up differing in their structure from area to area – some as private companies limited by guarantee, others by extension of the local authority. Although the idea had been that they should be business-led, the freedom came back to bite them. They were continually reviewed by the government, because the rigid structure Whitehall wanted was at complete odds with how they had emerged originally. In 2017, 2018, 2022 and 2023, a succession of ministers and non-executive directors continually examined their funding, role and functionality. In 2014, a nationwide LEP network was started to help the schemes work better and communicate with each other – but once again, Whitehall took a hands-off role.

In total, some thirty-eight organisations came into existence, employing 1,000 people across the country before they were integrated into local authorities. My first memory of LEPs is the conversation I had with the chairman of one, who said, 'There's just me and a secretary.' This indicated the worst sort of doctrinal conservatism. I believed that the LEP commitment had been made originally to provide an answer to the question as to why the Business Links support arrangements I had established in the 1990s were to be dismantled. The original concept of LEPs was no more than a fig leaf behind which to hide a non-interventionist dogma. LEPs as they were designed, forming public and private sector partnerships based on each local economy, made sense. Such a concept is sadly a cause for disagreement within my party.

A core part of LEPs were the Growth Hubs, designed to be free at the point of delivery to provide a service for local small- and medium-sized businesses. Whitehall never appreciated their potential and they received minimal funding – £12 million a year for the thirty-eight Growth Hubs, just enough to cover their minimal running expenses.

From 2015, after the Conservatives had taken over the reins from the coalition and were governing alone, Greg Clark, Secretary of State for Communities and Local Government at the time, was keen for LEPs to develop local industrial strategies; he recognised that industrial strategy and strategic economic plans go hand in hand. Central government had to be an essential partner in the process, otherwise each LEP could claim to be pre-eminent in the same specialist field. Such a conflict could only be resolved by a government's decision over the allocation of research funding. In short, it was a contract between local agencies and central government. But when Greg left the Department for Business in 2019, the scheme lost its sponsor.

One of the best measures of how successful LEPs were emerged during the Covid pandemic. Many of the thirty-eight organisations stepped up to fulfil crucial roles in their communities. To help mitigate the effect on employment, the Growth Hub network engaged with 2.2 million small- and medium-sized businesses – much larger than the reach of the British Chambers of Commerce or the Federation of Small Businesses. They proved to be an integral part of local forums across the country dealing with impacts of Covid.

Independently, LEPs undertook a range of initiatives to support individuals and businesses impacted by the pandemic. The Humber LEP set up a service – Humber Jobs Fuse – to help those who were made jobless because of Covid, helping people get back into employment while supporting key regional employers with staffing gaps due to the pandemic, especially in the care sector.

Meanwhile, the Coast to Capital LEP – covering much of the area from London to the Sussex coast – set up a £2 million fund to provide grants to small businesses and social enterprises. The fund helped around 400 organisations impacted by Covid, particularly in vulnerable sectors such as the aviation supply chain, tourism, hospitality, leisure and the service economy. The D2N2 Growth Hub in Derby, Derbyshire, Nottingham and Nottinghamshire funded a 'RESTART' programme designed to help businesses in the East Midlands return to operation following the impact of the pandemic. The Heart of the South West LEP helped lead regional economic recovery post-Covid, with the Nuclear South West public–private partnership teaming up with regional business organisations to help companies capitalise on key nuclear sector projects.

Further to this, the £2 million Pivot and Prosper Grant Fund was launched by the Greater Birmingham and Solihull Local Enterprise Partnership (GBSLEP), which gave businesses the opportunity to apply for matched funding up to £40,000. This LEP also launched apprenticeship and employment triage services to help employers, apprentices and individuals impacted by the pandemic – creating a service to help employers continue training employees who had previously worked on apprenticeships but had been furloughed.

The Oxfordshire LEP helped drive the work of their life sciences cluster in fighting Covid and was used by the Department for Transport to build the national investment strategy as part of the government's recovery planning. The Hertfordshire LEP, Hertfordshire

Opportunities Portal, set up a dedicated channel for local people and employers to set out a raft of guidance and support measures, listing job vacancies by sector and supporting people with careers advice. The Berkshire LEP and Enterprise M3 LEP worked with Pinewood Studios to initiate 'ScreenSkills', a programme that gave participants information on how their expertise in aviation and its supply chain could be used in the film, television and gaming industries.

The Marches LEP in Shropshire injected nearly £1.6 million into local tourism and businesses affected by Covid, using a grant support for strategic tourism and business initiatives following consultations with the area's business boards. And the Buckinghamshire LEP made £2 million of Covid emergency funding available to support local businesses, whose cash flow and future viability were impacted by the pandemic. They also supported Buckinghamshire businesses that were switching operational practises and production schedules to support the local and national resilience programme.

These multiple examples demonstrate the potential of LEPs. Like the Regional Growth Fund, they were a continuation of what I have always believed about government being active in laying the foundations for a thriving private sector. They were plugged into their local economies and engaged with local people. The expertise they build up over a decade in existence will not be easily rebuilt or regained. When the decision was made in 2023 by Michael Gove to scrap LEPs in favour of mayoral-led deals or fusion with local government, local resilience was damaged and the expertise fragmented.

Where there were combined authorities or devolution deals, the LEP functions should have been integrated, but where there wasn't, we should have retained the LEP until such time as there was and the LEP should continue to be funded in the meantime. When LEPs were first established, they received £500,000 each – £19 million in total between the thirty-eight organisations. That was reduced to £375,000 in 2022 and reduced further to £250,000 in 2023. Funding was due to be withdrawn entirely in 2024. Despite the relatively reduced core funding, some LEPs have built considerable balance sheets through investments in their local economy and the wise use of recyclable loan funds.

LEPs didn't make many friends with the local politicians or MPs. Their boards were excellent at stress testing and sifting out vanity projects that delivered little economic benefit but were often the recommendation of elected politicians.

Inevitably the Treasury itself was a major barrier to LEPs and wanted to end them. Ministers had lost sight of what they delivered. Jeremy Hunt, who was then Chancellor, seems to have steamrollered through the decision and just forgotten about LEPs in places where there wasn't a devolution deal. Leaders of LEPs might have hoped for a more friendly approach from the Conservative Party and its business ministers. Yet many felt they struggled to get that level of attention. It is a lesson that shows Conservative dogma is still powerful enough to override any serious and practical examination of results.

LEPs were to play a fundamental role in the numerous reports that each of them published, outlining proposals to regenerate their local economies. To stimulate this formulation of local strategies, they were able to submit applications for grants to facilitate their proposals and thus carry out the purpose of the Regional Growth Fund. I was able to summarise the essence of this relationship in the annual monitoring report, covering the work of the fund up to 2014. Deals had been concluded with each of the thirty-nine applicants, as a result of bids based on the priorities that local people had identified. This was, thus, an unprecedented process in the normal decision-making of government. In a formal review assessing its impact, the Department for Business concluded £2.8 billion had been allocated and had created 345,863 years of new employment. Private sector investment stimulated by the Regional Growth Fund came to a total of £11.4 billion.

I was strongly supportive of this local empowerment, which the Regional Growth Fund had played a clear role in: plans designed locally, significant input from central government, a competitive process and long-term growth as a result. The fund's closure was announced in October 2016, but there would be an emergency fund using money allocated but not used in earlier rounds.

CHAPTER 12

NO STONE UNTURNED

In 2012, hard on the heels of the 'Rebalancing Britain' report, David Cameron, encouraged by his aide Steve Hilton, asked me to extend my analysis of Liverpool across England. The 'Rebalancing Britain' report had assessed the opportunities for growth in the Liverpool city region and now I would do the same for the rest of the country. We agreed that I would be given an official from each government department to work at my discretion, without any attempt to restrain the recommendations that we might make. It was a most generous offer and it was of great excitement for me to have the resources of the civil service at my disposal once again. The outcome was the report 'No Stone Unturned: In Pursuit of Growth', one of the most important publications not only of my post-ministerial life but of my whole career.

Reflecting on my adult life since I first came to London as an articled clerk in 1955, it is clear that there are continuous threads running through all the jobs I have had, which come together in the conclusions set out in that report.

A small but significant dialogue arose over the terms of reference at the start of the project – the 'Heseltine Review', as it was initially known. I wanted to include the words 'industrial strategy' as part of the remit, but David Cameron was anxious about the effect of these words on some Conservative MPs. A compromise was reached: I was able to report about growth, referring to industrial strategy in other countries. It avoided the inevitable tensions among some of his backbenchers but highlighted an ideological split that remains in the party to this day. The review was announced at the end of March 2012, with a remit to report back to Chancellor George Osborne and Secretary of State for Business Vince Cable in the autumn.

The first meeting of my thirty civil servants was scheduled for 4 April 2012 at the Department for Business, Innovation and Skills. Full of expectation, I turned up to find a meeting room with only nine people in it. I was confronted with a very simple challenge: Whitehall does not take this regeneration challenge seriously and if I let them get away with it, that will be the end of the endeavour. So I apologised to the nine officials present, explained there must have been some mistake and adjourned the meeting.

Immediately afterwards, I wrote a letter to the Chancellor George Osborne, copied to the Cabinet Secretary, expressing my deep unhappiness at the lack of engagement. The meeting was shortly reconvened; this time there was a full complement of thirty officials in the room and I had stamped my tiny foot successfully at the cynicism of Whitehall.

The remit of these meetings ranged very widely, and I was determined we would not be subject to the special pleading of officials from every department coming with their departmental brief. I therefore divided my thirty officials into ten teams of three. The consequence was that each official first had to discuss agenda items with two other officials from different departments. I believed that this creative tension would have the effect of subjecting departmental advice to the intelligent criticism of other civil servants and therefore would produce a much more open and balanced dialogue – and so it materialised.

I was fortunate that each department had chosen a very high calibre of official, as has been shown by the promotions that followed after my group finished its work. Debbie Gillatt went on to hold various director posts in the Department for Business, Energy and Industrial Strategy and retired a few years ago. Jo Shanmugalingam went on to become second Permanent Secretary at the Department for Transport. Chris Carr is now director at Better Regulation. Chris Southworth is secretary general at the International Chamber of Commerce. Sarah Jenkins is managing director of Global Public Affairs at CPP Investments. Vicki Brown is head of data flows policy at the Department for Science and Innovation; Sam Hollister is head of energy economics, policy and investment group at LCP Delta; and Ben Pledger, my private secretary, is now deputy director for affordability, strategy and policy at the Department for Energy Security and Net Zero.

We set to work and the title of the report indicates the approach we took. The pattern so often adopted in Whitehall when faced with a problem is to draw in the great and the good, the high fliers, the excellent, and seek their advice. Britain has plenty of such people, with so much experience. We are world leaders in many fields, but that was not our problem. Our problem is to be found when you look at the averages. The challenge we faced in our report was how to influence the bottom end of the scale: the underperformers, the underachievers, the low standards, the untrained, the unskilled.

In order to do this, you had to ask uncomfortable questions of both the public and the private sector. Why was it that although we were good at innovating small businesses, we were poor at encouraging them to become significant businesses? Why was it that so many of our businesses did not export and therefore were not subject to the competitiveness of the world marketplace? Why was it we trained too few people at too inadequate a standard? Why was Ofsted still talking about a tolerance of failure in too many schools in the Midlands and the north?

In order to illustrate the problem, we invented the caricature of 'Uncle Bert' to exemplify a particular type of company. Uncle Bert was a nice guy – he had been running the family business since he inherited it in the late 1990s. Yes, he was a bit older now. Yes, sometimes he was to be found on the golf course on Thursdays. He was much admired locally, a pillar of the local Rotary Club. The company had not expanded that much – but then, did he want to be liable for higher estate duty? You couldn't say he is not interested in exports. He was the one who got in touch with Hank, that nice American who knew his father during the war and who has been buying from the company ever since. It's true, Uncle Bert is a bit sniffy about Europe. The French don't keep to the rules and, well, you know about the Germans. He's a good, loyal father and grandfather. We owe it to him to let him enjoy his later years.

Someone from the Confederation of British Industry told me my report would be damned out of hand if such language ever featured in it. Despite this, I told the story to a group of people from the West Midlands and one of them said, 'Yes, I know exactly what you mean. They are the stock in trade of my business. I am an official receiver.' I told this story to the Prime Minister and he replied, 'My constituency is full of them.'

Reluctantly, I decided to avoid the risk of undermining the reception to my report, but Uncle Bert became a recurrent theme in our investigations and a cartoon of him and his family was presented to me by officials when our report was published.

The central theme of the report was that too much power and too much money had accumulated in Whitehall. Unlocking this was the key to unlocking economic growth and potential. It called for the creation of a Single Local Growth Fund, from which local regions could bid for money for transport, housing and skills. LEPs would then be empowered to bid for funds to stimulate growth in their local areas, working more closely with local stakeholders and businesses. We called on LEPs to have the best possible leadership and some extra direct funds to improve their local strategy.

The report also made the case for legislation to allow all local authorities to have a directly elected mayor should they wish. It called for a more joined-up approach towards growth across Whitehall, with annual departmental business plans and strengthened roles for non-executive directors of ministries. It called on the government to streamline its management of EU investment funds. The report asked for more employer engagement with schools, particularly to ensure further education policy was pursued effectively. All of these recommendations were accepted.

George Osborne and Vince Cable referred to my report as 'compelling' with, at its heart, a passionate case for decentralising economic power from central government to local areas and leaders, who were best placed to understand and address the opportunities for and obstacles to economic growth in their own communities. The government agreed with this – just as strong local leadership is what built our cities and made the UK successful in the past, it also has the potential to transform our competitiveness in the present and future.

The coalition government was generous in the detail of their response, which was published in March 2013, and comprehensive in their coverage of the eighty-nine recommendations. Some sixty-one were accepted, twenty accepted in part, three had to await the subsequent spending review and five were rejected. A summary of these was helpfully provided and is included as an annex in the report.

Natural curiosity instinctively focuses on the recommendations which were rejected. One was that I wanted the LEPs to review their boundaries to ensure that they reflected the realities of their local economies. Opposition to that from neighbouring counties was predictable – particularly from Warwickshire, whose refusal to incorporate any part of its area into Greater Birmingham contributed to the subsequent loss by Andy Street of the mayoral election in 2024.

I fail to understand why, after the initial term for the Docklands Development Corporation expired in the late 1990s, its remarkable achievements were not replicated through Kent and Essex to the coast. This would have been controversial as there was already a new mayoral team at work in part of the area. Very shortly after this decision, George Osborne asked me to look again at the Kent–Essex area, which at least indicated that he may not have been totally happy with this decision. It was a missed opportunity.

In another recommendation that was rejected, the concept of empowering the Chambers of Commerce movement fell on deaf ears. The obvious international comparisons outlining the much greater effectiveness of chambers on the continent were too remote to influence the instinctive non-interventionist wing of the Conservative Party. This rejection must, however, be seen against the response that included very firm support for the LEPs and their involvement in local decision-making.

The third rejected recommendation was my suggestion that the UK should follow international examples, led by the US, to consider our national self-interest in foreign takeovers of our companies. I had faced this issue when, as President of the Board of Trade in the early 1990s, I was advised to cancel the government's 'golden share' in Rolls-Royce and British Aerospace, on the grounds that its existence was a serious impediment to the successful quotation of those companies. I flatly refused and the situation remains untouched to this day. But my proposal to adopt similar mechanisms more widely in British companies was too much for the non-interventionist elements in the Tory Party.

Finally, I had been persuaded that the shortage of airport capacity in the south east should be addressed and that a new airport to the east of London could provide a solution. The government instead opted for a third runway at Heathrow, which has yet to be built.

Only George Osborne himself can explain which of all the factors before him tipped the scales and persuaded him to take the devolution agenda seriously. What is certain, however, is that the Chancellor's determination to change the relationship between central and local government coincided with the publication of the 'No Stone Unturned' report.

I was fortunate that he was being well advised by Lord O'Neill of Gatley, a Mancunian who worked for Goldman Sachs from 1995 until April 2013, spending most of his time there as chief economist. He had given much support to Sir Howard Bernstein, the chief executive of Manchester City Council. Howard was one of the outstanding local authority executives of his time. He was rightly dismayed by my abolition of the metro counties after 1979, which I can only defend by pointing to the deep local hostility they created and the cost-cutting agenda that the government had no choice but to adopt. My legislation abolished the legal framework, but Howard used his position as chief executive to persuade the leaders of the other nine conurbation councils to preserve the partnership in their working relationship, albeit on a voluntary basis. The glue that held his project together was to persuade each of the leaders to take an interest in a specialist sphere of influence, not just in their own borough but across the conurbation as a whole. The concept of the conurbation remained effectively intact until the government's response to my report made it clear that not only was a framework to be restored but that within it there would be a substantial devolution of power and resources.

To achieve this new status, councillors had to accept another of my proposals, the concept of a directly elected mayor – something George Osborne forced through the Cabinet despite opposition from many senior ministers. Each mayoral deal was different and some were more comprehensive than others. The delivery momentum came from the Secretary of State for Business, Greg Clark, and was so effective that by May 2024, there were elections for mayors in virtually every English conurbation.

Of particular significance was Osborne's willingness to create a single pot of money by top slicing different departmental budgets. The government's response to 'No Stone Unturned' rejected my proposal that outside the conurbations, single-tier, unitary, county-based authorities should replace the jumble of some 200 unitary, district and county authorities. Such a concept was based on the Redcliffe-Maud map of 1969.

The hostility among Conservative MPs and councillors reflected the same opposition that the Redcliffe-Maud Report had generated on its publication. Despite this hostility, the government revealed its understanding of the reality of local economies because at the

With David Cameron in Liverpool in 2006. David asked me to join him on this trip shortly after he became the leader of the Conservative Party. The trip was followed by an invitation to chair a policy group and come up with a series of action plans for urban regeneration.
© Andrew Parsons / PA Images / Alamy Stock Photo

At the ceremony where I was awarded the Freedom of the City of Liverpool. *From left to right*: Lord Mayor Frank Prendergast, Max Steinberg, me, my daughters Annabel and Alexandra, Anne and Mayor Joe Anderson. Source: Liverpool City Council

With Greg Clark at the 2015 Conservative Party conference. I worked closely with Greg as his adviser when he was Secretary of State for Communities and Local Government.
© Colin McPherson / Alamy Stock Photo

The cover of my report 'Empowering English Cities'. The report was published in 2019 and set out my recommendations for further devolution after I found that many of the UK's major cities had been underperforming economically for decades.

The cover of my report 'No Stone Unturned: In Pursuit of Growth'. I consider this report one of the most important publications of my entire career and I remain immensely proud of it.
Source: public sector information licensed under the Open Government Licence v3.0

The team that worked on 'No Stone Unturned' planting a tree in celebration. Andy Gregory, my long-term driver, is holding the dog. Debbie Gillatt, the team leader, is planting the tree.

The Isle of Dogs in 1979. By the time I took up my first Cabinet post in the 1980s, the docks were dead. They had gone from being 'the hungry mouth of the British Empire' to being rendered obsolete by the advent of globalisation and container shipping. © APS (UK) / Alamy Stock Photo

Canary Wharf today, changed beyond belief. By 2030, it is calculated that there will be more people working there than in the city of Manchester. This growth story is unique in modern London in its scale. © Brave Heart / Alamy Stock Photo

Cantril Farm Estate in 1981. The estate had been very poorly managed and had become a dumping ground for homeless families. When I first visited, in the aftermath of the Toxteth riots, decline had taken hold, with the police struggling and people and businesses fleeing the area. © Professor Miles Glendinning

Stockbridge Village – a community reborn. I worked with Jim Lloyd, the Labour leader of Knowsley Council, to create a public–private partnership and transform Cantril Farm into Stockbridge Village. © Knowsley Council

Hulme Estate in 1990. This area of Manchester was made infamous as the subject of Friedrich Engels's study 'The Condition of the Working Class in England'. Unfortunately, poorly planned rebuilding of the area in the 1930s meant the new 'deck-access' housing blocks quickly became unfit for human habitation. © Jim Hutchison / ANL / Shutterstock

Hulme Estate today. Following its successful application for City Challenge funding in the 1990s, work began on a huge regeneration project and thousands of new homes were built by housing associations and private builders.
© Martin Bond / Alamy Stock Photo

Of all my visits to Teesside, the most spectacular was an invitation from Ben Houchen, Mayor of Tees Valley, to blow up the remains of the SSI steelworks site. Source: Tees Valley Combined Authority

In place of the old steelworks, several companies, such as BP and Shell, are developing a £3 billion carbon capture plant under the net zero programme. There will also be a facility which assembles wind turbines for the North Sea. The opportunities now emerging in Tees Valley will be regarded as a model of the kind of leadership and process that can turn industrial disaster into thriving business activity. Source: Tees Valley Combined Authority

Addressing the People's Vote demonstration in Parliament Square in 2019. I told the thousands of activists, 'What cannot be in doubt is our responsibility to our young generations to pass on to them a country richer, more powerful, safer than that we ourselves inherited. Our partnership with Europe is that destiny.' © World History Archive / Alamy Stock Photo

Our family, including our children, their partners and our nine grandchildren, at my ninetieth birthday party at the Savoy in March 2023. © Alex Deverill

Anne and me at her ninetieth birthday party at the National Gallery in 2024. © Alex Deverill

same time it published a map of the LEPs, which, ironically, largely reflected the Redcliffe-Maud recommendations. The debate about devolution rumbled on until the 2024 election, but even where local politicians were pressing for a much extended devolution deal, such as in Essex, such was the fragility of the government's political position that even the smallest number of local MPs could quash any enthusiasm for such change. With the election of the new government, the devolution agenda has taken on a new dimension. As I write, we await a government white paper on the matter. Informed leaks that have appeared in *The Times* talk of dozens of district authorities being abolished.

• • •

I was deeply grateful for the response to my report and I believe it made a major difference to our national conversation. I remain deeply committed to the restoration of the power and prestige of our great urban economic centres. The great cities of this country made us what we were, in partnership with London.

Every experience I had in Liverpool convinced me that the lessons apply equally to the rest of the country – not just some parts, not just the urban areas. They apply equally to the challenge to make life more meaningful, more successful and more economically dynamic for citizens and their communities right across the land. Communities do not end at the urban fringe. Rural communities depend on their relationships with urban centres.

As 'No Stone Unturned' was about to be published, I was advised by John Browne of BP that it needed a cover that would stand out. We obliged with an illustration of my search under every rock. One of my team obtained a suitable drawing for our purpose.

I remain immensely proud of the report, as a comprehensive attempt to produce a detailed agenda to transform this country's performance. It was based on experience and practice in a variety of different jobs, which developed and reinforced the interdependence of the public and private sectors and central and local governments, as well as the need for identified, clear and empowered leadership.

There are no short-term or easy solutions to unlocking the whole country's economic potential. A clear strategy and a determined programme of implementation is not compatible with five different Prime Ministers in eight years, frequent changes in Cabinet ministers, and deep philosophical divisions not just between Conservative and Labour governments but within the Conservative Party itself about the way in which economies work best.

Public opinion is largely driven, as Harold Wilson once said, by the pound in your pocket. This is the reality for people every day: another bill to be paid, another need delayed, another desire frustrated. Politicians have to counter that feeling of resentment and do it with words that promise change, delivered quickly and avoiding the impression that people have to individually change as part of the process. Obesity and the crisis in the health service, truancy and low education standards, for example, don't stand a chance against simplistic promises to 'stop the boats' or cut taxes.

CHAPTER 13

DEVOLUTION: THE CASE

When David Cameron invited me to speak at the Conservative Party conference of 2007, I had never expected to again have the pleasure of addressing the party en masse. I used the speech to outline the problems caused and sustained by the gross over centralisation of our economy and political machinery. I warned the assembled crowd of how it is the root cause of the woes we face as a country. 'It creates an intellectual straight jacket,' I said.

> Solutions are devised, rules drawn up, circulars issued, guidelines promulgated in London. Each city has a different history, different strengths, different opportunities. Just as we praise the strength of individualism in people and the private sector, let us recognise the same spirit of independence and pride in the governance of provincial England.

In that speech, I recommended a radical increase in the autonomy of cities, the establishment of directly elected mayors with powers over education, transport, housing, planning, policing, regeneration and skills. I also outlined a competitive process for distribution of capital funds, in which cities could outline any scheme they desired and funds would flow based on the merit of their proposals. Cameron agreed with the principal recommendations in his speech, pledging that a Conservative government would 'tear up the rules and all the ring-fencing and auditing and actually say to our local councils, "It's your money, spend it as you choose and get judged in the ballot box by the people you serve."'

After the 2010 election, I found myself returning to an old maxim: success in politics is about moving up, moving on and moving out. I was drawn back in to reconsider the issues I had tried to influence and determine over four decades. Throughout my career, the central theme has been devolution – moving power away from the entrenched bureaucracies of Whitehall and closer to people, through local government structures new and old.

Looking back to the day Ted Heath became Prime Minister in 1970, he gave me my first job in government – as a junior minister in the Department for Transport. A few months later, the transport ministry was merged into a new, larger Department for the Environment – and within the new structure, I moved from John Peyton and transport to Graham Page and planning. I was fortunate enough to return to that department twice more as Secretary of State and once more after that, not quite in government but in the corridors of power and covering the same policy areas. Between 1945 and 1997, the average minister of Cabinet rank had just over two years before being moved to another department or back to the oblivion of the back benches. To revisit the same territory on four separate occasions must be unprecedented.

This unique occurrence gave me two opportunities. The first was to look back over those four periods and to see whether my actions actually made any difference. Did any of my reforms last, or did all that effort, like the fallen leaves of autumn, eventually fade away? The second opportunity, easily the most tantalising, was to deploy the lessons I have learned in my long career, both inside and outside government. Looking back at the longevity of my previous work, the omens are not good. When I look at the things I did that I believed to be necessary, which I hoped would be permanent, one by one I saw them being undone.

This is not recrimination against the Labour Party. Some of my most cherished achievements bit the dust with the return to power of a Conservative government – Urban Development Corporations, garden festivals, City Challenge, Enterprise Agencies, Business Links, the Audit Commission, English Partnerships, Regional Government Offices, the Competitiveness Agenda and the Management Information System for Ministers (MINIS), which I designed and introduced into several departments. All are now gone or struggle on as such pale imitations of their former selves as to be unrecognisable. Yet it may be wrong to focus on the names of the organisations if the philosophy behind so many of them has become, or is now becoming, mainstream. The agencies I advocated for may have disappeared, but the ideology that drove their creation is in many cases alive and kicking.

In 2024, a fifth of citizens in England could vote for a directly elected mayor. Unitary authorities are now commonplace and privatisation is a largely irreversible part of the body politic. Public agencies that I transferred to the private sector are now part of the market economy, engaged in competitive business. The concept of public–private partnership is now deeply ingrained and the ability of public sector investment to lever in private sector spending is now recognised and welcomed. But most importantly, our cities are being transformed in what must be one of the most exciting periods of urban renaissance in our history. Devolution is now accepted as a mainstream part of our political progression.

Britain's cities once led the world. Manchester, Liverpool and Newcastle were at the forefront of the Industrial Revolution, each with their own industrial specialisms, entrepreneurial energy and powerful local government. Mancunians would boast, 'What Manchester says today, the world does tomorrow.' The grand Victorian town halls of these cities attest to an age of municipal pride, when people looked to their city, not Westminster, for solutions. When Joseph Chamberlain took up his seat in Parliament in 1876, he worried, 'Unless I can secure for the nation results similar to those which have followed the adoption of my policy in Birmingham … it will have been a sorry exchange to give up the town council for the Cabinet.' The men and women who drove our great cities to success, whether from the Chamber of Commerce or City Hall, were essentially entrepreneurs, committed to the creation of wealth, who saw their job as helping their city to compete for trade within the global British empire. They drove the Industrial Revolution and exploited the huge, protected imperial market of empire to their advantage.

Over time, however, the remit of local administration has slowly eroded from one of entrepreneurial activity and wealth creation to the crucial but passive delivery of social services. Nowadays, local government is seen by the political class as either a training ground for ambitious young things with an eye on Westminster or a noble retirement activity for those long in the tooth. Westminster and the south east are indisputably the centre of economic gravity, around which the 'provincial' cities revolve. Bristol is the only city outside London with a GDP per capita higher than the national average. On the same measure, Leeds is only the forty-third most prosperous city in Europe, while Birmingham ranks fifty-sixth, Manchester fifty-seventh, Newcastle fifty-eighth and Liverpool sixty-first. How we sank into this poor state of affairs is an indictment of the actions of a series of governments from both the left and right, stretching right back at least to the Second World War.

Prior to the development of the modern welfare state, local public services and welfare programmes had been delivered by a mishmash of quasi-governmental boards, charities and friendly societies. Over the course of the nineteenth century, these were slowly aggregated under the control of democratically elected local governments.

However, the creation of the welfare state by the post-war Labour governments brought about a significant shift in the division of responsibilities. Poverty relief, education, hospitals and housing were all brought under the control of central government, which alone could provide the funds necessary to ensure standard services throughout individual local authorities, with very different levels of their own financial support. These authorities became steadily more dependent on central government grants. In 1929, councils lost their power to tax agriculture and most of their power to tax industrial property. Then in 1949, their financial autonomy was further undermined when their ability to revalue properties to determine local tax rates was taken over by central government. Unsurprisingly, Westminster politicians subsequently proved reluctant to increase tax rates for which they saw no revenue benefit. It became a widespread belief that no government that conducted a general revaluation of property for rating purposes would survive the subsequent election.

At its simplest, the general view developed in Westminster and Whitehall was that local government was not up to the job. Rather than address the real question of how to improve the professionalism and performance of local government, national politicians decided simply to take away or constrain local powers. As a member of Margaret Thatcher's government of the 1980s, I'm afraid I played a part in this. A mixture of ideological commitments and monetarist economics inspired the government to cut down on public spending. Combined with the rise of the hard left on city councils, it made local government a prime target for reform.

During this era, a whole raft of local authority services were either privatised (buses), centralised (hospitals), put into arms-length quangos (skills) or made autonomous (schools and housing). By 1984, the winds of centralism were blowing so strongly that the relevant Secretary of State was given the right to unilaterally impose caps on the budget of any local authority they thought to be 'excessive'. The cumulative effect of these reforms was significant. Back in 1930, local government raised three quarters of its income locally. By 1993, this had fallen to just under a third. Despite being an early advocate of localism, Tony Blair's government continued to reduce the autonomy of local government, submitting it to an ever-increasing number of ring-fenced grants and guidelines.

As a new Cabinet minister back in 1979, I had to agree with the Treasury a total budget for my department in the public expenditure round. Once agreed, I had the flexibility to move the cash from one part of the budget to another. My ability to move cash was a major help in tackling the rebirth of Liverpool in 1981. After my time, the Treasury increasingly insisted on ring-fencing their grants of money into tightly defined compartments.

There are many other reasons why local government lost out. The decline of local newspapers dramatically reduced the visibility of local councils, to the point where few people today can recall the name of their local councillor, let alone the leader. National politics also has the comparative advantage of being professionalised. MPs were given salaries just over 100 years ago and ministers have received additional compensation for their responsibilities since 1934. Councillors, on the other hand, still do not formally receive a salary but are instead given a meagre 'allowance' of around £11,000 a year. Although local authority leaders and Cabinet members receive additional money, their remuneration doesn't compare to national politicians, let alone the private sector.

Most local authority chief executives are paid two or three times the amount that the political leader of the council receives for a job that will probably occupy much of their life. The leader of Bristol City Council is paid just over £50,000 a year, for example, while the chief executive receives £190,000. Turnout at local elections reflects the low status of local government – usually around 30 per cent in years with no general election. Those that do turn out tend to use their vote to deliver a verdict on the national government rather than local issues. This is no way to run our cities.

Unfortunately, this long process of centralisation does not only affect the way we are governed; it also has consequences for how well we are governed. Effective local government should perceive policy challenges as they actually are – tangled knots of interrelated issues embedded in a particular place. Westminster approaches policy challenges along departmental lines, treating 'individual' problems as if they can be addressed in a vacuum. This departmental tunnel vision is best described as 'monopolistic functionalism'. Civil servants in the Department for Transport assess the merits of a proposed bus lane in Birmingham, civil servants in Homes England assess a site for a new science park in outer Birmingham. Another set of civil servants plan post-sixteen skills provision for the West Midlands, while yet another group in the Department for

Culture, Media and Sport decide where to install a new high-speed broadband hub. The most extreme and silly example of this recently was a £100 million fund set up to enable local authorities to clear discarded chewing gum from their streets.

Nowhere in Whitehall is anyone asking questions like, 'How can we create a well-connected new centre for high-tech employment in Birmingham with a ready supply of highly skilled labour?' Only when you have a structure of government taking care of all these angles at the same time can you unlock the economic potential of an area and forge a truly entrepreneurial local government – creating the conditions for economic growth and proactively helping cities to flourish. Monopolistic functionalism, on the other hand, is a recipe for dysfunction. The same is true of social policy. The eradication of poverty and the sense of hopelessness in sink estates or deprived areas is seriously hampered by the lack of coherence between spending departments in Whitehall and their local branch offices embedded in municipalities.

But centralism doesn't just choke the engine, it deprives it of fuel. By hiving off the crucial economic tools of transport, infrastructure investment, regeneration and house building into separate central government departments and satellite quangos, the process of revitalisation of our cities is deprived of the biggest single energising force available to it – democratic accountability. If city governments were once again empowered to become entrepreneurial investors in their own future, voters would be able to hold politicians' feet to the flames and drive them to deliver better outcomes. Communities of voters thus become geographically and electorally closer to the politicians responsible.

Most people know the name of the Mayor of London, but the average voter doesn't even know that Homes England exists. Radical reform can be achieved by unelected bodies, but local democratic accountability would provide a powerful boost in restoring entrepreneurial government to our cities.

When I reflect on how I became involved in local government reform in my first ministerial job, I can see now how policy in this area has developed over time and how, after the Redcliffe-Maud Commission hit on a solution more than fifty years ago, we are now inching towards a set of proposals that, ironically, look similar to Lord Redcliffe-Maud's original plan to restore entrepreneurial self-government and municipal pride to our cities.

The 1966 general election was a disaster for the Tories. Significant numbers of Conservative MPs left the House of Commons, some voluntarily, others dismissed by the voters. Forty-seven seats were lost to Labour and three to the Liberals. Of those Conservative MPs that had secured re-election, a significant number planned to use the period in opposition to return to other interests outside Parliament and replenish their coffers. For the eleven Conservative MPs who had secured a Commons seat for the first time, including myself, this provided plentiful opportunities for involvement in supporting the activities of our front bench.

Arriving at Westminster was comparable to one's first day at school. There was a sense of apprehension and awe and an inevitable disorientation brought about by the unfamiliarity of the surroundings. But there is also a big difference: from the moment tearful parents eject their offspring through the school gates, there is somebody to give orders, to organise, direct and instruct. When I arrived at Westminster, nobody appeared to care if you had arrived or not, let alone whether you knew what you ought to be doing. On your own and overawed by your surroundings, it was easy to forget for a moment that sense of confidence with which you enlisted the support of thousands of your constituents just days before. On election day you were a hero, an all-conquering victor. Upon entering the Palace of Westminster, you were firmly reminded that you are barely a footnote in British history.

Most new arrivals probably know other, longer-serving MPs. I was fortunate that Patrick Jenkin, then the MP for Wanstead and Woodford, took pity on me and gave me an extended tour of the facilities. But I will never forget that sense of being on one's own, expecting something to happen, waiting for an indication of how one's new role will play out. In practice, nothing does, but gradually one gets into the swing of things. Constituency correspondence started to arrive the day after I was elected. Initially the bulk of the post was congratulatory, but the balance soon shifted to the everyday problems and complaints of constituents. In those early days, my time was shared between the things that kept me at the Palace of Westminster and the demanding job as chairman and chief executive of Haymarket Publishing Company.

It was almost a year before Peter Walker, then shadow spokesman for transport, asked for my assistance. His proposal was very simple; he was planning a tour of the West Country and wondered if I would like to organise it. I knew enough about politics to realise that Peter, an ambitious and rising star, was interested in projecting his image as widely as possible across the region and in particular the local constituency parties. I set about the task with enthusiasm and secured for Peter significant attention from the local press and media over the course of the weekend. On our return to London, Peter thanked me for what he perceived as a success and asked if I would like to join him in the work he was doing in opposing Barbara Castle's transport bill. He was to become a good friend and mentor over the years, perhaps the politician from whom I have learned more than any other.

After the 1970 election, in which the Conservatives returned to office, I was given the job of assisting Graham Page with his responsibilities for local government and planning briefs in the newly created 'super' Department for the Environment. Peter Walker, in his new role as Secretary of State at the department, introduced a ministers' meeting. He understood the art of delegation; he remained in close touch with responsibilities that were placed upon him, but the day-to-day work was delegated to people in whom he had absolute trust. Every morning at 9 a.m., he would chair a meeting including his three ministers of state, Julian Amery, Graham Page and John Peyton, and the three junior ministers, Paul Channon, Eldon Griffiths, and me. Peter would allocate tasks to his team, and the junior ministers assumed a degree of responsibility which, though more common these days, was almost unheard of then.

The biggest single item in Peter's in-tray was the Redcliffe-Maud Report, properly referred to as 'The Report of the Royal Commission on Local Government in England'. The previous Labour government had taken a hard look at the bewilderingly complex structure of local government in England and concluded that serious reform was required, appointing a Royal Commission to do the heavy lifting.

At the time, there were 124 county and county borough councils and around 1,000 district councils outside London. The county borough councils were mostly in big cities and were 'unitary authorities' with responsibility for delivering the full range of local government services. In all other areas, responsibilities were split between first-tier (top-level) county councils and the various second-tier district councils within them. The district councils were either urban districts, covering urban centres, or rural district councils, which covered the surrounding areas, often in a 'doughnut' shape. As Lord Redcliffe-Maud pointed out in his introduction, English local government is in a sense a random growth. It has not been planned systematically in light of what it has to do and the social and geographic conditions of each place. The Royal Commission, set up in May 1966, was the first-ever attempt to examine the government of our towns and countryside from top to bottom and plan a radically new start. In my view, it is still by far the best.

Redcliffe-Maud was commissioned to make recommendations on the type, size and function of local government across England, 'having regard to the size and character of areas in which these can be most effectively exercised'. His report, released in 1969, was an exemplary piece of analysis, fastidiously researched and carefully argued. It is worth reproducing the reasoning in some detail here.

The commission took evidence from some 2,000 witnesses and investigated the issue for nearly three years before developing their proposals. Redcliffe-Maud maintained that a modernised system of local government must do four things: deliver a wide range of important public services, attract and hold the interest of citizens, be strong enough to deal with national government in a valid partnership and adapt itself to changes in the way people live. It will be clear to any observer of local government that the present system fails miserably on at least three of these fronts.

Redcliffe-Maud went on to highlight four flaws in the existing structure. Local authorities did not fit the pattern of life and work of modern England; the division of places into small authorities along urban or rural lines made the planning of spatial development and transport very difficult; the division of responsibilities between county and subsidiary district councils made the coordination of closely interrelated services more difficult; and many local authorities were too small to discharge their functions efficiently. Again, local government aficionados will recognise many of these weaknesses in the contemporary system. The question that Redcliffe-Maud set out to answer was intimidatingly broad in scope. His brilliance came in the way he employed a set of evidence-based principles to arrive at such an elegant conclusion. The crucial principles were:

1. Local authorities should be defined in a way that allows citizens and elected representatives to have 'a sense of common purpose'.
2. The areas must recognise the interdependence of town and county.
3. Services concerned with the physical environment (planning, transport and major development) should not be split between different authorities, so that residents share a common interest in their environment 'because it is where they live, work, shop and find recreation'.
4. Personal services (social services, education and health) 'closely linked in operation and effect' must also not be divided between separate authorities, to allow proper coordination.
5. There must be a minimum population size for authorities to ensure efficiency; on the basis of the evidence submitted, the commission put this lower band at about 250,000.
6. Authorities should have a population no larger than 1 million, in order to ensure elected representatives do not become too distant from their constituents.

This followed neatly from Redcliffe-Maud's principle that any relatively self-contained economic area that had a population of between 250,000 and 1 million people and could be looked after democratically by one council should be administered by a single, all-purpose, unitary authority. Large conurbations would need to have a universal top tier responsible for environmental services and multiple lower tiers responsible for personal services.

The commission recommended the complete abolition of the previous system and the introduction of fifty-eight new, all-purpose unitary authorities, largely based around major towns. There would also be three new metropolitan areas to cover the big city regions, which were so big they violated Redcliffe-Maud's principles. These would be created in what we would now call Merseyside, Greater Manchester and the West Midlands, and each of them would be subdivided into metropolitan districts charged with delivering social services. The reforms would have reduced the raw number of local authorities by a factor of ten, down to just eighty-one. The combination of larger units, more financial autonomy and more powers would have put our cities in position to shape their own future once more and, crucially, put them on a more equal and sustainable footing with central government. Redcliffe-Maud had come up with a comprehensive, rational and workable solution to the riddle.

The politics of it, however, were impossible. While in opposition, Peter Walker held a series of conferences to ascertain the Tory Party's grassroots opinion about local government reform. They were overwhelmingly hostile and a highly critical motion was passed at the 1969 Conservative Party conference. The idea of redrawing historic boundaries was anathema to the average party member, and Conservative councillors, most of whom would have lost their seats under the reforms, were particularly hostile. Redcliffe-Maud's proposals would have alienated the entire party rank and file at just the time they would be called upon as the foot soldiers in the forthcoming election battle. As a result, the Conservatives fought the 1970 election pledging not to make any changes to the existing two-tier system.

The Local Government Act 1972 did just this. It was drawn up with the help of the council associations but still proved controversial in Parliament, suffering multiple revisions and near-defeats. The legislation also provided for 'metro counties', recognising that in certain parts of the country there were great conurbations, which were made up of individual boroughs but had problems with issues such as waste disposal and transportation that transcended local authority boundaries. It fell to me to define the frontiers of these new metropolitan counties. I recall spending hours listening to interminable arguments for drawing the boundary this or that side of various satellite towns and suburbs. Eventually, I gave up hope of making progress through this method and instead chartered a light aircraft. We flew over the big conurbations and I made a judgement about whether particular towns were really just parts of the conurbation or were genuinely distinct entities.

Whatever the merits of the structure we created, the politics of it worked well. By 1977, I was shadow Secretary of State for the Environment and responsible for the local election campaign of that year. We launched Operation Clean Sweep with the intention of winning every county. We failed by five, but we secured majority control of thirty-four of the thirty-nine English county councils and ended up with control of every local government association: county councils, district councils, London boroughs and metropolitan counties. When I became Secretary of State for the Environment in 1979, the Conservatives even controlled the normally red metropolitan counties of Greater Manchester, Merseyside, the West Midlands and West Yorkshire, alongside great swathes of traditionally blue rural England. It was the high watermark of Conservative power in local government.

But by the early 1980s, considerable scepticism was emerging about some aspects of Peter Walker's reforms. Many of the new authorities that had been created – Avon or Herefordshire, for example – were deeply unpopular with residents who felt no natural affinity with other parts of the authority. The 'two-tier' structure in the metropolitan areas was also seen as wasteful when the government was putting considerable efforts into bringing public spending under control. I remember a notable Conservative councillor on the Greater London Council coming to see me in the late 1970s to seek my advice as to what I thought the council should be doing. Although I may have not said it to him, my reaction was instinctively, 'If you don't know it doesn't seem to me there's much point in the Council existing.' On another occasion, after the 1979 election, I was discussing future plans with the chief executive of the Merseyside conurbation and when I asked about one aspect or another, he said, 'We are still trying to identify our role here.'

The situation was not helped by the fact that the 'loony left' were in the ascendancy across the metropolitan authorities, many of them openly committed to non-democratic practices through their affiliation to Labour's Militant Tendency and wilfully engaged in unconstitutional practices by refusing to set budgets. The coup orchestrated by the hard-left Ken Livingstone at the Greater London Council (GLC), just one day after the London elections, served to harden conviction that the top-tier authorities had to be done away with. I was wrong. The decision I took to scrap the GLC, the

Inner London Education Authority and the metropolitan counties seemed right at the time, but with hindsight it should have been possible to reform them in a more constructive way. It would have saved future Labour and Conservative governments time in recreating virtually all of them.

I moved from the Department for the Environment to the Ministry of Defence in 1983 and then left the government in 1986. My period on the back benches after 1986 enabled me to travel and provided me with some valuable time to think. I had been commissioned to write a book explaining Japan's economic success by William Rees-Mogg on behalf of Pickering & Chatto. I returned to government in 1990 before I could finish the book, which turned out to be a lucky escape as Japan's economic fortunes deteriorated dramatically just at the time that my rather bullish assessment of its strengths were influencing my line of thought.

In 1992, the Conservatives won a fourth election, this time under the leadership of John Major. I returned to the Department for the Environment and this time I was clear that I wanted unitary counties. In Scotland and Wales, we achieved this by legislative fiat, halving the number of authorities in each. There was little opposition and there were no Conservative councillors to unnerve our MPs. Unitary authorities became the standard in both countries and there have never been any serious efforts to change this.

In England, the familiar obstacles re-emerged. The councillors in rural areas were highly active in the Conservative Party and close to MPs. There was no option of bringing about reform on a general basis; the only way forward was to set up a commission, which would go around the country looking at individual areas and making specific recommendations. I believed this would gradually lead to unitary authorities also becoming the standard in England and that the drip-drip process of change would make the reforms easier to steer through Parliament.

I asked John Banham, who had done an excellent job as the first controller of the Audit Commission, to become chairman of the Local Government Commission for England, set up to look into the issue. Banham soon realised it would be impossible to come up with a set of proposals that the cross-party members of the commission could agree on. To solve this problem, the commission relied heavily on surveys of local residents, who were inevitably averse to redrawing of the existing boundaries. As a result, and despite evidence from a specially commissioned case study which found that district councils were too small to be efficient, the commission only recommended the creation of four new unitary counties and fifty new small unitaries drawn tightly around city boundaries. For all the other counties, no change was again the order of the day.

Part of the problem with securing this controversial reform was the reluctance of the county councils. Despite the fact that they stood to gain additional powers from becoming unitary, they gave only lukewarm support to the proposals. This can partly be explained by the fact that many district councillors also had a seat on the county council.

Over time, however, attitudes have begun to change and under Tony Blair's Labour government, county councils began to wake up to the benefits of becoming unitary. Large unitary councils have been created in Cornwall, the Isle of Wight, Wiltshire, Herefordshire, Shropshire, Cheshire West and Chester, Cheshire East, East Yorkshire, Durham and Northumberland. Of England, Scotland and Wales's 206 local authorities, 110 are now unitary. At the time of the 2010 election, Devon, Suffolk and Norfolk were also in the process of becoming unitary counties, but the issue was bogged down in the courts under judicial review and the Conservative Party pledged that, if elected, they would reject the bids.

Redcliffe-Maud saw the importance of governing areas in the way that people live in and experience them – as one, integrated community. The long and tortuous process of local government reform thus brought us closer to implementing these original proposals, but we are still a long way from finishing the job. Small unitary authorities in our big cities remain too small to effectively wield the powers required for entrepreneurial local government, with the result that the levers required for urban renaissance remain out of reach in quangos and central government departments.

What is the solution? Here are six ideas to create a real sense of partnership between central and local government with an entrepreneurial, wealth-creating purpose:

1. The powers and responsibility required for entrepreneurial local government (transport, big infrastructure investment, regeneration, skills, planning, culture and tourism, environment and inward investment house building) should be returned from central government departments to single-tier local authorities.
2. The creation of large unitary authorities along the lines proposed by Redcliffe-Maud should be completed. This is a crucial step in enabling central government to devolve the powers required for entrepreneurial local government (what Redcliffe-Maud referred to as 'environmental' services) to local authorities.
3. City-region authorities (metropolitan counties, if you like) have been created for virtually all conurbations. Their creation followed detailed negotiations about their devolved powers, which vary from place to place. This process needs to be completed to

ensure they have both the resources and powers appropriate for the task.

4. Directly elected mayors serving four-year terms should be introduced for all unitary authorities. This will boost accountability, allow clear leadership and improve the prospects of attracting high-calibre people to the post. It would also provide cities with a well-known champion who could be the single point of contact for potential investors. The mayors' electoral mandate (which would rank among the largest in the country) would finally put local government on an equal and more stable footing in holding back the ever-present forces of centralisation. Serving as a successful mayor of a big city could become a stepping stone to Parliament, and ex-Cabinet ministers should see the opportunity to run a great city as one probably more stimulating and satisfying than half the offices within Whitehall.
5. Local government should be given more robust financial autonomy. Capital funding, currently channelled through central government departments and quangos, should be returned to local government – partially as an unconditional grant, the remainder allocated by challenge funding in an open and competitive process. There are opportunities for local museum charges and tourism taxes.
6. Local government should be able to raise money by issuing its own bonds.

After the 2024 general election, *The Guardian* invited me to comment on the result. Sir Keir Starmer was scheduled to meet England's mayors and I was pleased to address Angela Rayner, the new Deputy Prime Minister and the minister responsible for levelling up, with my views about the task she faced, reflecting on my lifetime of experience. I noted that the importance of levelling up is now understood across the political spectrum and I pointed out there are no easy wins for the new Labour government if it is serious about its commitment to urban renewal. With directly elected mayors in most of England's conurbations, we finally have a framework for growth in city economies, in valuable contrast to more remote regional groupings.

I advised Rayner to extend powers to these authorities to ensure that they have effective control of the economic policies that influence growth, including skills and employment. Some of the most dynamic parts of our country are situated in areas where the exercise of leadership is divided between some 200 authorities, with thousands of councillors elected at different times. The present position is incompatible with a coherent, properly led, local partnership with government. If Labour is serious about its intention to grow the whole economy, I argued they should legislate in their first term to create directly elected mayoral authorities across the rest of the country and ensure their involvement in local growth planning.

I also suggested Rayner should examine unlocking investment. The new Labour government should work to tackle the current lengthy planning and consultation process. My proposals recognised the acute financial challenge we face. I realise that the capital programmes are already contracted for the next year or so. But the initiatives themselves send a clear signal and unlock further investment, as local mayors are able to use their flexibility with capital programmes to attract additional investment from other sources.

My advice to Rayner is based on a lifetime engaged in urban renewal. Her appointment meets the first priority, in that there is now a senior member of government responsible for driving the devolution agenda. She will presumably chair an appropriate committee of the ministers involved. She should also recreate the regional offices of government under a senior civil servant, to ensure that Whitehall sees the full picture and gives the issue high priority.

In terms of levelling up, there is one key question Angela Rayner and the new government must answer and quickly. Were their words mere electoral slogans or will they herald a determination to make radical changes? Having first examined this question in 1966 and revisited it over more than fifty years, I hope that the Labour government's promises will be delivered. For more than half a century, it has become ever more clear to me that if our cities are to compete again on the world stage, they must first be given the tools to do so.

We must unleash a new entrepreneurial localism. It is long overdue.

PART IV

REGIONAL GROWTH

CHAPTER 14

MANCHESTER

In 1988, one of my successors as Secretary of State for the Environment, Nicholas Ridley, used the powers I had put on the statute book to create a development corporation in Salford under the chairmanship of Felicity Goodey, which was to reclaim nearly eighty-six acres of derelict land and attract over £300 million of private finance over the next eight years. My close involvement with the city of Manchester coincides with, over time, the city council abandoning a policy of hostility and defiance towards the government and instead embracing the idea of a private–public partnership that is central to pro-market activism. The city has progressed from being a hopeless mess, stumbling from one crisis to another, to becoming a visionary local authority.

During the early 1980s, the perennially Labour-controlled Manchester Council had been taken over from within by a new generation of Bennite socialists. They ran for election on the promise of not making any cuts or redundancies, while pledging to undertake big public investments at a time when Manchester's economy was struggling.

This put them on a collision course with central government, which was attempting to cut local authority spending, partly by curtailing their tax-raising powers. The city lurched from one financial crisis to the next and by 1985, was simply refusing to set a budget in a last-ditch standoff with central government. Manchester was broke yet still retained a principled opposition to working with the private sector or releasing any of their sizable stock of land for development.

Graham Stringer became leader of the council in 1984, the relationship changed and I worked with him when I returned to government in 1990. In the words of Sir Richard Leese, who would become leader of the council in 1996 after Graham went to Westminster, 'We were all puritans. Antipathy about working with the private sector actually sprang from the ideological view that capitalism wasn't a good thing.' As I have said, abolition of the metropolitan counties was wrong, but it was understandable against the political backdrop of the time, when councils such as Manchester maintained their stubborn attitude.

When I returned to the Department for the Environment in 1990, among my priorities was a determination to build on the success of Stockbridge Village and apply the lessons learned in Knowsley after the Liverpool riots to the rest of England.

The policy that emerged in 1992 was the City Challenge. The story of one of the winners, Hulme in Manchester, provides a vivid case study of the fluctuating fortunes of a particular area and the role that pro-market activism can play: central government catalysing a broad-based local response and local government working closely with the private sector to put an area back on its feet.

Hulme was made infamous as the subject of Friedrich Engels's study 'The Condition of the Working Class in England'. It expanded rapidly in the nineteenth century on the back of Manchester's industrial boom, as migrant labourers poured into the area to take up jobs in the new factories and found cramped housing accommodation of poor quality. By the early twentieth century, the housing stock had deteriorated further, but Hulme remained a centre of employment. Dunlop rubber and Rolls-Royce were the most famous firms there, and historical accounts reveal a tight-knit, working-class community, with a vibrant culture based around the music halls, theatres and cinemas.

After the First World War, a huge programme began to improve the quality of the nation's housing stock – 'homes fit for heroes' as the government's slogan went. Inner-city communities were encouraged to move out to newly built suburban towns to allow slum clearance. In 1934, the Manchester Corporation purchased the whole of Hulme, some 300 acres, and declared their intention to rebuild it from the ground up, making it the biggest slum clearance scheme in Europe. The corporation wisely decided to avoid the high-rise blocks that proved so unpopular elsewhere and instead opted for huge 'deck-access' housing blocks laid out in four giant crescents, apparently modelled on the Georgian crescents in Bath, each of which housed around 900 families.

Unfortunately, this housing quickly became unfit for human habitation, let alone homes for heroes or Georgian aristocrats. The flats and communal areas deteriorated due to poor management and the inadequate heating systems forced residents either to pay extortionate heating bills or turn the heating off all together, leading to problems with damp. The high decks were unsafe for children, meaning they had nowhere to play and tended to concentrate anti-social behaviour right outside residents' front doors. They also helped with the spread of vermin. Just three years after the completion of the

'Hulme Five' block, some 96 per cent of its residents wanted to be rehoused.

The council began moving families out, and too often the people willing to move in were those with no other options – hard-up students or unemployed adults with their own set of problems. Tenant turnover was sky high and the management all but lost track of who was actually living on the estate. Heroin and Valium addiction became a serious problem and brought with it an increase in crime. By 1978, you were thirty times more likely to be mugged on the Hulme estate than the average for the UK.

By the time the application was made for City Challenge funding in the early 1990s, Hulme was at rock bottom. One third of properties were empty and it was impossible to collect the rent on another third.

The last thing Manchester could afford at this time was the financial black hole of the Hulme Estate, let alone its disastrous social consequences. Graham Stringer, the increasingly pragmatic Labour leader of the council, realised that City Challenge represented the only opportunity to do something about it. However, regeneration would require big private sector involvement as a condition of the concept.

Graham set up a meeting with Alan Cockshaw, chairman of AMEC engineering, who he had asked to address the Labour council group to discuss the situation on the grounds that many of them 'had never met a capitalist'. Graham frankly explained to Alan that the costs of the estate, both the maintenance and the barrage of public services required to support its residents, were bleeding the city dry. Something had to be done and he needed help. Alan agreed to work with Manchester to establish a standalone organisation including councillors, local authority officials and leading private sector representatives. AMEC seconded staff to help administer the project. As Alan puts it, it was the 'end of isolationism in Manchester'.

The plan for Hulme involved improving the housing stock, attracting new residents and new retail outlets – Tesco had recently moved out – and capitalising on its central location in order to attract major new employers. The big deck-access blocks, which had become the symbol of Hulme's decline, were knocked down and thousands of new homes were built by housing associations and private builders. One third of the remaining housing stock was comprehensively refurbished.

Hulme Park, which was eventually completed in 1999, was the first new park to be completed in Manchester for over fifty years and included 4.7 hectares of well-designed public green space. Hulme Community Garden Centre was established to nurture the sense of community that had previously been so conspicuously absent. It still exists today and while paying only a peppercorn rent to the council, draws over 5,000 visitors to the area every year. By the end of the project, a public investment of £37.5 million had helped attract a stunning £81.5 million of private sector money, with investment continuing long after the end of the City Challenge.

When Tesco had vacated the site in Hulme, the land had been worth nothing. Six years later, it was climbing towards £2 million an acre. Surveys after the refurbishment found that net 34 per cent of residents thought the area was now a 'little' or a 'great deal better' as a place to live. Again, the most telling statistic is that nearly two thirds of Hulme house buyers surveyed in 1997 had moved in from outside the area.

Male unemployment also fell slightly faster in Hulme than in Manchester as a whole, though it remained high. Tempting big employers into the area proved tougher than expected, however, and it took some time to let some of the units in the business park and the smaller units in the shopping centre.

Writing in 1998, Rob Ramwell and Hilary Saltburn, in their excellent history of Hulme, summed up the results of City Challenge:

> At the end of City Challenge, many residents are still poor and live in difficult circumstances. But one recurring comment from many people has been about dignity … the provision of a decent new home has brought about a central stability to their lives that has enabled them to plan and think to the future. Hulme has in many respects become normal. Children and cats can now be seen on the streets instead of packs of stray dogs. Ice cream vans ply their trade, and for the first time in years, milk and newspapers are now delivered.

Now, Hulme's close location to the city centre – a mere fifteen-minute walk thanks to the Hulme Arch Bridge erected in 1997 – means it has become increasingly popular for younger families and professionals.

In all, thirty-one partnerships from across the UK won a total of £1.14 billion of City Challenge funding. A remarkable £4.4 billion of additional private sector investment was leveraged on the back of this money, significantly boosting its impact. The scale of the change was remarkable: 110,000 dwellings were constructed or refurbished, 8,700 businesses were helped to start up, 3.6 million square metres of office space was created or refurbished and 130,000 qualifications were secured by residents.

The official evaluation had some limitations in terms of measuring which outputs were genuinely 'additional' versus what would otherwise have occurred but did conclude (based on its best guess) that these outputs had been secured at lower cost than the average for comparable regeneration exercises. Analysis conducted for the evaluation suggested that somewhere between 4,800 and 5,500 people were removed from the unemployment register as a result of the 'City Challenge effect' and that about two thirds of the jobs created went to people residing in City Challenge areas. This macro analysis is, in a sense, misleading, as each of the City Challenge winners adopted their own approach and enjoyed their own levels of success. Each also has their own lessons for urban regeneration.

Distributing capital funding by competition requires a strong nerve and a detachment from party loyalties that can so easily undermine it. The autonomy it allows, however, unshackles a dormant creativity and energy that some communities seem to have forgotten they possess. The challenge element also helps catalyse cooperation across many bureaucratic boundaries, which would normally be as impermeable as castle walls. It is the essence of a hand up rather than a hand out. What is unquestionable is that the City Challenge experience created relationships between the public and private sector in Manchester that were fundamental in the devolution agenda and owed so much to early developments and personalities in that city.

Looking out over Hulme after the regeneration was complete, with Alan Cockshaw, Richard Leese and Howard Bernstein, I said, 'Could any of us have imagined it would turn out as good as this?'

• • •

On 15 June 1996, a Ford Cargo van carrying 3,300 lbs of homemade explosives was detonated by the IRA in the commercial heart of Manchester. It was the largest bomb ever to explode in peace time on the UK mainland, spreading debris over half a mile in either direction and a mile up into the air. The shockwave shot along the streets at 2,000 metres per second, ripping out windows and mangling the concrete pillars of shops and offices. Large shards of glass came crashing down followed by bigger debris – metal, brickwork and huge chunks of concrete – and then a rain-like blanket of fine glass dust. The explosion set off a grim chorus of car and burglar alarms right across the city centre. A bomb threat had been received by police shortly before the explosion and, fortunately, the evacuation was already well underway when it detonated. Incredibly, no one was killed, but the bomb injured 200 people, displaced 670 businesses and caused £300 million of physical damage. The destruction was devastating, but it had the effect of bringing people together.

There was, of course, immense pressure to get Manchester city life back to normal as soon as possible, in order to allow businesses to reopen and begin trading again. Many traders feared for their survival. In Ray King's history of the Manchester bombing, he records how Howard Bernstein, then a senior council officer, took the extraordinary step of calling together the local banks and asking them to promise not to foreclose on any businesses without first discussing it with him. At a meeting a week later, Bernstein, and Richard Leese, now leader of the council, gave the business community a full update on progress made and outlined the plan for the coming weeks. They ended up leaving the hall to a standing ovation. In Bernstein's words, 'It was remarkable to see the business community applauding a Labour council leader and a town hall deputy chief executive like that.' A 'Lord Mayor's Appeal' was established and local businesses large and small, as well as charitable foundations, gave hundreds of thousands of pounds to help with the rebuilding process.

I was Deputy Prime Minister at the time and knew Manchester as well as most Cabinet ministers, having been involved in many projects there since 1979, including the constructions of the Manchester Velodrome and the Bridgewater Concert Hall. I travelled to see the damage for myself and meet with local leaders. It quickly became apparent that the terrible events in Manchester had opened up an opportunity far larger than an orthodox repair job. In the 1960s and 1970s, Manchester city centre had been the subject of a massive redevelopment, which had cut off the ancient heart of the city around the cathedral from the main shopping area. The grim concrete facade of the old Arndale Centre and the dull grey market square had failed to stand the test of time. The city centre population had been in decline for years and now faced the threat posed by the imminent opening of the giant out-of-town Trafford Centre shopping mall.

I put it to Richard Leese that we should see this as an opportunity to reshape and redesign the entire city centre. An international competition should be run to find the best architects for the job and the project should be delivered on the same model as Hulme, with a standalone organisation, comprising both public and private sector partners, tasked with the delivery. To my pleasant surprise, he completely agreed.

Within three weeks after the explosion, Manchester Millennium Ltd (MML) was established for just this purpose. To my delight, Alan Cockshaw agreed to chair the board, on the condition that they had an office separate from the council. Richard Leese would co-chair with him and Howard Bernstein would become chief executive. MML set up on the fifth floor of an AMEC building in Manchester and Bernstein was stationed on the floor above, allowing them to work very closely.

Following my agreement with Richard Leese, the design competition was launched on 17 July with twenty-seven entries submitted that August, from which five were chosen for further consideration.

It was then announced that a consortium led by Ian Simpson, the selected architects, were the winners. In a paper produced by Howard Bernstein on 26 October, he set out the likely costs and the potential sources of revenue. With appropriate qualifications, he calculated a total cost of £430 million, of which £335 million would come from the private sector, leaving a deficit of £75 million to be funded by the public sector. He pointed out that this indicated a ratio of 4.7:1, which was good value. The new master plan for Manchester city centre was developed in close consultation with local businesses and residents. Cockshaw claimed that even before the process started, he knew the chairman or chief executive of every business with a building in the area, enabling him to draw in MML staff from NatWest and KPMG and ensure the masterplan was developed in close consultation with local businesses. Marks & Spencer, whose store had been badly damaged in the attack, was able to move into brand-new, purpose-built premises. The scheme also opened up and reconnected the city centre by cutting a brand-new pedestrian route through its centre, New Cathedral Street. Today it is some of the most valuable retail spaces in Manchester and boasts a range of ultra high-end brands.

The redesign proved to be just the first phase in a process that would see more than £2 billion of private and public money invested into Manchester following the bombing. I was present at a press conference in February 1997 to report progress by Alan, Richard and Howard and to announce a government grant of £43 million to add to the £20 million from the European Regional Development Fund.

As with Liverpool, a series of warehouse conversions and new builds has drawn students and young professionals back into the city centre. In 1991 only a few hundred people were living in Manchester city centre; today the number is 60,000. What is more, the whole area is governed by CityCo, a permanent, standalone organisation with a board composed of senior councillors, council officials and private sector representatives from leading property and retail developers such as Argent, Bruntwood and Milligan, the leading law firm Cobbetts LLP and the chief executive of Marketing Manchester.

The defeat of the Conservative government in 1997 appeared to end my relationship with Manchester. With the exception of its decision to create a directly elected mayoral authority in London, the Labour government placed its emphasis on devolution elsewhere, focused on regional concepts. These became as bogged down in controversy, just as we had experienced wherever we tried to change boundaries or functions of local government. It is not the purpose of this book to write about the experiences of the Labour government, but it is worth noting that Regional Development Agencies were established in 1998. Then, in 2008, the government negotiated fifteen multi-area agreements, including one with Greater Manchester. But in practice, the consequences were very limited.

Manchester has made close public–private partnership into something of an art form. In late 2010, Greater Manchester was among the first wave of places to secure a Local Enterprise Partnership, which included senior local politicians and executives from major private sector organisations including TalkTalk, the Co-Op and the Arup Group. Meanwhile, Manchester Combined Authority commissioned the groundbreaking Manchester Independent Economic Review from a panel of leading academic economists and business leaders to create an evidenced-based agenda for economic development in the city region. This work would be sustained by the Greater Manchester Economic Advisory Panel, which included very senior figures from private sector organisations including McKinsey, KPMG, FTI Consulting and Rothschild & Co. It was chaired by Jim O'Neill, who was born in Gatley, Manchester. None of them receive any remuneration for their efforts and all work in partnership with local government, deploying their considerable abilities for the benefit of a city they love.

Another great example of this partnership is the North West Evergreen Fund, a privately managed but publicly capitalised venture capital fund administered by a large consortium led by Manchester City Council. The largest of its kind in Europe, the idea is that the fund lends money, at competitive market rates, to projects struggling to raise money in conventional commercial capital markets, stepping in where the credit market has failed and making the most of this opportunity both for the public purse and the local economy. The return from these loans will then be recycled back into the fund to finance new projects, hopefully in perpetuity, while providing a return for local authority pension pots. The fund plans to support commercial and light industrial regeneration opportunities that will contribute to economic development and business growth in the north west. To ensure that investment decisions are based strictly on commercial grounds, they will be made exclusively by a team of politically independent and highly experienced fund managers overseen by a board of banking, private equity and venture capital hot shots. Although the fund is currently in its early stages, it is hoped that it will eventually attract additional private capital, thus further increasing its financial firepower.

In the space of thirty years, Manchester has gone from a position of ideological opposition to the very idea of the private sector to a place where working in intimate partnership with the private sector is now second nature. That the same Labour administration is now investing its own pension funds in a privately controlled venture capital fund, set up to exploit commercial opportunities while also achieving economic development, shows just how far they have come. In Manchester, the public and private sectors recognise just how interdependent they are, each bringing to the table a unique set of capabilities, resources, powers and links which, when combined, are worth infinitely more than the sum of their parts. Just as importantly, they have established institutional forms that allow them to exploit these complementarities, working in concert for the benefit of the city. Pro-market activism par excellence.

The redevelopment of Salford Quays is another example. The docks there closed in 1982 and the following year, Salford City Council acquired 220 acres from the Manchester Ship Canal with the aid of a derelict land grant. The brand 'Salford Quay' originates from that date. Its first task was to improve the water quality to enable the introduction of 12,000 coarse fish. Public and private funds brought about a transformation in the waterside over the years that followed, including a grant of £64 million from the Millennium Commission in February 1996 to build the Lowry Centre, celebrating the work of Salford's most famous son. That was one of several grants chosen by the commissioners as significant awards in different parts of the country to balance in some way the cost of the Dome in London. The gallery and exhibition space was opened by Queen Elizabeth II in 2000 and in 2005, MediaCity was launched by the Secretary of State for Culture Tessa Jowell – a partnership between Central Salford Urban Regeneration Company, Peel Holdings Ltd and Salford City Council. It is now home to the University of Salford, Granada Television and major BBC studios.

Manchester has also been a trailblazer on mayoral devolution. When I had abolished the metro conurbations back in the 1980s, Howard Bernstein maintained the concept of cooperation between Manchester's boroughs, even if the legal structure was abolished. He urged individual council leaders to specialise in a different responsibility, such as housing or transport, and look at it across a wide-scale conurbation. Thus, he encouraged a wider perspective. The 2010 Conservative manifesto contained proposals for directly elected mayors in large cities. These proposals were reinforced by my 'No Stone Unturned' report, which contained recommendations for stronger devolution. When the new coalition government began to examine how to implement these ideas, it was natural that Manchester was in a lead position for the first decisions. It was particularly beneficial that Jim O'Neill was a minister in the Treasury with George Osborne.

In November 2014, the coalition government announced the most comprehensive conurbation authority deal to date. Osborne declared that Greater Manchester would be the first city to be given a significant package of new powers and elect a mayor for the city region, giving them the tools necessary to take greater control of their own economic prosperity. The powers to be given to Manchester's first directly elected mayor would include:

- Responsibility for a devolved and consolidated transport budget, with a multi-year settlement to be agreed at the next spending review.
- Responsibility for franchised bus services (subject to consultation by Greater Manchester) and for integrating smart ticketing across

all local modes of transport, plus urgently exploring the opportunities for devolving rail stations across the Greater Manchester area.

- Powers over strategic planning, including the power to create a statutory spatial framework for Greater Manchester. This would need to be approved by a unanimous vote of the mayor's cabinet.
- Control of a new £300 million housing investment fund.
- The reform of the 2012 City Deal arrangements to create a '£30 million a year for thirty years' investment fund for Greater Manchester. This in turn enabled the Trafford Metrolink extension to be funded.
- Take on the role currently covered by the police and crime commissioner.

During a debate in the House of Lords in June 2015 on the Cities and Local Government Devolution Bill, Lord Goddard of Stockport, who was the leader of the borough at the time, explained what the change looked like from the position of a local authority leader:

> There was no referendum in Liverpool because the government offered Liverpool more powers if it did not have one … Greater Manchester did not, in principle, want an elected mayor but the deal was that if you wanted full powers that was the price. Looking at the full deal, the ten leaders felt that it was a price worth paying. For the avoidance of doubt for anyone else, I say that you will get limited powers from the Chancellor. If you want full powers, the caveat is that the elected mayor is the cornerstone of that. I am afraid that is the top and bottom of it.

In July 2016, I went to Manchester to discuss their bid, which reflected their ambition to establish Greater Manchester as a financially self-sustaining city at the heart of George Osborne's Northern Powerhouse project. It was both interesting and encouraging. It was not necessary to agree with every part of the proposals, but what stands out is how far cooperation between local government and the private sector had moved once policy making had been focused on local strengths and opportunities and upon partnership across the stakeholders in the locality. They had had to focus on the real world. However much the dynamics of party discipline demand that the public face continues to utter the language of a different world, in private, behind closed doors, agreement is close at hand.

Andy Burnham symbolised the power of devolution when he became Manchester's first directly elected mayor in 2017. He was the first former Cabinet minister who decided to make the journey home. Later, in 2024, he co-authored a book with Steve Rotheram, his mayoral counterpart in Liverpool, called *Head North*. The book was a rallying cry for a more equal Britain, and I was deeply touched by the personal dedication he added that said, 'We will always be grateful for your role in starting the turnaround of the north west. We salute you.'

Manchester's devolution journey has continued apace. In March 2023 the city was given a 'trailblazer devolution deal', creating a path to devolution by giving it much more flexibility to spend across departmental budgets. Over the last forty years, Manchester has grasped not just the opportunity of post-industrial regeneration but gone beyond it and started building a whole new economy. It has re-established itself as an outward-looking, internationally connected, successful city. This generational transition has been characterised by long-term shared vision, dynamic yet stable public sector and political leadership and a deep commitment to partnership.

As I was preparing this book, I was very anxious to share my memories with Sir Howard Bernstein, with whom I had worked for so long and in such detail. I knew that he was not well in June 2024 and became concerned that two appointments to discuss all this were cancelled on the day on the grounds of his ill health. He died in the early hours of 22 June 2024. He was a quite exceptional local authority official – certainly one of the most significant of his time. I have no idea if he had a political preference. My clearest memories of Howard are of endless practical decisions that affected Manchester. My earliest memories were of admiration of his administrative abilities, which rebuilt the Hulme estate, and of the pride with which he later took me to see it. Howard, Sir Alan Cockshaw and Sir Richard Leese were the team that restored the city centre after the bomb. Howard managed all this on a day-by-day basis and deserves the gratitude of his city. On Tuesday 12 November 2024, I attended a memorial concert for Howard. The tributes and the thousands of people who listened demonstrated just how widely this is recognised.

CHAPTER 15

LIVERPOOL

The story of the riots in Liverpool in 1981 is now well known and is, in many respects, uncomfortably similar to the riots that broke out in Tottenham in 2011 and across the UK in 2024. Relations between the police and local residents, many of them ethnic minorities, in and around Toxteth were already tense. An economic downturn, combined with large government spending cuts, had caused a big increase in unemployment in an area that had been struggling for some time.

Then, in the heat of the summer, one particular instance of police brutality against a young black man prompted community anger to erupt. Cars were torched in protest and pitched battles ensued between gangs of young men and riot police. The violence spread with alarming speed. Police were belatedly drafted in from around the country, but the violence re-emerged night after night. Hundreds of cars, businesses and homes were destroyed by fire and looting. For days, the entire city was gripped by fear and shock. Other cities, including the capital, underwent similar experiences, but there was something about Liverpool that demanded attention.

What went wrong in Liverpool? The short answer is, almost everything. In the early twentieth century, Liverpool found itself, both literally and metaphorically, on the wrong side of historical change. The city had flourished on the back of imperial expansion and its cotton trade with Egypt and America. After the 1920s, however, the UK's trade with Commonwealth countries in Africa and the Caribbean began to decline and the UK economy slowly but surely turned towards Europe, favouring cities on the east and south coasts. The port was also slow to respond to the containerisation revolution, with poor management and consistently belligerent trade unions hampering much-needed modernisation. Underinvestment also led to the loss of the express and deep-sea passenger liner trades to southern ports.

The workforce in the docks declined from 20,000 in 1920 to just 4,000 by 1980. At the same time, many of the Liverpool-based banking, business and financial services companies were gradually taken over by larger, London-based companies and then consolidated into their London operations.

The wider industrial belt of the city region also suffered with the loss of steel production, electronics and coal mining. Important local manufacturing companies merged and moved their bases elsewhere; few now remember that the 'Beecham' in SmithKline Beecham (now GSK) and 'Lever' in Unilever began life in the Liverpool area. By 1981, unemployment was above 20 per cent and the city's population had declined by 40 per cent in as many years. The exodus of business, encouraged by a simultaneous downturn in manufacturing, industrial and other blue-collar work, had blown a huge hole in the local economy. Just a mile from the city centre, 1,000 acres of waterfront land covered in decaying, toxic waste stood as a monument to the city's decline.

This is the story of how Liverpool became the testing ground in which the philosophy of pro-market activism began to be developed.

• • •

As far back as I can remember, Liverpool has been a part of my life. In 1941, at the age of eight, my mother, sister and I passed through the middle of a Liverpool air raid on our way to join my father, who was stationed in Dundrum, Northern Ireland.

After the war, when I was at Shrewsbury School, they had a mission to Liverpool, where I was taken for a brief visit in 1948. Later, as a junior member of Peter Walker's ministerial team in 1968, I became involved in his task to implement the Conservative government's response to the Redcliffe-Maud Commission on the structure of local government in England. It fell to me to resolve the fraught issue as to where the boundaries of the new conurbation authorities in Manchester and Liverpool were to begin and end. I organised local meetings and invited representatives of those arguing to be included or excluded to put their case in front of each other and in front of me.

The arguments were often complicated and opinions were deeply held. As I listened, one subtext was always in the air: wealthy people, who worked in the city and lived in a prosperous village or suburb outside, wanted nothing to do with the high-spending, typically Labour-controlled urban boroughs. The most controversial example of this was the case of Wilmslow in neighbouring Manchester, which in any view was a part of the conurbation, despite the protests of its inhabitants.

I made the best judgement I could with the aid of maps and, in at least one case, in a light aircraft. Before my decisions were finally implemented, I was promoted to be Minister for Aerospace, leaving my successor to figure it out. I have often wondered if the two events were linked.

My next involvement with Liverpool came in 1979, when Margaret Thatcher appointed me Secretary of State for the Environment and I inherited the chair that Peter Waker had filled in an earlier Cabinet. Before the election, I had shadowed this portfolio and worked closely with my party in local government, as Operation Clean Sweep swept us to power in every level of authority.

It is important to remember the political climate that surrounded us when we came to power. The Labour Chancellor, Denis Healey, had to call in the International Monetary Fund to bail out his mismanagement of the economy. Jim Callaghan's government had been fatally undermined by the worst outbreak of strikes since the war. Inflation was rampant, in part as a consequence of the oil price increases made by the Organization of the Petroleum Exporting Countries. High on our agenda was the promise to control public expenditure.

My relationship with Liverpool took a dramatic step forward at the outset of my new responsibilities. Peter Shore, the outgoing Labour Secretary of State for the Environment, had introduced an innovative idea to link himself and each of his ministerial team to a named local authority with particular urban problems. I was asked if I wished to continue the idea and, specifically, whether I wanted to take over Shore's relationship with Liverpool. I agreed.

Among my first instructions to officials had been to search out papers and advise how to set up a development corporation to take over responsibility for the planning of the South Bank of the Thames. I then announced my intention to proceed with the legislation to take over not only 6,000 acres of east London but 600 acres of derelict and toxic land on the north bank of the Mersey in central Liverpool.

Two further decisions followed. The Albert Dock in Liverpool was threatened with demolition in 1980, which I prevented by listing it. The second decision was to organise a garden festival for a short period before making the land available to the private sector for development. The festival set new standards for the fast and effective reclamation of derelict land against a tough backdrop. Incredibly, a court order had to be taken out to stop further waste being deposited on the site even as it was being cleared. Around a quarter of a million plants were placed in the sixty different gardens, including the famous Japanese garden with its pagoda.

The festival itself was an enormous success, not least with Liverpudlians. More than 3 million paying visitors passed through the gates in the months it was open, making it the most popular visitor attraction in the UK that year. In the judgement of Basil Bean, the chief executive of the Liverpool Urban Development Corporation, the festival 'helped enormously to improve the image of the area and restore some of its lost confidence' just three years after the Toxteth riots.

As Andrew Theokas writes in his brilliant book on the garden festivals, *Grounds for Review*:

> Perhaps, in more human terms, there can be no greater testimony to the degree with which an emotional connection was made with this site than the requests made, and granted, to permit ashes of deceased Liverpudlians who had worked on the project to be scattered over the festival grounds after it had closed.

I have my own very special memento. I had visited an Italian nursery, which had supplied some of the plants for that country's contribution. On learning of my interest and my arboretum, they asked me if I would like to have their trees, which otherwise they would have to clear away after the festival. Perhaps it would have been wise to check the cost of transporting large oaks from Liverpool to the Midlands before I accepted, but I didn't, and both are now proud possessions in my collection.

In the summer of 1981, the riots broke out in the Toxteth area of the city. It came as a profound shock and I felt a personal responsibility as a consequence of my ministerial duty for Liverpool. 'Give us jobs, not trees!' was a shout I heard across the street when I visited the city shortly afterwards. My first reaction was to support the police in their determination to restore law and order. But I told Margaret Thatcher that I thought a deeper response was justified, and I proposed to spend some time in Liverpool listening and talking in order to better understand what had led to such an event.

This experience had a profound effect on me. I had no previous dealings with local government. My background was that of a middle-class, public school-educated, private sector person who had served for some years in London's powerhouse in Whitehall.

One overwhelming theme became apparent, as I spent my first three days in the city. Everyone knew exactly who was to blame, but it was always someone else. There was no one in charge and local organisations were mesmerised by this great city's chronic economic decline. The local authority was a collection of branch offices of Whitehall departments, tightly controlled in what they could do and what they could spend but with no effective coordination of their responsibilities and powers.

The initial reaction to my arrival was courteous and cooperative, even if punctuated by the observation that it took a riot to bring me there. I faced a dilemma: listening to the people of Liverpool was the relatively easy part of the response, as there was a genuine welcome to the fact that someone was at last here. Inevitably, the mood changed within a few days as the predictable questions came: what was I going to do? It would have been possible to escape back to the safety of London, but already two clear impressions were in my mind. Against the prevailing sense of hopelessness, a list was forming in my mind of what needed to be done. Just as serious was the conviction that there was no one and no system with which to grip these opportunities.

At the press conference to signal the end of my visit to Liverpool, I produced a list of projects that I believed would demonstrate, with the right leadership, the fortunes of the city could be restored. I announced a task force of civil servants and secondees from the private sector who would work with me, and I would take personal interest in driving the projects forward.

I began on the most interventionist journey of any minister of which I have knowledge. I not only admit this but am proud of what I did. I was intervening in order to breathe the life of enterprise and self-reliance into an economic situation in apparent terminal decline. Derelict land, polluted to the point that no one would build on it. Breakdown in communication between the public and private sectors, between which, apparently, no bridge existed. Council estates laid waste by vandalism, empty buildings and rat-infested public spaces where even the local authority had given up.

I wrote the report 'It Took a Riot' in my own hand for the Cabinet. Years later, it was suggested that in discussing my report, Geoffrey Howe, Chancellor of the Exchequer, proposed that Liverpool should be left to its own devices and allowed to go into 'managed decline'. I do not remember any serious discussion along such lines, although inevitably Geoffrey would have been briefed by the Treasury to watch out for the pennies.

The only judgement of any validity to me is that for eighteen months after that meeting, Margaret was aware that I was visiting Liverpool every Thursday and Friday to lead a team of officials and private sector secondees as we set out to prove that things in Liverpool could work. There was never a hint of criticism from her, nor any attempt to limit my activity. Indeed, in the middle of 1982, she told her Chief Whip, Michael Jopling, that she thought I was her natural successor. Europe, at that point, had not raised its head.

As it appeared in 1981, here is the list of all the projects I pursued in Liverpool. Each Thursday, the first task was to check progress:

- The creation of the Merseyside Task Force under the direction of Eric Sorensen.
- The establishment of the Financial Institutions Group.
- The creation of the Mersey Basin Campaign.
- The reclamation of the Liverpool riverside.
- The announcement of the Tate Gallery in Liverpool and the extension of the Maritime Museum.
- The creation of the Bootle Industrial Area.
- The completion of the Derby Road scheme.
- Work in Wirral, including the restoration of the river wall at Secombe and the re-engineering of the Scotts Field and Morpeth Dock areas.
- The upgrading of the Liverpool city centre and M62 link.
- Faster new ferries across the Mersey, with a new landing stage at the Dingle and improved terminal facilities at Woodside.
- A new riverside walk between Otterspool and Pier Head.

- The creation of the Eldonian Village on the site of the closed Tate & Lyle factory.
- Refurbishment of Wapping Dock and creation of industrial units at South Brunswick Dock.
- Establishment of an international architectural competition to design the Anglican Cathedral project and carry it out.
- Housing Associations to improve older housing in Toxteth.
- Agreement with Knowsley Council to regenerate the Cantril Farm Estate with the help of the private sector.
- The compiling of land registers in Knowsley and St Helens to identify derelict land.
- The establishment of the Wavertree Industrial Park.
- The refurbishment of Lime Street Station.
- Agreement with large local firms each to create 100 local training vacancies and to offer job opportunities to people from local black communities.

These projects were not just good practical interventions. Taken together, they were the essential tools needed to address a city's renewal. This required the intelligent use of what is there by building on the city's great assets, turning those assets from a liability to a benefit, encouraging entrepreneurship and business development, targeting investment to provide clear and timely outcomes, and building community resilience and self-help. This was all part of the determination to restore hope and pride in the city.

The budgeting disciplines at that time were such that once you had agreed the total with the Treasury, you were free to move cash from one part of the budget to another. This flexibility enabled me to top slice funds from the very large Housing Corporation budget in order to finance individual projects on my list.

Early in 1983, I was promoted to be Secretary of State for Defence. Liverpool left my agenda and Patrick Jenkin was left to cope with the disastrous emergence of Derek Hatton and the hard-left Labour council. With my new defence responsibilities, I realised I should not become involved for fear it would provoke headlines suggesting the government was about to deploy troops in the city. There never was any such prospect – indeed, as I listened to Patrick discuss in Cabinet the possibility that he would have to put commissioners in to run the city, it occurred to me that I might be qualified for the job. The moment passed and it was decades later before I was once again in the headlines over Liverpool.

Fortunately, the Hatton experience had been relatively short-lived, and in 1998 the Labour government had asked the architect Richard Rogers to examine the challenges of urban deprivation. I was happy to discuss the issues with him and agreed with his proposals to create urban regeneration companies (URCs) to lead and coordinate the regeneration of the area.

I recognised the precedent for this in what I had done with the original task force in 1981 and with the City Challenge in 1992. The critical point was to recognise the need for a collective approach – to involve both public and private sectors, to consult the people involved and to provide effective leadership. URCs were a more sophisticated mechanism of the development corporations I had created in 1979, but the concepts were the same. Published in 2000, the Strategic Regeneration Framework for Liverpool was ambitious, far-sighted and led the way for the city's successful bid to be the European Capital of Culture. It encouraged business development, argued to reinforce city communities and included a list of achievable projects. The original UDC was wound up in 1998 and it is incomprehensible to me that it was not extended to the derelict area downstream.

Grosvenor Estates, the organisation that handles the Duke of Westminster's property assets, began work as consultants in 1997, which led to a competition in which developers would submit proposals to develop a 42-acre site in Liverpool City centre known as the Paradise Street Project. Grosvenor won the competition with a project later known as 'Liverpool One', and they then invested the best part of £1 billion in this redevelopment. They rejected the simple option of one large office block in favour of a comprehensive, environmentally attractive concept linking the banks of the Mersey and the Albert Docks with the city centre.

I discussed the project with Jeremy Newsum, then chief executive of Grosvenor Estates. They were experienced developers in urban renewal, but they had a special relationship with Liverpool, born of the close proximity of the family estates in Cheshire. The then Duke of Westminster was not only deeply involved in all that went on in Liverpool and the area surrounding it, he was the most senior Territorial Army officer in the land – a major general – and many of his soldiers were Liverpudlians.

There are never simple explanations when major projects such as this exceed their original budget. Inflation, the inevitable discovery of omissions in the specification, unanticipated costs involved in executing compulsory purchase agreements and, ironically, the tight time scales imposed by the need to comply with the timetable put forward by the Capital of Culture Award all contributed. It became clear – and there were warnings – that the project would incur serious cost overruns as it progressed. The financial partner, Henderson Group, pulled out in 2002, leaving Grosvenor with a clear choice. It was to Liverpool's immense good fortune that the trustees – under the chairmanship of the duke – decided that they would deliver what they had promised. They started work in 2004 and completed the project five years later. Everyone working on the project felt a personal pride in what they were creating, a feeling reciprocated by citizens on the street.

In strictly commercial terms, the investment cost £250 million more than its commercial value. From Liverpool's viewpoint, its value is priceless.

The conclusion that emerges from all these different initiatives is that, over a quarter of a century, the face, performance and reputation of Liverpool had been transformed. The Merseyside Development Corporation rejuvenated much of its site and the Albert Dock from an empty, if architecturally distinguished relic to a magnet of activity attracting 6 million visitors a year. Liverpool's universities had invested millions in improved facilities and expanded student places. Liverpool Vision, the local authority's regenerative vehicle led by Max Steinberg, pioneered project after project. LEPs and other private sector bodies, such as The Peel Group, added to the potential.

Reflecting now on the thirty-year gap, it is impossible to overstate the difference between the Liverpool to which I returned in 2011 and the city with which I was involved at the time of the 1981 riots. Instead of being given a long list of other people who were at fault, which is what had characterised my earlier visit, this was a community of people who had clear ideas about what needed to be done and who should be in charge. They just wanted the chance to get on with it.

David Cameron asked me, together with Sir Terry Leahy, to revisit the issues set out in 1981 in my report 'It Took a Riot'. Now all we had to do was to prioritise the avalanche of ideas available to us, with an army of people willing to finance and manage the projects. Our report 'Rebalancing Britain: Policy or Slogan?' was published in October 2011. I cannot overstate the warmth with which our endeavours were welcomed. I hope and believe it was accepted that we were there to help.

All doors were open when I returned to the city in 2011. However, these memories are disturbed by one door that remained firmly closed. Anyone with any knowledge of Liverpool must remember the great Atlantic passenger trade, when Cunard's great liners sailed back and forth between Liverpool and New York. These liners were symbols of a certain majesty and excellence. A vital component of this trade was the Adelphi Hotel adjoining Lime Street Station. Any casual examination of its facilities, particularly the grandeur of its public rooms and its history as a transatlantic terminal, would see it as the five-star hotel that it had once been. However, there are still no five-star hotels in Liverpool and it is questionable whether even now the demand exists, although the significant growth of the number of four-star hotels is symptomatic of the city's changing fortunes.

I discussed the possibility with hotelier Rocco Forte that he might enter a deal with the Adelphi to restore and upgrade it. He said he had looked at it, but it would mean having to charge guests a minimum of £200 per night and he didn't think the market to do this existed.

The present Adelphi operates as a three-star hotel and I felt that it would be worth exploring with the owners what their plans are, given that Liverpool is now self-evidently enjoying a significant economic revival. Times change, markets disappear, and the Adelphi had had little option but to seek a cheaper market at the time. But I wanted to understand whether the chairman of Britannia Hotels, the company that owned the hotel, felt the new circumstances that were leading to the construction of new four-star hotels in the city could encourage him to change the Adelphi back closer to its earlier glory.

Despite repeated requests for a meeting, every call was refused. Eventually, a meeting was offered with his finance director. I learned a long time ago that to make progress, you need to talk to the person in charge. In my entire experience in public life, and particularly in Liverpool from the 1970s to now, I have never been confronted by a refusal to even engage in a dialogue with somebody whose only interest was the welfare of the city and whose only purpose was to understand the long-term plans of the owner of a major Liverpool asset. I was later to learn that Joe Anderson, then the Mayor of Liverpool, received the same treatment. It is little wonder to me that Britannia Hotels is regarded as one of the worst chains of its sort in the country.

In the 'Rebalancing Britain' report, Terry Leahy and I acted more as presenters of other people's ideas than originators of our own. This new confidence and ambition was the striking difference between the Liverpool of 2011 and the one I remembered some thirty years ago.

Terry and I each contributed one proposal for action. He made the important point that across the world, there is a large diaspora of Liverpudlians who might well be willing to help their parent city if someone indicated what they could do to help. For my part, I returned to a theme I had first explored in 1981 in the campaign to clean the Mersey. This had already produced significant improvements in water quality and the local environment, highlighted by the return of salmon and seals to the river, but its momentum had come to an end after its 25-year lifetime.

I believed, and still do, that water quality is an issue that will increasingly be of concern to the public; people are not going to put up with inadequately regulated sewage discharges into their urban rivers. I suggested that Liverpool restart the campaign with an announcement that after twenty-five years, no untreated discharges would be permitted. In the case of the Mersey, this timescale had the advantage of ensuring that virtually all of the capital equipment already doing the job would have to be replaced in the normal course of events. By setting such absolute standards well in advance, those presently discharging would have plenty of notice. This could be set up as a world model of what could and should be done.

The potential was there for all to see. Consultancy firms would emerge to set the pace. Manufacturing companies could locate close to the new market they wished to serve. Cities across the world would send delegations to monitor progress and learn lessons. Improving standards of water quality could generate new leisure and hospitality industries, and Liverpool would have staked a claim to be the city with the cleanest water in the world, just as populations were demanding better care for the environment.

• • •

At an extraordinary meeting of the city council in March 2012, in the presence of the Lord Mayor and fifty-two Labour councillors, Mayor Joe Anderson proposed that I should be granted the Honorary Freedom of the City and six days later, the conferment was celebrated at the town hall. It was a particular pleasure that my wife and daughters, Annabel and Alexandra, were there. They must have felt many times that Liverpool was just another reason why I was away from home so much. I hoped that the evening's event left a clearer message.

In my speech, I said that I had come first to Liverpool in the 1960s and '70s as a partisan member of the Conservative Party. I paid tribute to my Labour predecessor, Peter Shore, for introducing the concept of partnership between central and local government and said that I had set out to extend that sense of partnership to include the private sector and other local stakeholders. Joe Anderson told the audience that there were tears in my eyes when he first told me of the proposal. I said that I made no apology for that; a part of me will always be in Liverpool. The eighteen months during which I visited the city weekly turned the practices and theories of politics into a living experience of people and circumstance.

I said that there had been tears on other occasions. I was standing outside a council house one Saturday lunchtime when the tenant returned from work to find that his home had been trashed. Every single thing he owned was ruined. I shared his grief. It was a scene unrecognisable from the world in which I live.

I told the audience of the night in August 1981 when I looked out from my suite on the top floor of the Atlantic Tower hotel at the Mersey below – majestic, ever running, the lifeblood of Liverpool's history but now an open sewer flowing through a scene of utter decay. There had been a tear that night too, but there was also a vision and a determination – to clean the Mersey from the source to the sea. It was with pride that I saluted Liverpool's reassertion of its rightful place as a city recognised across the world as a place of culture, a font of enterprise, proud of itself and ambitious for its future. I concluded that Liverpudlians had done all this before – and because you did, you can.

At this time, Greg Clark, as the responsible minister, was pressing to carry out the government's commitment to establish mayoral authorities. Joe Anderson, while appreciating the benefits of a conurbation-wide structure, was anxious to negotiate an exclusive deal for Liverpool. It was agreed that an initiative for this purpose would have to come from the authority itself and Joe was anxious to conclude such a deal before his council meeting on 18 June 2011. The initiative was duly forthcoming and Joe became the elected mayor in the following year.

In January 2013, the vice-chancellor of Liverpool University wrote to tell me that in the year before, they had established the new Institute for Public Policy, Practice and Place to undertake research and related activities, largely focused on work in the north west but also nationally. In recognition of my success in working with the area and of my becoming a Freeman of the City, the university had proposed that the faculty should be renamed the Heseltine Institute and he asked if I would agree to this. Of course, I accepted this great honour enthusiastically. The staff and visiting fellows, holding senior decision-making posts, have extensive experience and expertise in public policy, local and regional economic development, devolution and urban governance. They have led research, collaborated with decision-makers and influenced the national policy debate on three broad themes – the future of cities and city regions, regional inequalities and public service reform. In July 2013, I was also awarded an honorary fellowship from Liverpool John Moores University.

In the autumn of 2014, the Liverpool city region became deeply involved in negotiations for their own mayoral deal. They held meetings with Greg Clark, and in a letter to the Chancellor George Osborne, signed by Phil Davies, chair of the combined authority, and Robert Hough, chair of the City Region Enterprise Partnership, it was quite clear that they were very conscious of the progress towards such deals elsewhere and were desperate to catch up.

I helped to advise them on how to prepare their bid in a meeting on 21 October with the council leaders of Wirral, St Helens, Sefton,

Knowsley and Halton, as well as the Lord Mayor of Liverpool and the chair of the Local Enterprise Partnership. The order implementing the deal was laid before Parliament in December 2016, with Joe Anderson, as chair of the Liverpool City Region Combined Authority, canvassing members for their support.

No one was surprised when the first incumbent as mayor, Steve Rotheram, came from the Labour Party. Steve was re-elected in 2024, as was his colleague Andy Burnham in Greater Manchester. He and I enjoyed a cordial relationship and I was particularly pleased when one of his first decisions was to announce plans to clean the Mersey of sewage by 2030.

On 22 November 2017, Professor Michael Parkinson of the Heseltine Institute organised one of the most extraordinary events of my life. Anyone who has ever been in public life is all too familiar with the sensationalist headlines and the vicious criticism that the media and one's opponents utter, while the more restrained language of one's friends disappears in the small print. 'You Liar!' was plastered across the whole of the front page of *The Sun* during the Westland affair. This event was billed as 'Lord Heseltine's contribution to the nation, its cities and Liverpool', which was somewhat different!

In his opening remarks, the professor generously said:

> Nobody knows what might have happened if Michael Heseltine had not done what he did after the riots in Toxteth in 1981. But I'm sure Liverpool would be a very different place from what it is today – less successful, less self-confident. We owe him a great debt of gratitude.

He had also persuaded a number of Labour politicians, led by John Prescott, and the leaders of Manchester and Liverpool councils, alongside civil servants and others with whom I had worked to recount their experiences at the event. When Lord Prescott died in 2024, I recounted my gratitude that he had taken the trouble to travel all that way just to salute an old opponent. In his speech, he said that we had both started at opposite ends of the social system. Over the years we had learned from experience to meet in the middle ground of politics. In thanking him, I said that if we went on thinking like this, we could end up forming a coalition and he could be Deputy Prime Minister.

But all was not smooth sailing. In December 2020, Liverpool's mayor Joe Anderson was arrested as part of a far-reaching investigation into allegations of fraud, bribery, corruption and misconduct in public office. In April 2024, I raised the question in the House of Lords about the time that had elapsed with no charges being brought: 'He has lost his job, his income and his reputation. Is this justice?' I was very disappointed by the ministerial reply, which effectively left the matter in the hands of the police. I hope to raise the matter further. In the protection of any citizen, there must be a proper ministerial opportunity to ensure that justice is done within a reasonable timescale.

There is, of course, still much more work to be done in Liverpool. Regeneration and renewal programmes have had a major impact, improving the quality of social housing and the physical environment in the most deprived areas. Despite this, on many streets a majority of households remain completely unemployed. The employment rate in parts of Liverpool is 63.5 per cent compared to a national rate of 74.5 per cent. Converting those statistics into human terms means that about 200,000 extra jobs are needed to bring Liverpool in line with national levels. While people of all ages need gainful employment, of particular concern are the effects of inactivity on school leavers who fail to establish the routine and confidence that work, training and education instil. Business density is also far too low; there are only thirty-two businesses per 1,000 people in greater Liverpool compared to an average of forty-two per 1,000 nationally.

Such statistics demonstrate that there is still more to do, but regardless, you can sense the change from the Liverpool I first came to know forty years ago. There is a renewed sense of pride and no shortage of people with the determination to further the changes and build on the opportunities. There is an effective political leadership anxious to assume more responsibility and work in partnership with the central government. That is the real transformation, in which I was fortunate enough to have played a part.

CHAPTER 16

LONDON

After school, I set out to qualify as a chartered accountant, but rejected the option of five years articled to a local firm in Swansea, my home town, in favour of three years at Oxford University followed by three years articled in London. So, after Oxford, I duly presented myself on 5 January 1955 at the offices of Peat Marwick Mitchell in Ironmonger Lane in the City of London, neat as a pin with suit, tie, waistcoat, bowler hat and furled umbrella. Shortly afterwards, I was dispatched to tick the books of the slaughterhouses of the Fatstock Marketing Corporation in Islington.

Some seventy years later, I sat with my wife outside the offices of Deloitte, our tax consultants and a giant firm of accountants, watching the city's workers enjoy their midday break. Everyone was casually dressed with not a tie to be seen and there were as many women as men – a cosmopolitan workforce from every part of the world, passing their lunch hour in one of the world's most multiracial and multicultural cities.

No one could have predicted such a complete change over that time. And I could not have imagined the speed and quality of the transformation of parts of the city, a mere two miles from where we sat, when I first became involved in London Docklands in 1979.

The Royal Docks, centred on the iconic loop in the River Thames to the east of the Tower of London, were developed in the nineteenth century to accommodate the booming commodities trade that grew up on the back of our imperial expansion. It has been said that the Docklands were 'the hungry mouth of the British Empire' – consuming coffee, sugar, spices, fruit, tobacco and hundreds of other items from all over the world.

In the 1960s, when I first entered Parliament, traffic in the Royal Docks reached an all-time high. But by the 1980s, when I took up my first Cabinet post, the docks were dead. A new wave of globalisation, spurred by the advent of container shipping, had dramatically redrawn the trade map. Containerisation is a paradigm of disruptive innovation; it dramatically reduced the cost of transporting goods and, at a stroke, rendered many previously successful shallow-water ports such as London obsolete. The business of unloading containerised goods destined for the British market moved to Felixstowe, Southampton and even Rotterdam. Unemployment on the Isle of Dogs soared to 40 per cent.

My first involvement with the Docklands came about entirely by coincidence. In the early 1970s, as Minister for Aerospace, I was responsible for drawing up plans for a new London airport off the Essex coast. I chartered a light aircraft in order to survey the proposed site of Maplin Sands on the Foulness Island mudflats. The airport was never to be, but the trip was far from wasted. Flying across London in 1973, the immense tracts of dereliction left by the loss of the docks industry were laid out below me. The abandoned Docklands were a huge, ugly scar on the landscape to the east of the capital, some 6,000 acres of crumbling Victorian warehouses and toxic, methane-emitting dumps. The land was owned by a mixture of publicly owned utilities, local authorities and private companies. None of them had any appetite for cleaning up the land. Each of them was waiting for the other to find a buyer, hoping that they would then be the last person holding on to their land in order to get the best price for it. The result was a stalemate; a never-ending game of 'after you'.

In 1971, during my first ministerial posting in a planning department, I had been so appalled by the piecemeal and incoherent development of the South Bank of the Thames that I asked my officials to prepare plans to set up a single body to take over and control the planning and development of that area. It would be modelled on the specific planning authorities used to develop the new towns after the war. Unfortunately, I was moved on before the plans came to anything.

On my first day back in the Department for the Environment in 1979, over lunch at the Connaught Hotel, I handed my new Permanent Secretary, John Garlick, an envelope, on the back of which was my wish list of priorities. It included a development corporation for the 6,000 acres of redundant dockland. My plans were not revolutionary; development corporations were single-purpose agencies with wide powers over planning, land assembly and regeneration under the direction of a team, drawn from both the public and private sectors. And so, the idea of the Urban Development Corporation (UDC) was born. We took control of 55,000 acres of east London and began the task of breathing economic life back into Docklands.

Sir Geoffrey Howe, then Chancellor of the Exchequer, was keen on the concept of an enterprise zone. I was sympathetic to his arguments, which could incorporate fast-track planning, a local tax holiday and, crucially, the right to offset capital construction costs against profit on other projects. However, successful urban regeneration requires more than just tax incentives, particularly land acquisition and planning powers and resources to stimulate the work.

Therefore, the legislation which created the London Docklands Development Corporation (LDDC) also designated the Isle of Dogs – a small part of the corporation's land portfolio – as an enterprise zone. The LDDC was run as a distinct body under the chairmanship of Sir Nigel Broackes, chairman of Trafalgar House, with Bob Mellish, a former Labour Chief Whip, as his deputy. While maintaining a majority of members from the private sector, I made sure that each of the Labour leaders from the affected boroughs were also members. The UDC was able to compulsorily purchase areas of derelict land, use public money to clean them up, bring them to a marketable state and sell them on in consolidated chunks to allow buyers to assemble land for coherent, large-scale development. The relaxed planning controls meant that whoever bought the land could be confident that delays would be kept to a minimum. This model was to prove extremely effective.

The thinking behind the UDC was never that bureaucrats should attempt to construct a new economy on the Isle of Dogs or in any of the other thirteen places where they were eventually established. The philosophy was clear: faced with the accumulated detritus of long-dead industrial life, with its consequent pollution and toxicity, no developers would ever take on the cost of reclamation when cheaper, more profitable options were available for their investments. Our ambitions were large both in terms of the scale of the area being regenerated and our desire for significant coherent development projects, but they were also limited in the sense that we never had a 'plan'. The government should stimulate, not predict, and support to compete.

The dilemma the enterprise zone concept faced, however, was the lack of quality control. If the intention was to attract substantial new investments of high-quality projects, investors need reassurance that they are not going to be surrounded by sheds erected by cowboys who had been attracted by the tax concessions. Investors know that the local environment was critical to the value of their asset and, particularly, the security of their staff. Reg Ward, the first chief executive of the UDC and an outstanding public servant, insisted on quality as a condition of the flexible planning regime.

Despite my belief in the approach we took, it did require a considerable leap of faith to rely on a positive response from the business community. Whom could we persuade to move to this somewhat inaccessible and barren peninsula five miles from the centre of London? At the time, we had no idea, and looking back at the remarkable chain of events that followed, there was no way that we could have guessed what would happen next. If, on second reading of the legislation in 1981, I had outlined a plan that included Canary Wharf, London City Airport, the ExCeL Centre, the Olympics and the Millennium Dome – all serviced by HS1 and Crossrail – the House would rightly have fallen about with laughter.

The shape that the development would take would depend on the efforts of private investors, responding to the opportunities that we were going to provide. The opportunity for office development on the Isle of Dogs was first spotted by Michael von Clemm, the chairman of Credit Suisse First Boston. He had witnessed firsthand the expansion in demand for ultra-large trading floors in Boston and realised that the move to electronic, screen-based trading meant the traditional small, wood-panelled offices of the City would need to be replaced with larger, open-plan trading floors. On a visit to London to look for a storage facility for the famous Le Gavroche restaurant, of which he happened to be chairman, he spotted the potential of the Isle of Dogs.

In Boston, a similar ex-dockland area had been redeveloped into a new financial centre for the city. As it happened, the dockside warehouses in Boston had been constructed by the same companies as those that had built on the Isle of Dogs, because they were at either end of the same shipping route. The traditional area of the city was already crowded and the City of London Corporation was unwilling to allow the construction of new high-rise towers in place of the historic buildings with their small cubicle offices that made up the Square Mile.

Von Clemm introduced a colourful Texan property developer, G. Ware Travelstead, to get the first modest four-storey development underway. After three years, however, it became clear that Travelstead could not raise enough capital. The idea of creating a financial outpost two miles east of the City appeared to be dead in the water, but then Margaret Thatcher got wind of the problems and took a long shot at reviving the project.

The Prime Minister contacted Paul Reichmann, the co-owner with his brother Albert of the world-renowned property developers Olympia & York, and she made him a blunt offer. Thatcher explained to Reichmann that Olympia & York, who were at the time rebuilding the new World Trade Center in New York, were the only organisation in the world with the ability and the resources to develop the site. She pledged that the government would deliver an extension of the Jubilee Line from the centre of the city right into the heart of the development, bringing it within easy reach of all of London, if he took on the project.

Paul Reichmann had a vision of tomorrow and he thought on a scale to match it. He is most easily described as a classic Jewish patriarch. A deeply religious man, committed to the traditions of his faith, he was far removed from the cut-throat world of international property development. He spoke in a voice so quiet he was difficult to hear. Paul also had an uncanny talent for spotting market opportunities. He and his brother Albert started their career running a small importing business in the US. While looking for new premises they decided to build their own, which they achieved at half the market rate. They created a new company, York Factory Developments, and thus Olympia & York was born.

In response to the Prime Minister's phone call, unknown to each other, he sent members of his team individually to London to look at the site and consider the opportunity. Each of them saw the isolated site, accessible only by a single road, unconnected to the transport network and lacking in even mains gas and water and reported back to Reichmann with their findings. Five opposed involvement in the project; only one was in favour.

The advice they received from their British contacts was even more negative. Nobody would even consider renting or buying office space east of Tower Bridge. But, in a truly remarkable move, Paul decided to come to London himself over a weekend and, as a result of his visit, he went against the weight of their advice and signed a contract to go ahead and buy the entire Canary Wharf site. Thus was born the plan for the development of several huge skyscrapers, offering 50–60,000 sq. ft of trading floors. This was several orders of magnitude more ambitious than anything von

Clemm and Travelstead had conceived. The government then agreed to build the Docklands Light Railway (DLR) to connect the new Canary Wharf development to the City, as I announced to the 1982 Conservative Party conference, as well as promising to connect the West End by extending the Jubilee Line into the heart of the development. But it wasn't all plain sailing: Canary Wharf's plans were met with the same hostility that I had experienced originally over the UDC itself. Put simply, local people were demanding bigger public subsidies and additional service provision for a community that was already almost entirely dependent on such handouts. The young, their children and grandchildren had gone off in search of jobs and new homes.

The UDC was a vehicle for transforming the economy, not for providing additional subsidies, but local residents were angry that they had not been consulted about the fast-tracked development. At one point, though well before the Canary Wharf row, protesters had cut off access to the two road bridges that connected the southern half of the Isle of Dogs, declared it an independent country and even began printing their own money. At the Canary Wharf launch ceremony itself, protest groups hid in an old dockyard overnight and then released a herd of sheep among the guests!

I have always regretted that I did not enter into a dialogue with the local authority tenants at the time. Certainly, I learned my lesson and took a very different approach when confronted with the riots in Liverpool. Consultation with local people then became a central feature of my approach to regeneration more generally. I remember I had thought at the time that there would be no point in holding local discussions because I knew the sort of things they would say and there would be no meeting of minds. There was some truth in that – but I was wrong. I was proposing to authorise significant changes to the place they called home, and the least I could have done would have been to explain why and to what purpose.

One Canada Square was completed in 1991 and was, at the time, the tallest building in the UK. However, all was not well with the project. Transport for London was suffering serious difficulties with the crucial DLR link. Poor track design, endless delays and inadequate capacity brought frequent closures and the need to replace rolling stock. There were occasions when Canary Wharf sales executives were bringing potential clients from the City via the new rail link to view the development and it was actually breaking down with them on board! This even happened when the Queen paid a visit.

The government had also been far too slow in committing to the Jubilee Line by presenting the necessary legislation to Parliament, which delayed matters until the necessary legislation allowed the go-ahead in mid-1992. They insisted that the promised £400 million from the Canary Wharf development must be contributed before construction would begin, despite the fact that the line was six years late and the necessary legislation had not even been introduced into Parliament.

By this time, Olympia & York had invested £2.5 billion of their own money, but slower sales than expected meant that they were no longer able either to service their debt or to pay the £400 million. They filed for bankruptcy; Ernst & Young were called in as administrators. There is no doubt that the cumulative delays were a major cause of the bankruptcy, but the Reichmann brothers never claimed compensation.

Ownership of the DLR eventually had to be removed from Transport for London, which had a very poor performance record. It was transferred to the Department for the Environment. John

Major and I visited the site in 1993 and looked in despair at this huge investment, which was still being served by a railway that did not work. So, I invited Peter Levene, whom I had first brought into public service in 1983, to transform the out-of-date procurement process in the Ministry of Defence and take on the responsibility of rescuing the situation. He worked miracles. Within six months the line was operating at near full capacity, and shortly after that it was recognised as one of the best-performing lines in Europe.

In 1993, a new company was formed called Canary Wharf Limited. Peter Levene was installed as chairman and chief executive, and he appointed George Iacobescu as construction director. Under this new management, the company quickly became highly profitable and successfully let most of the available space.

The shareholders then put the company up for sale and it was bought by a large consortium led by Prince Al Waleed from Qatar, Paul and Albert Reichmann and others. After 1996, it was run by Sir George Iacobescu as chairman and chief executive.

Under the new arrangements, the £400 million was paid – contributed by Olympia & York when the company came out of bankruptcy. There is a letter setting out this arrangement, but I could not persuade Sir George to let me see it.

The Jubilee Line also finally got underway, opening just in time to convey passengers to celebrate the turn of the century at the new Millennium Dome.

Ownership of Canary Wharf is now divided between the Qatar Investment Authority and Brookfield of Canada, and there are now 100,000 people working there. By 2030, it is calculated that there will be more people working there than in the city of Manchester. It has evolved from providing first-class offices for financial services to become a new city area with a wide variety of businesses, one of London's largest shopping destinations, an enormous range of bars and restaurants and a cinema and entertainment location, with many new homes and more being built. The opening of the Canary Wharf station on the Elizabeth Line in 2022 added to this growth story, which is unique in modern London in its scale and nature.

Canary Wharf is by no means the only offshoot of London Docklands Development Corporation. Reg Ward, chief executive of the LDDC, wasted no time in establishing the feasibility of building an airport in the Docklands. Before the end of 1981, Mowlem had submitted a proposal for a short take-off and landing airport running along the thin strip of land in the centre of the King George V dock. London City Airport was built and owned by Mowlem PLC and officially opened in 1987. In its first full year, it handled 130,000 passengers.

I had the pleasure of approving the expansion of the airport in 1991, and in 2005 the London City Airport extension of the DLR opened, bringing the airport within twelve minutes of Canary Wharf and twenty-four minutes of Westminster. It now handles around 3 million passengers a year and contributes around half a billion pounds a year to the UK economy. It is now owned by a consortium.

The ExCeL centre was another major success. The centre encompasses 90,000 square metres of exhibition space situated on the opposite bank of the King George V dock. It has three dedicated DLR stations, five on-site hotels and, since opening in 2000, has received more than 5 million visitors. In 2012, it hosted more than 150 events for the London Olympic Games.

Housing on the Isle of Dogs was also dramatically improved. Labour councils had, over many years, concentrated almost exclusively on social housing. A direct consequence of this was that in order to get their feet on the property ladder, the young, aspiring members of the East End community had to move out of the area. Private house builders wasted no time in putting forward ambitious proposals for new housing. Some 20,000 additional houses were built in the area, at least 40 per cent of which had to be offered at affordable prices, and local people were given preferential loans of up to £10,000 to use as mortgage deposits by the development corporation. The Canary Wharf Group envisages that the number of people living on Canary Wharf itself will rise to around 15,000 in the next ten years, bringing with it a further expansion of affordable housing.

There can be no doubt that the Docklands has been totally transformed, with multiple world-class developments, all linked by the DLR. There is, however, still a question that needs to be answered, and it is whether all this development has been of benefit to the local communities.

The polished glass towers rising up among one of the most deprived communities in the country is itself a stark vision of the inequality that persists. It is too easy to deride the idea that creating a global investment banking hub could ever help impoverished local residents struggling to recover from deindustrialisation, often lacking in basic skills or even the ability to speak English. As with all caricatures, however, this grossly misrepresents the reality.

Any modern office employs a large proportion of its staff in 'support' roles. For example, half of the people employed by J. P. Morgan are not bankers. ONS's employment survey data show only 59 per cent of employees in Canary Wharf and the immediate surrounding area work in finance and insurance, professional services and public administration. A further quarter of jobs are in administration, retail, catering, transport and storage, with another 16 per cent recorded as 'other'. One tenth of people employed in Canary Wharf live in Tower Hamlets, and this figure does not include the wider network of local businesses supplying the wharf.

The Canary Wharf Group also has a dedicated team working to help local small and medium enterprises secure contracts for painting and decorating, photocopier repairs and such like. The delivery authority for the 2012 Olympic Games specifically required contractors to provide jobs for local residents, and the London Legacy Development Corporation continued this practise in the contracts they let for redevelopment and new construction after the games, as well as continuing to support local economic activity on a wider scale. This included a recruitment and training centre, which actively works to help local residents qualify for jobs available on the wharf. The airport's management also has specific initiatives to offer employment opportunities to local people.

So, the answer to the question is resoundingly 'Yes'. It clearly has done so, not least because there was not much of a local community left by the early '80s. No doubt there will still be a few elderly members of the original Docklands community dreaming of yesteryear, but whichever way you look at it, the East End is a place transformed. There are still massive problems, which remain to be addressed, but the direction is forwards and the prospect is hope.

My main regret with the Docklands Development Corporation is that we did not go far enough. The Docklands make up only a small part of the much larger Thames Gateway region, which stretches for forty miles along both banks of the River Thames as far as Southend and Sittingbourne. At the same time that the dock work was disappearing from Docklands, car manufacturing and other industries were moving away from the Thames Gateway. The area contains several pockets of severe deprivation – including three of the six most deprived local authorities in the UK. I can vividly remember the moment in 1979 when I was persuaded to leave out the derelict sites south of the Thames in Greenwich and Lewisham and concentrate only on the north bank. In a moment of weakness, I agreed, but even at the time, I suspected I had made a mistake.

• • •

In the mid-1990s, it came as a bolt from the blue when John Major invited me to become a millennium commissioner and work on the celebrations for the turn of the century. I was delighted to accept. It is very rare in life that you are given the chance to spend £2 billion on a party! The Millennium Commission was funded entirely by proceeds from the newly created National Lottery, and we planned to support a wide range of projects with one big central exhibition to mark the event.

We distributed the money following two guiding principles: funds would only be given towards capital investment and not as a substitute for revenue, and we would fund no more than half of the capital for any particular project. Matched funding proved particularly effective and grants of £1.26 billion ended up contributing to £3 billion worth of projects. I had first used this concept of gearing when confronted with the opportunities of regeneration in Liverpool in 1979.

The 1951 Festival of Britain was the closest parallel to what we wanted to achieve with the millennium celebrations. It had signalled a determination to break out of the wartime mindset, to make a statement about rebuilding Britain and to provide a chance for the nation to get a glimpse of what the future might hold, whether scientific or cultural. I remembered visiting the festival as a young man and that provided much inspiration during our preparations for 2000.

The 1951 festival was extremely controversial, just as the millennium celebrations would prove to be. Britain was then just coming to terms with the extent of post-war austerity and many complained that it was a frivolous waste of public money. Winston Churchill famously dismissed it as 'three-dimensional socialist propaganda'.

In drafting the terms that created the Millennium Commission, a lurking suspicion about government's ability to manage anything effectively had caused conditions to be inserted that prescribed the need for competitive bidding from the private sector and, worse, to invite separate bids for location and content. Problems began when we considered the bids for the millennium celebrations; the best proposal for content came in one bid and from another, a proposal for the most suitable site.

There were four serious contenders for the location of the main millennium exhibition: the NEC in Birmingham, Pride Park in Derby, Stratford in east London and Greenwich. The most attractive bid for the content relied on using the NEC, but police advised us that the local roads were simply not up to the job. After much deliberation, the chance to build a unique structure, which would simultaneously symbolise the celebrations and achieve the regeneration of a long-derelict patch of land, swung the vote in favour of Greenwich.

The governance for the project was, to say the least, complicated. The Millennium Commission was responsible for soliciting bids and distributing money. Initially, a private company, Millennium Central, was tasked with delivering the project; this was quickly replaced by the government-owned New Millennium Experience Company. The land was owned by British Gas and would be purchased by

English Partnerships, the national regeneration agency. To add to the complexity, the site lay within the Royal London Borough of Greenwich and they, of course, took a close and legitimate interest in its future. There was also an array of anxious private sponsors who had agreed to finance individual parts of the contents and who had to be kept happy.

To compound this difficulty, the project would have to survive the transition between three different Secretaries of State for National Heritage and the prospect of a change in government. By 1996, the emerging plan for the Millennium Dome was attracting significant criticism in the press and it was by no means certain that Labour would support it. The directors of the New Millennium Experience Company were being advised that committing more money before receiving a guarantee that Labour would continue with the scheme, should they take over the reins, would expose them personally to liability.

Tony Blair eventually announced that he would continue the project, subject to a complete review after the election should Labour win. Shortly afterwards, however, a report from the National Audit Office was released, which warned in stark terms that the New Millennium Experience Company had inadequate operational experience, no marketing strategy and no contingency plan should the dome project fail for any reason. On top of this, Eric Sorensen, the Millennium Commission's chief executive, felt obliged to make a statement that the visitor number projections were grossly overoptimistic.

Treasury officials were, needless to say, decidedly twitchy about the whole endeavour, which was not helped by the fact that lower than expected ticket sales necessitated additional transfers of funds from the Millennium Commission amounting to around £200 million. The press remained sceptical, to the point that shadow culture spokesman Peter Ainsworth declared that 'attacking the Dome had become the nation's favourite sport'. The fact that the entire press pack and many other visitors were left waiting in the cold on opening night only served to reinforce their distaste.

In the end, the Millennium Dome opened on time and, technically, on budget. Six and a half million people passed through the turnstiles that year, an impressive number but nevertheless 3.5 million less than was needed to break even – and significantly less than the original 12 million target. Although critics complained about the lack of coherence of the exhibits, the public reaction in the end was largely positive. A total of 85 per cent said they were satisfied with their experience and the spectacular Millennium Dome Show proved popular.

It is crucial to remember that no taxpayers' money was spent on the dome itself. Although some public funds were used to detoxify the land, further long-term benefits would flow from that.

Initially, there were problems finding a buyer for the dome after the exhibition closed. An attempt was made to attract the public with demonstrations by companies illustrating where new technology was taking us. There were also more conventional entertainment offerings, one of the last of which ended in disaster. Such was the atmosphere inside that it created its own microclimate. The presence of tens of thousands of concert goers stimulated this and it actually started to rain on the audience! By February 2002, the government was incurring large costs to look after the site.

In 2004, English Partnerships, Meridian Delta Ltd (MDL) and AEG Europe entered into an agreement whereby AEG would be responsible for the redevelopment of the Millenium Dome and the dome waterfront area, while MDL would be responsible for developing the neighbouring land on the peninsula where English

Partnership, the UK government's national regeneration agency, was the principal landowner.

MDL, owned by Trinity College Cambridge, granted a 999-year ground lease of the land for the Millennium Dome and the dome waterfront area to AEG Europe, who agreed to spend at least £120 million on regeneration of the Millennium Dome within two years. Bon Jovi performed at the first public concert on 24 June 2007. The dome, renamed the O2, was to become the world's most popular live entertainment venue, with the public purse receiving a share of the profits. My first experience of an event there was in response to a plea from my granddaughter, Gusty, who was determined to see Taylor Swift on her first appearance there in March 2011.

Meridian Delta Dome took on the rest of the land in a deal worth around £160 million to the taxpayer. The 1.4 million square metre planning proposal was among the biggest ever submitted to a local authority in Britain, including plans to build 10,000 new homes (38 per cent of which would be affordable), a new business district, two new schools and a medical centre, creating an estimated 25,000 jobs in the commercial and retail sectors. There would also be forty-eight acres of parkland.

Considering that just ten years earlier I had been reliably informed that the site was so toxic that two guard dogs had died as a result of poisonous gas releases, this was quite an achievement. I was in touch with Philip Anschutz, the owner of AEG, while these negotiations were in progress. One evening, I gave a dinner for him in Wiltons to introduce him to members of the British press. Many years later, he remembered for me his feelings at the time:

> When considering the development of a modern arena in London, I was presented with an opportunity to pursue a site

opposite Canary Wharf where the Millennium Dome, as it was then called, was located.

The idea to build an arena on the Greenwich Peninsula was much different than what I had been thinking – something along the lines of the West End but with less location risk if a site could be found. Upon further analysis, it became clear that the Millennium Dome location offered substantial acreage to work with but also carried with it the burdens of considerable cost, meaningful location and political risks and negative perception of the area, attributable to some of the reputational baggage of the Millennium Dome. Despite the potential pitfalls, I have always been an unapologetic Anglophile, and with the conviction that, with the British government as a partner, we could develop creative solutions to the problems at hand, I decided to pursue the project further.

The ability to work with Lord Heseltine, along with other senior members of the British government, was admittedly the deciding factor on my final decision to move forward to a final contract. In retrospect, it was indeed the right decision and I believe has contributed to making a meaningful and lasting favourable impact on London, the development of east London and the South Bank of the Thames and the acceptance of the whole region by sport and entertainment fans who attend the O2 and the development around it.

By any standards, Philip's company was huge and widely dispersed into fields as far apart as port operation and entertainment. He had foreseen that performers would become increasingly part of an international market. He was already operating stadiums across the US and it was an obvious step to extend the concept overseas. As a result of Philip's vision that entertainment would become increasingly international, he now owns many stadiums across the world and organises world tours for many internationally renowned stars.

His first choice in this country was not just the dome. He explored the use of Battersea Power Station and Wembley Stadium, only to find that planning restrictions would prevent any change to the configuration of the former, as it is a listed building, while in the latter the seating arrangements in connection with the swimming pool were not to be moved. There were constraints associated with the dome as well. They could not touch the dome roof, which meant they had to build a stadium within the structure itself, a roof on the floor and hoist it into position.

Despite these considerations, the Millennium Dome is an excellent example of successful regeneration. Five years on from the takeover, there had been 30 million visitors and the dream of creating London's foremost entertainment district had become reality.

By 2011, AEG were able to show that the O2 generates over £405 million of additional income for London annually. It attracts over 8 million visitors a year – which exceeds the number of international tourists received by Australia per annum. It has already generated an economic impact which amounts to more than double the original investment in the whole project, while providing a range of additional social, environmental and commercial benefits.

The dome has created the equivalent of 8,500 full-time jobs and most of those who work there live locally. The millions of people who visit the dome area have helped to showcase the rich heritage and historical significance of south east London and the Royal Borough of Greenwich.

During a breakfast meeting in the House of Lords in July 2024, I met someone whose story gives us a fascinating example of how a small company can play a very significant part in the growth agenda. Sean Collins was an apprentice in east London and started full-time work at Canary Wharf in the early stages of the development. He witnessed the ups and downs, including the collapse of Olympia & York, and he was made redundant in 1993 when the project to connect the Docklands with central London by River Bus went out of business. However, he felt sure that the overall project would flourish and that the Docklands would need a river bus service. The LDDC had erected piers on the Isle of Dogs, in the Surrey Commercial Docks and at Canary Wharf, which were still there should there be another attempt to launch one.

In 1999, with his business partner, Alan Woods, he bought one of the three original river buses and took an option on the other two. Operating as Thames Clippers, they ran a service into central London from the three piers eight months before the Jubilee Line began to operate. The prevailing view was that they were mad, as the underground and the DLR would, in time, scoop up most of the passenger traffic.

They stuck to their view that they could provide a faster, more efficient journey between Docklands, the City and central London – Westminster, Chelsea and the West End for example – given the intensity of the developments and the number of extra passengers that would be generated as a result.

Within three years, Thames Clippers had extended their routes to serve Royal Arsenal at Woolwich. By 2006, they had expanded their fleet to seven vessels carrying 1 million passengers a year. They were looking for a partner to help them expand even more, and it was no surprise when Philip Anschutz of AEG took a majority stake, which enabled them to double the fleet and include the dome in their service.

The business was sold to a Canadian investment fund in 2022, but Sean has retained an equity holding and continues to run the business, which now carries 5 million passengers every year between twenty-two piers, using a fleet of twenty-three vessels. Operating under the brand of Uber Boat by Thames Clippers, they are now pioneering electric-powered vessels.

• • •

Unfortunately, not all of the major public investments in the Docklands were a success. The saga of the Thames Gateway Bridge is a sorry tale, which shows beyond doubt that governments cannot successfully deliver vital infrastructure projects alone.

The lack of any road crossings east of Tower Bridge has long been an impediment to the development of east London. There are nineteen road and rail crossings over the River Thames in west London and only three east of Tower Bridge – leaving a ten-mile gap between the Blackwall Tunnel in Greenwich and the Queen Elizabeth II Bridge and Dartford Tunnel complex. Transport for London has repeatedly highlighted the problems this causes: huge congestion throughout the whole area and severe limitations for anyone who lives there and may want to look for work on the other side of the river.

As far back as 1979 there had been a proposal to build a road bridge just east of the King George V dock, from Thamesmead to Beckton. The initial proposal proved controversial because it included a new road through the 8,000-year-old Oxleas Wood in Greenwich. A public inquiry had to be held, which lasted for several years. By the time permission was granted, the bridge had to be redesigned to accommodate the flight path for the new airport. The new design brought further objections, which meant there had to be another public inquiry.

Full go-ahead for the revised bridge was finally given in 1991, some twelve years after the initial proposal. Protests continued and a huge campaign developed, which many leading national environmental groups joined. Local residents were encouraged to 'adopt' individual trees and protecting the wood became a cause célèbre. Following a High Court challenge, the scheme was dumped in 1993 by John MacGregor, the Secretary of State for Transport. The bridge was finally removed from road building plans in 1997.

In 2004, the Mayor of London, Ken Livingstone, gave his agreement for a replacement crossing on the same site. This time it was consciously branded as a 'local crossing' rather than part of a new regional trunk road development, and Livingstone was careful to ensure he had the support of the relevant local authorities. The new bridge would cost £380 million and consist of a dual carriageway, a pedestrian walkway and a public transport lane. A consultation was held in 2003, but the plan was subsequently criticised for not giving enough information about the development or considering alternative options. It also failed to include an environmental impact assessment.

Howls of protest followed and, once again, a public inquiry was called in 2005, which led to the planning inspector rejecting the bridge. A fresh wave of protest and the emergence of 'new evidence' led Hazel Blears, Secretary of State for Communities and Local Government, to reopen the inquiry in 2007.

In 2008 Boris Johnson, who had by now been elected Mayor of London, cancelled the whole project. A year later, Johnson appointed consultants Mott MacDonald to make recommendations on a new crossing and, in 2012, he promised to build a new £700 million tunnel within ten years.

The result of this perpetual procrastination is that, after thirty-three years of almost continuous work, not a single brick has been laid for an east London river crossing. Anyone wanting to travel the three kilometres from Thamesmead to Dagenham by car faces a journey lasting somewhere between thirty and sixty minutes, depending on the traffic. The people of Greenwich and Bexley had every right to protest as they did, and Oxleas Wood is a beautiful and ancient site, which should not be interfered with lightly. Nevertheless, the question remains why, after thirty-three years, has government not been more determined to find a way around these obstacles in order to unblock fully the potentially huge opportunities which would accrue to east London?

The failure to build any sort of road crossing is the result of two features of our system of government, which can be dangerous in isolation but are disastrous when combined. The first is the system of planning laws and consultation requirements that surround major infrastructure projects. These processes are important but by their nature, they take too long and often give objectors and dissenters opportunities to, for example, raise wider environmental issues that are not strictly relevant to the proposal in question. They can also too easily serve merely to repeat arguments that have already been heard and rejected.

The second is a lack of consistent commitment from central government, often as a result of the high rate of turnover of ministers responsible for such projects. Between 1979 and 2006, there were no fewer than fourteen separate Ministers for Transport (and as we have seen, they are far from being the only relevant politicians in such matters). Every time a new minister arrives, there is a risk that they will lose their nerve in the face of protest, or they simply don't understand the importance of the project, or they might be politically vulnerable to one of the groups protesting. There are always easier alternatives for them – to announce a further inquiry (by the end of which they might have moved on) or even to cancel it altogether.

The benefits of big infrastructure projects are usually spread widely, but the costs are invariably concentrated in a small area. The result is that vocal opposition groups often face no counterbalancing support and so governments are left alone with the uncomfortable obligation to fight for projects considered to be in the national interest.

This disastrous combination was seen with the failure to deal with the major airport capacity problem in London and the south east. Since 1998, no new runways have been built anywhere that serves London. Heathrow is now operating at 98 per cent of capacity and Gatwick at 95 per cent, seriously hindering their ability to recover from unexpected events such as freak weather, accidents or terrorist attacks, which in turn has a huge impact on average delays. Stansted and Luton still have some spare capacity, but the Department for Transport forecasts show that, without further runway availability, London's airports will all be operating at full capacity by 2030.

In 2009, in the run-up to the forthcoming election, David Cameron announced that the Conservatives would not support the creation of a third runway at Heathrow, but in 2012 he set up an independent Airports Commission, led by Sir Howard Davies, the chairman of NatWest Group, to work out how and where to expand our airport capacity. In the run-up to the 2015 election, the government went no further than a pledge to respond to any conclusions.

In July 2015, the Airports Commission's report strongly supported the need for a third runway, and Chris Grayling, Secretary of State for Transport in Theresa May's government, set out the procedures to achieve this. There was a vote in the Commons in favour of a third runway in 2018, but a reduction in air traffic during the Covid pandemic led to further delays, and uncertainties still remain.

Heathrow is already running at full capacity, and marginal extensions to the other London airports cannot solve this problem. With its growth capped, it is all but inevitable that Heathrow will slowly lose its capability to remain as a European hub and through traffic will switch to airports on the continent. Serious economic consequences will follow, perhaps the most important being the limitation of our ability to open new routes to emerging markets.

For reasons that seem to me inexplicable and unjustifiable, the London Docklands Development Corporation that was established in 1981 was abolished in 1998. A consortium of east London boroughs attempted to persuade the Labour government to foster the regeneration opportunities of the London part of the Thames Gateway.

In the event, what emerged was the new London Thames Gateway Development Corporation. It was financially underpowered, only covering a part of the proposed area, and was wound down in 2012. When I was working for Greg Clark in 2015, an official reminded me of my interest in this part of London, which led, after a conversation with George Osborne, to an invitation to chair a commission that would explore where the London Thames Gateway Development Corporation had left matters by looking at the development of east London all the way to the coast, including Southend and Canterbury. As a result, the Thames Estuary 2050 Growth Commission was born in March 2016 and launched in July that year at the Queen Elizabeth Olympic Park.

This was essentially a short-term exercise to undertake a comprehensive survey of the strengths, weaknesses, opportunities and threats throughout the Thames Estuary region – stretching some forty miles from north Kent and south Essex to the east of London – and then to propose effective action. The research acknowledged there were severe pockets of deprivation but also huge opportunities to boost economic growth. Six areas were chosen for research: creating high productivity clusters, boosting connectivity, building new homes and communities, securing investment, harnessing innovation in the built environment, and creating centres of excellence. The commission examined existing major infrastructure projects on roads and rail, including work done by local government and Local Enterprise Partnerships.

Before I could complete the work, I was abruptly sacked by Theresa May over Brexit and Sir John Armitt took over the responsibility. His report was published in June 2018 with the following recommendations:

- The creation of a structure of five 'productive places', based on existing areas and their assets, with a clear vision for each area, a tight focus on priorities and stronger, streamlined governance.
- A robust, locally led review of governance arrangements within six months of the report being published.
- A single voice for the Thames Estuary through a strengthened and streamlined Thames Gateway Strategic Group.
- The development of statutory Joint Spatial Plans in Kent and Essex.
- A revision of the geographical boundaries for a south east Local Enterprise Partnership.
- Development corporation(s) with planning and compulsory purchase powers to drive the delivery of homes and jobs, aligned to major infrastructure investment.
- Strengthened governance arrangements for the River Thames itself.

- Revenue-raising powers and tax incentives to be granted to the Thames Estuary.

The overall report was much in line with my expectations and received a favourable response from the government. James Brokenshire, then Secretary of State for Housing, Communities and Local Government, announced £1 million for a new Thames Estuary Growth Board, under the chairmanship of Kate Willard, the former chief executive of Southend Airport, with a balance of members drawn from the public and private sectors. It has a budget only just sufficient to cover running costs. It is empowered to talk but has no other powers and – crucially – no other money. There can be no comparison with the powers entrusted to the original development corporation, without which none of the transformational changes would have happened in the first place. It ranks high on the list of examples of how not to make progress.

I still believe there is terrific untapped potential in the Thames Gateway yet the government has failed to exploit it. If I had my way, I would convert both Essex and Kent into unitary mayoral counties. In the case of Essex, I would incorporate the vitality of the southern part of the county with both Thurrock and Southend into a Greater Essex, within which they would have a profound influence over the wider economy and not just the microcosms over which they have power today. I would create an overarching body, similar to a conurbation authority, incorporating the two proposed unitaries of Essex and Kent, the Port of London Authority and other appropriate bodies. Above all, answerable to this body, I would establish a development corporation with roving powers, as opposed to designated boundaries. This would enable it to intervene only where action was needed, leaving the vast body of services in the hands of the unitary counties.

The answer to the question why more has not been achieved in the Thames Gateway is simple. Every independent review of the project has been heavily critical of the complex and fragmented governance arrangements.

Whitehall's response to such criticism has traditionally been to create yet more partnership arrangements and joint boards. Although it has since been simplified slightly, the original responsibility for the whole project rested with over forty different agencies, departments and authorities. Accountability is so dispersed that, in effect, nobody is accountable at all. The only way to achieve shared ambition, collaboration and visionary leadership is to actually put somebody in charge.

The Thames Gateway is of huge importance for the continued health of the south east, not least in relieving the chronic housing shortages. Only when the governance arrangements are reformed will the necessary progress be made, and only then will the Thames Gateway be able to achieve its true potential as one of the main engines of our economy.

CHAPTER 17

BIRMINGHAM

Even before Joseph Chamberlain was elected to the House of Commons in 1876, his reputation for municipal leadership and national prestige was firmly established. It was these combined factors that persuaded me to choose Birmingham Town Hall as the venue for the launch of my 'No Stone Unturned' report in 2012. Some years later, in June 2018, I was invited to deliver the first Chamberlain lecture in his memory. While preparing for this, I realised the extent to which I was reversing the transfer of power to London that his reforms had inevitably led to.

He was one of a generation of local leaders faced with the breakdown of social provision driven by the pressures of the Industrial Revolution. If you wander around the town halls of our municipalities, the portraits of the Victorian gentlemen who adorn the walls often carry the names of the companies that were the engines of local growth.

In delivering the lecture in June 2018, I described the process that replaced these fathers of the Industrial Revolution with the early structures of today's social provision. The demands for improving standards and services that Chamberlain had promoted soon outstripped the funds of church, parish and charity combined. So, the taxpayer had to take on that responsibility, but those funds were distributed by central government to national standards of social provision. The growth of democratic accountability ensured that the local industrialists who made their brass were replaced by managers of public services. Throughout my career, I have made efforts to restore something of that entrepreneurial dynamic to England's local economies.

Chamberlain's agenda was essentially a social concept. He wanted effective solutions to urgent problems, coupled with financial prudence. His preoccupation with education, his ambition to enrich the cultural quality of Birmingham and his determination to construct buildings and streets to environmental standards ahead of their time were part of that vision. The rapid growth of the country's population and the inadequacy of public provision or adequate infrastructure, together with the often appalling living conditions of the people, created a clear agenda. Chamberlain tackled these challenges with gusto and proved that municipal government can make a real difference.

At the party conference in October 1991, I had announced the proposal to build High Speed 1 (HS1), a fast rail link between London and the Channel Tunnel. I had been involved in the discussions about the best form of cross-Channel travel in 1981 when Margaret Thatcher made the decision and opted for a tunnel. I had been arguing for a bridge and tunnel combination. There was a moment when, sitting in our embassy in Paris, I thought she would make such a choice, but the moment passed.

During the later detailed workings, the Department for Transport's preferred route was to come into London via Waterloo station. I intervened to persuade John Major to bring the route into St

Pancras, through the East End of London, and to provide a stop that would help with the regeneration of Stratford. This line was later sold to the consortium London and Continental Railways, who made it a condition that there should be no such stop. The acceptance of this diminished role was justified in that the sale proceeds were thus enhanced. It ultimately fell to Labour's John Prescott to ensure the successful completion of the project in 2007.

It was perhaps this early association that suggested to Lord Adonis, Secretary of State for Transport in the Blair government, that he should invite me to his office in 2009. He wanted to talk about a proposal to build what became High Speed 2 (HS2), a rail link from London to the north. My immediate fear was that he wanted to break the news to me that the line would threaten our Grade I listed home in Northamptonshire. For six years at the Department for the Environment, I had presided over planning appeals time and again, wrestling with the trauma that the decisions I had to take would inflict on property owners. Would it now be my turn? That turned out not to be the case, but the line as proposed would cut through a great swathe of the local countryside and create deep and understandable opposition. At much the same time, a neighbouring village, Farthinghoe, needed a bypass and one of the two potential routes crossed our land. I concluded that I would not object if the local authority opted for the route across our land, which I believed would be the better choice.

It was inevitable that the HS2 proposals would be deeply controversial. The initial plan to start construction on the fringe of London, at Old Oak Common, and build the link from there to Birmingham gave the opponents a potential field day. One of the most powerful arguments for the project was its ability to link the north of England more tightly to the prosperous south. Saving just fifteen minutes' travel time between outer London and Birmingham did not present a substantial contribution to such a vision.

Later, an old friend and former colleague, Patrick McLoughlin, became the new Secretary of State for Transport in the coalition government. In December 2012, he wrote to tell me of his intention to announce in late January the second stage of the project to connect Birmingham to both Leeds and Manchester and thus demonstrate the government's commitment to build the entire line. He invited me to discuss what help I could give him in support of the project.

In a speech to the Royal Town Planning Institute, I referred to the scheme as a 'really imaginative project' to expand the prosperity of London and the south east of England northwards by better linking Birmingham to London, with further extensions to Manchester and Leeds. Spreading wealth more evenly would reduce some of the pressure on the south east, which was growing faster than the rest of the country.

I suggested that the construction costs could be shared with the private sector, which could provide the trains and build the stations. I was helped by a letter from the owners of HS1, who explained their interest in a similar purchase of the completed HS2. I mocked 'the guys with slide rules' who were sceptical about the project for assuming that they could make any realistic calculation of the benefits of such an investment so far ahead.

Andrew Adonis, out of office by this point, delivered the Lunar Society lecture in Birmingham in March 2011, where his picture of Birmingham was far from encouraging. He rightly recognised the great strengths of the city – its location at the heart of England, the strength and pride in ethnic diversity and an instinctive internationalism with great cultural institutions. He praised Birmingham

City Council leaders such as Mike Whitby, Albert Bore and Dick Knowles for the success under their leadership of the major reconstruction projects such as New Street Station, Symphony Hall, the canal district, the International Convention Centre and the National Indoor Arena.

His more general view, however, revealed a very different story. A falling population, unemployment rising at twice the national average, low productivity and an increasing reliance on public sector jobs. Underlying all this, he emphasised the most worrying statistic of all: Birmingham almost topped the league of low-skilled cities. His view was clearly expressed that it all came down to ineffective leadership and a lack of any strategy.

Andrew concluded his lecture by returning to a theme I knew only too well. What Birmingham needed was a second Joseph Chamberlain. He quoted Chamberlain, who had once compared his city council to the Duke of Wellington's army, who would 'go anywhere and do anything'. Birmingham needed a modern mayor in his image to unleash the huge potential of this great city and its people once again.

By 2015, an agreement was struck to create the West Midlands Combined Authority, with Albert Bore, leader of Birmingham Council, playing a key role in creating a metro mayor for the region.

Greg Clark was now Secretary of State and had immediately invited me to join him as his adviser. As such, I was much involved in the negotiations and although I don't remember believing that I was marching towards the sound of the drums, I did believe that we were on the verge of a historic constitutional reversal of the country's power structure. The creation of the West Midlands mayoralty eventually produced the platform for fresh leadership that the region so desperately needed to change its fortunes.

Andy Street became the first chairman of the Greater Birmingham and Solihull Local Enterprise Partnership when it was launched in May 2011. I first got to know him in 2012, when presenting my 'No Stone Unturned' report. He brought to the role not only his personal dedication as a local boy but all his commercial experience as managing director of John Lewis – a renowned company with serious local commercial interest and a long-established reputation for establishing good relationships with the communities they served.

Andy was at the heart of the changes that were to fundamentally reshape the local forces at work in the regeneration of the West Midlands. His LEP was governed by a board drawn from a wide representation of local stakeholders. This was localism in the truest sense of the word, with representatives from some of Britain's major companies, local authority leaders and the vice-chancellor and the principal of Birmingham Metropolitan College. They brought a perspective to the conurbation's strengths and weaknesses that no one in Whitehall could possibly have matched. Within two years, the locally based inspiration, stimulated by the LEP, was evident in a number of reports and initiatives.

'No Stone Unturned' was about a major reordering of the dynamics that drive this country. I was advocating the restoration of power to the great cities and local economies, in partnership with the central government. If there was one man in history associated with such ideas, it was Joseph Chamberlain. I hoped, as I spoke at Birmingham Town Hall in October 2012, that he would have approved. I told the assembled audience that there was no sharper contrast between the reality of public administration in this country and the very different model I was recommending. The reality in which we lived was one where officials in central government departments or independent quangos worked on their specialist transport, housing, education, skills or environment projects in concert with their opposite number in each local authority. Most government officials change their jobs every two or three years, which leads to a limited collective memory and lack of experience.

Much more damaging was the absence of any effective coordination within this decision-making process. There was nowhere where questions could be asked about the nature of the local economy as a whole, with its very individual characteristics, strengths and weaknesses. The proposals that I was advocating would be locally prepared by people in charge of the engines of the local economy and the composition of the community. These people not only lived and worked there, they were in touch with a large number of other local players and, usually, would have been around for a significant period of time. They were uniquely placed to know the priorities that can best serve the area and, critically, what can be added to any expenditure the government might make available.

The examples are legion, but I emphasised that local organisations could commit investment to designated areas made available by coordinated transport and housing development, universities can attract investment in science parks if they can match the investment provided by their research funds and the provision of skilled labour, and hospitals can offer sites to firms or laboratories anxious to draw on their particular specialisms.

Above all, I spoke of the fact that all of this is not just some airy-fairy pipe dream. The past fifty years have demonstrated the benefits of local coordination and initiative in parts of this country, to say nothing of learning from the experience of similar economies overseas.

The most significant progress in this area was the single consolidated grant of £12 billion over six years announced by George

Osborne in 2013. The spending departments, whose budgets had been proportionally cut as a consequence, got their money back and the Treasury reasserted its nit-picking supremacy. Labour has replaced this initiative with a National Growth Fund, albeit with about one third of the spending power of Osborne's decision.

Following the launch of 'No Stone Unturned', the Greater Birmingham and Solihull LEP asked me to explore how the report's recommendations could be applied to the West Midlands conurbation. Andy Street agreed with No. 10 that Birmingham could be a test bed to demonstrate what the recommendations might achieve in practice. So, in January 2013, a steering group met in KPMG's offices in Birmingham, which included Caroline Spelman, the MP for Meriden; MEP Phillip Bennion; council leaders Albert Bore, Ken Meeson and Richard Grosvenor; David Eastwood of Birmingham University; Christine Braddock of Birmingham Metropolitan College; and Andy and Steve Hollis from the LEP. The group appointed Steve as project director and set a three-month timescale to illustrate how Birmingham might respond if the Chancellor offered to allocate funds to LEPs from a single capital grant.

We set five priority areas: business support, existing strengths, skills, improved connectivity with markets and better use of available land. In my preface to the 'Greater Birmingham' report, I wrote that the M42 economic corridor around Solihull presented a 'fantastic opportunity' not only for the region but also the rest of the country. However, it required a development corporation-type approach to ensure the area could benefit not only from the extension of HS2 but also from the expansion of Birmingham Airport. There is a crisis over lack of capacity in airports across the country and Birmingham has the potential to expand passenger numbers from 9 million to 36 million over the next three decades.

The 'Greater Birmingham' report called for empowered leadership to help reduce duplication and promote a collaborative approach to link the physical assets, development sites, inward investment support, skills programme, areas of worklessness, research and innovation together to unlock significant growth. We were hopeful that a single consolidated grant from central government would be transformative. There had been significant educational improvements in the Greater Birmingham and Solihull area over recent years, which needed to be matched by a greater local influence towards skills funding.

We noted that there were currently separate funding pots provided for broadband infrastructure roll-out, each with its own application criteria and monitoring processes. The nine local authorities within the LEP area had considerable procurement budgets, totalling over £1 billion per annum but lacked the ability to work together to stimulate local economic growth.

In 2012, a number of other reports were published that pointed to the scale of local initiative in Greater Birmingham. Their existence proved that the building blocks were available to those charged with responsibility for the city.

Nothing created in Whitehall can begin to act as a comparable starting point. At the start of 2013, an entrepreneurial group of young professionals, in partnership with Warwick University, published their report 'Choose Work, Choose Life, Choose Birmingham'. Then, in March, the Birmingham Chamber of Commerce published a report by Jerry Blackett, the CEO, indicating how the chamber movement might help to create a strong, locally based, private sector business support infrastructure if they were given a greater role. This report was particularly helpful in endorsing my long-held view that there was sharp contrast between the support available elsewhere in Europe for small businesses – particularly in export services – and the inadequately equipped organisations here.

In June that year, Paul Kehoe, the CEO of Birmingham Airport, sent me their response to the Airports Commission inquiry into the future of UK aviation. In 2012, they were handling just under 9 million passengers. Their report was designed to show how the airport could compete in the twenty-first century, with plans to handle up to 70 million passengers a year. The response was not just about runways – it was fundamentally about serving the community. The Covid crisis seriously disrupted their plans and it was not until 2023 that the passenger numbers returned to pre-pandemic numbers. The proposed expansion has yet to materialise.

Although Liverpool and London are the two cities with which I am most closely linked, I was delighted to accept an honorary doctorate by Aston University in 2013, followed by another from the Birmingham City University in 2014 when I opened the Parkside Building – a new home for the Birmingham Institute of Art and Design and a key part of the regeneration of the city's Eastside region. I am pleased to have played a small part in helping empower another of our greatest cities.

Patrick McLoughlin, then chairman of the Conservative Party, invited me to introduce Andy Street to the 2016 party conference held in Birmingham that year, but before I began my speech of introduction, I could not resist a small diversion. William Hague was sitting there. It was nearly fifty years since, as a young Conservative, he had made one of the most outstanding conference speeches of our time. Pointing generally in my direction, he had told the conference in 1977 that 'half of you won't be here in thirty or forty years'.

I took my revenge: 'You got many things right, William, but not that one.'

I then turned to Andy and explained to the conference how, since the early 1980s, we had developed the concept of partnership with and within local communities. He had built his career climbing the ladder of one of our most successful companies, John Lewis. He had spent his life satisfying customers' demands for quality and now he wanted to bring the same obsession to improving the quality of public service. In his role at John Lewis, he had not only had to satisfy customers but, in the unique structure of that business, his fellow employees as well. They collectively own the business and come from all communities, regardless of race or creed.

As chairman of the LEP, he had demonstrated an ability to work successively with George Osborne, Greg Clark and Sajid Javid in government but also with local leaders from the major parties. I concluded by asking the question as to why he would give up a salary that would make even local football heroes gasp with envy to do this job?

'Because he is a Brummie,' I told them. 'This is home. He was born here. He grew up here. He loves it. He would serve it with the loyalty and duty that have been the hallmarks of every stage of his life.'

Andy went on to become Mayor of the West Midlands in 2017 and later asked me to produce a report outlining the progress of the devolution agenda within the six combined authority areas that had gained a mayor since then. I warned him that as a consequence of being sacked by Theresa May in 2017, linking my name to the project could be detrimental. He brushed this aside, persuaded his five colleagues to open their doors and made clear that the report would be mine.

The report, 'Empowering English Cities', was published in July 2019 and made clear that many of the UK's major cities 'have underperformed economically for decades'. In it, I suggested the following ideas to further the devolution journey:

- The creation of a Department for the English Regions and the relocation of all government policy offices outside London into regional offices.
- A review of local authorities with updated boundaries; all local elections should be held at the same time.
- Select committees should be set up in both Houses of Parliament to comment on, advise and review the devolution process.
- Combined authority mayors should meet the Prime Minister and Chancellor together at least twice a year.
- Quangos – such as Homes England, Highways England, Network Rail and the Environment Agency – should be under a statutory obligation to cooperate with combined authorities.
- The government should publish a report explaining the structure and powers of the world's twenty most prosperous cities.
- The power of mayors should be enhanced by combining their office with police and crime commissioners and by transferring to them the responsibility for affordable housing, schools performance, skills and unemployment matters.
- Mayors should be able to appoint unelected people with specialist expertise to serve in their Cabinets as advisers.
- Combined authorities should receive local tax revenues and charges such as vehicle excise duty, airport passenger duty, tourist tax and local cultural admission charges.
- The Chancellor should explore the issuing of local bonds.
- Mayors should develop five-year programmes, updated annually, to cover spatial infrastructure, the economy, transport, housing, education and skills and environmental improvement.

- A new single sum for funding capital projects should be created by top slicing existing budgets, using the model George Osborne had pioneered to finance projects developed within these programmes.

The *Birmingham Mail* reported my warning that the shadow of Brexit hangs like the darkest storm cloud over our body politic, while Whitehall, the powerhouse of our society, was paralysed by indecision. I responded that, whether we are in or out of the EU, the need to make our country competitive contains its own imperatives.

Andy Street said about my report, 'The inertia created by Brexit meant that key policy decisions, such as the future direction of devolution, were at risk of falling by the wayside, and I hope this document, with its bold vision, encourages not only similar ambitious thought but real action.' He added, 'Against the backdrop of the leadership election, here is an idea whose time has come.'

The Confederation of British Industry also welcomed the report, commenting, 'We've come a long way since the emergence of metro mayors … the government now must publish a devolution framework outlining what powers can be devolved, how and when.'

Launching the report at Birmingham Town Hall, I returned to familiar themes – starting with the lack of connection with their communities that was felt by too many people:

> 'Trust the people' is a phrase that has inspired the greatest of orators. It has also, sadly, been used at the street corner by tub thumpers for every manner of base purpose. Today, without apology, I present that exhilarating theme in an attempt to address the great challenge of our time. As change sweeps across the world, penetrating ever more deeply into every corner of our lives, people hunger for the chance to control it, influence it and

> play a part in it. To give meaning to those words, power must be restored to the communities where they live and where they work. Real power to real people means real democratic power in the hands of those people. I have devoted much of my political life to this purpose.

I warned that Britain can either 'go on in the same old way' or embrace the pace of change, because the management of our cities is crucial to meeting the huge challenges that the advance of new technologies such as AI are presenting. The full effects of climate change are as yet unknown, although what has already happened is already badly affecting the lives and livelihoods of millions of people across the world:

> Our future depends on the success of our great cities. They are the engines of our prosperity, the rocks of our stability. They made this country what it is. All our tomorrows are dependent on their strengths, are challenged by their weaknesses. We have to build on their pride. Trust them with the freedom to identify more clearly and pursue more energetically their own self-interest. London can never match the pride, motivation and, yes, self-interest of people who live in, work and enjoy their leisure in these places.

I pointed out that much of our post-war world enjoyed underlying economic growth rates that sustained a consistent advance in living standards. But Birmingham was an example of the divisions within our country:

> It is a tale of two cities. Two interwoven cities, linked, interdependent and entwined. There is the city of excellence. Great

entrepreneurs, world-class companies, excellent universities, outstanding public servants, dedicated carers, social cohesion. A nation prosperous and at peace with itself. But there is another city. A city of the postcode lottery, of the forgotten fringe, of the lurking shadow. There is that place on the other side of the road, so easy to pass by. The failed school, the excluded child, the gangland where the moralities to which most of us subscribe are a philosophy of contempt more appropriate for a television soap opera than the reality of everyday life.

In many of our great cities, the democratic deficit is being dealt with and, in addressing the big challenge I faced in Liverpool all those years ago, we have put someone in charge, locally elected, publicly accountable. But devolution is a 'job half done', with uneven powers, constrained leadership and Whitehall unreformed to acknowledge these changes:

> I want to unleash the ambitions of the British people. I want to empower them to rise to such an opportunity. We will never inspire such a vision with empty phrases or lofty exhortation. We need a plan of action. A call to arms. Detailed. Practical. Based on experience. It is a programme of national rejuvenation. We should start with our cities, embrace our towns and spread the benefits deeply into the countryside and villages.

I concluded that the mission should be to empower people to build on their own strengths. Only when our cities prosper can their citizens share in that prosperity. Then, ultimately, our country can flourish once again.

The attention of the Conservative government, however, with

its ever-changing leadership, was much diverted around this time attempting to cope with the Covid pandemic, the war in Ukraine, the energy crisis and Brexit.

Negotiations about the precise powers of metro mayors dragged on, but by 2023, such was the growing confidence that the evolving arrangements were working that agreement was reached with Prime Minister Rishi Sunak and Secretary of State for Levelling Up Michael Gove that, from the next spending review, Birmingham and Manchester would enjoy the flexibility of the single grant that George Osborne had pioneered years ago. These 'trailblazer' devolution deals marked the next step of prising power away from Whitehall. I hope the restoration of executive municipal authority will continue in the way Joseph Chamberlain would have approved of.

The opinion polls were already predicting the dire outcome of the forthcoming general election by the time of the mayoral elections in May 2024. One central focus of interest was whether the two Conservative mayors – Andy Street in Birmingham and Ben Houchen in Teesside – could buck the national trend and hang on. Both had strong records of achievement, measured in essentially local matters, that merited their re-election. But would local people notice?

I asked Andy whether I could help, conscious of the fact that my well-known pro-European views could have a negative effect on some voters. We agreed that I should write an article for the *Birmingham Post* stressing the importance of local policy and local achievement. The article was published by the Conservative Home website in the run-up to the election. I wrote that, when returning to public life under David Cameron, tasked with effectively creating more wealth, 'Andy Street was just the sort of leader I wanted to bring into public service'. I explained in the article why the West Midlands should re-elect him for a third term:

> His qualities – a pragmatism allied to principle, a gift for negotiation, eye for detail and presentational elan – have made him a perfect fit for the role he went on to win at the subsequent election and has retained ever since. And while I'm delighted he comes from the Conservative tradition this is, in a sense, incidental. The whole point of having strong mayors is that they can transcend the partisan and represent their region rather than party.
>
> It is for this reason that I very much hope the voters of West Midlands consider Street's record and prospectus first and foremost when they choose who they want to champion them over the next four years.
>
> They ought, in my view, to consider the improvements to transport, to housing and to the region's economy and reputation that he has brought about. Gains in each of these areas were achieved because the mayor used the power and money available wisely. And because the gains were so evident he won more money and more power from Whitehall to go on making better the everyday things on which people depend.

It was Andy's ability to work with the grain that had unlocked new housing – especially affordable homes on derelict sites – while his exceptional business acumen had driven up investment from across the world. The triumph of the 2022 Commonwealth Games was an astute harnessing of soft power and showed Birmingham was ready for its close-up inspection from the rest of the world. All of this was testament to his hard work since 2017.

With the national trend strongly against the Conservatives, I knew the contest would be close. I sat up for the result and was buoyed with optimism when a recount was announced. I hoped it indicated a high chance of success for Andy.

It was not to be, and he lost by the narrow margin of 1,508 votes in a turnout of 30 per cent. Had it not been for the Reform candidate, who took 34,471 votes, he would almost certainly have won a third term. The West Midlands lost a very able and strong champion who delivered the best of devolution, but I hope we have not seen the last of Andy Street in public life. Under Labour's Richard Parker, I hope that the Birmingham region will build on his successes and thrive well into the future.

CHAPTER 18

TEES VALLEY

After my appointment as chairman of the Regional Growth Fund, I travelled extensively in its support. One such visit, in September 2012, took me to Teesside to discuss bids for our funds from the Local Enterprise Partnership. Within Teesside there are five unitary authorities, which have a long history of working together: Darlington, Hartlepool, Middlesborough, Redcar & Cleveland and Stockton-on-Tees.

They had established a Tees Valley Joint Strategy Unit, which laid the foundations for the LEP under the chairmanship of Sandy Anderson, a former senior executive with ICI and chairman of the board of Teesside University. His team included a mixture of local authority leaders and chief executives from the private sector. As part of their regeneration agenda, they had already designated a twelve-site enterprise zone and been awarded over £40 million of grants in rounds one and two of the Regional Growth Fund. They had also been involved in schemes covering the north east more generally.

A new range of bids that could help Teesside were currently under consideration. I was briefed on the reasons for the region's eligibility for grants in the first place – including the relatively high number of people claiming Jobseeker's Allowance and the data that indicated a lack of skills in the local population. At the time, I was advised not to raise the issue of the problems at the SSI steelworks. Steel production had recommenced in April 2012 after its closure in 2010, but the company was in discussion with the government about acute cash-flow difficulties, even though the government's ability to help was restricted by state aid rules. Some 2,000 jobs were at risk.

Shortly after the eventual collapse of the steelworks in 2015, the Secretary of State for Business, Sajid Javid, asked me to lead a Tees Valley Inward Investment Initiative. We had only met on one previous occasion, shortly after he had taken up his post. We had lunch and a very friendly discussion, but I think both of us went our separate ways afterwards, aware that we came from different wings of the Conservative Party. Sajid, a former managing director at Deutsche Bank with a distinguished City career, had just been appointed to his new job, whereas I was the Tory industrial spokesman prepared to intervene before lunch, dinner and again the next morning.

I had been warned of the problems facing Tata Steel during my earlier visit. Then, the company had just been sold to SSI, south-east Asia's leading producer of hot rolled steel sheets in coils, who had taken out three loans from Thai banks. They had refinanced the project largely to supply their own mills. A range of problems, including technology and software issues, bad weather and industrial action, had delayed the restart, which led to debts of $60 million to UK suppliers, many of whom were small companies. The government was applying what pressure it could on the banks, but a serious risk of closure and job losses existed and there were already contingency plans to set up a task force under Sandy Anderson, the LEP chair, if the worst were to happen.

Three years later, in October 2015, production stopped and there was no prospect of another buyer coming forward. A local task force under the chairmanship of Amanda Skelton, the chief executive of Redcar and Cleveland Council, was created to scope and deliver support for the area. Sajid, on behalf of the Prime Minister, the Chancellor and himself, wrote to ask whether I would be prepared to work with ministers and with the Tees Valley Task Force to secure and accelerate inward investment into the region to speed up its recovery. In the same letter, he included a list of projects that had been announced or were seen as having potential.

One interesting statistic indicated nearly 200 projects over the next two years that could create or protect over 15,000 jobs. As a former salesman, I knew all too well the difference between a gleam in the eye and signed contracts, but this demonstrated the right approach and indicated that someone was at work locally. My judgement was reinforced by the announcement that £80 million was to be provided to help the families and communities affected, there would be funding to keep the site safe and a government company to take over responsibility for the site from the official receiver. Subject to the approval of the as yet unestablished combined authority, a Mayoral Development Corporation would be established as soon as possible to take on the leadership of the site.

I was, of course, delighted to accept. I had been invited to do earlier reports on regeneration by the government and had always assumed the remit included the opportunity to take a strategic view of the challenges and opportunities across local economies. I was provided with official help with the appointment of Gwen Wright to work for me. She proved invaluable in researching and drafting my report and then remained to help me more generally until my various responsibilities came to an abrupt end in 2017.

My reports became, in effect, an analysis of strength, weaknesses, opportunities and threats. Until now, Tees Valley had played virtually no part in my political career. It is an area easy to overlook when travelling north, which effectively meant going to Newcastle. Darlington is the gateway station, but there is little to alert you to the massive economy that lies to the east.

Influenced as I was by the headlines describing the loss of 3,000 jobs and the collapse of the steel industry, in my mind's eye there was, inevitably, an image of yesterday's industrial heartland – perhaps reinforced by the memory of Margaret Thatcher striding around an area of desolation in which one of my Urban Development Corporations had been created in the 1980s. I wanted to do for Tees Valley what I had done for similar areas in previous years.

My earlier visit had prepared me for the scale of opportunity which lay before me. Most of the Tees Valley has a modern, successful, multi-disciplinary economy. Driving east from Darlington to the SSI site reinforced my impression, left by that earlier visit, that the collapse of the steel industry was the last vestige of yesterday's industrial power structure. However powerful a product it may have been, however successful a facility it once was, it was now just a gigantic scar on a site of some 4,000 acres along the south bank of the River Tees. The surprise was not that it had closed but that it had survived so long.

The vibrancy of the local economy was admirably demonstrated by the efforts that local employers had made to find alternative work for the people whose jobs had gone. This, coupled with the schemes the government offered for retraining, had a consequence which must have amazed local people and certainly surprised me. The unemployment figures hardly reflected the collapse, and then only briefly, so great was the re-employment that took place. By December 2016, around 90 per cent of those who initially applied for unemployment benefit had ended their claim. A quarter of the former workers never registered at all. The report by the combined authority and the LEP, 'Tees Valley Strategic Economic Plan', was indicative of their determination to take a lead in organising their own recovery. The Industrial Strategy for Tees Valley 2016–26 was launched in December 2016 and a detailed report by the CBI titled 'Unlocking Regional Growth' was published at much the same time.

The unavoidable conclusion from all this is that there was no shortage of ideas or people to carry them out. What was missing was a framework in which decisions could be taken and the necessary resources deployed. This was a failure of central, not local, government, stretching back over many years. At the heart of government decision-making is what is known as the 'green rules', which guide Treasury thinking. In practice, they demand quantified calculations indicating the likely results in investment programmes. In my experience of urban regeneration, it is simply not possible to anticipate and therefore quantify what may happen when the process of regeneration is started. This lack of detailed information provides the Treasury with the opportunity to oppose the regeneration in the first place.

When I had persuaded Margaret Thatcher to proceed with development corporations in London and Liverpool in 1979, I had no investment rates of return. I simply had an idea and a vision, which she shared. One glance at the SSI site and I knew that here was an outstanding opportunity for regeneration. This was not about this site alone or the other scars that littered the area. My instinct, reinforced by all my previous experience, told me that what was needed was an organised, properly led, well-financed regeneration scheme to match the scale of the opportunity which lay before us. On the opposite bank of the River Tees was a fully occupied, vibrant and dispersed economy. That would be my answer to people who asked for statistics.

My report 'Tees Valley: Opportunity Unlimited' was launched at an event at Middlesbrough Football Club in June 2016, in the company of Secretary of State for Business Greg Clark and his junior minister, James Wharton. I began by recognising that the SSI site was part of a much bigger picture – located, as it was, at one end of some 4,000 acres stretching four miles along the south bank of the Tees. There were isolated examples of new investment by PD Ports and Northumbrian Water, but the overall picture was of desolation and a memory of industrial activity now long gone. So impressed was I by the local reaction that had led to the creation of a combined authority, the first Mayoral Development Corporation outside London and the commitment to a mayoral election in April 2017, I could have concluded that my job was already done.

I had, however, become so fascinated by the opportunities for the wider area, backed by the numbers, talent and energy of the local people from both public and private sectors, that, making no apologies for mission creep, I put forward suggestions to help the whole of the Tees Valley enjoy an exciting future. I asserted how it could break out from under the shadow of Newcastle, exploit its past, secure the interconnectivity of transport infrastructure, establish Darlington as its gateway and add an increasing range of new industries to those on which its past had depended.

I made recommendations over seven policy areas. Under the industrial and urban regeneration section, I advocated the collecting of a set of procedures to be followed in the future if substantial closures occurred and to make all relevant information available quickly. The South Tees Development Corporation needed therefore to be created quickly so that the ownership of the SSI site could be transferred, together with the necessary resources to maintain safety, and the regeneration could be started. The shadow board should, in the meantime, prepare an ambitious plan for the area within a year.

The section on growth opportunities and the wider regeneration included an examination by universities and employers of the possible contribution that one of Kenneth Baker's University Technical Colleges could make to the provision of skilled employees. I included a reference to the infrastructure regeneration plan, which at that time I was working on.

The local chamber of commerce should also visit their opposite number in Germany to learn from them about overseas organisations against which they would have to compete. This would be a prelude to bringing together all the business support organisations to give the best advice available.

The new combined authority should recognise an urgent need to raise standards in failing schools and should also cooperate with the Local Enterprise Partnership to increase the number of apprentices.

The energy economy was of great significance on Teesside, and I recommended that every effort should be made to cooperate with the government's schemes for carbon capture and, in particular, explore the suitability of the proposed new nuclear site in Hartlepool to house a small modular reactor.

On housing, I recommended there should be a greater emphasis on building more starter homes and the region should take the opportunity to participate in the government's new £3 billion Home Building Fund. Several road schemes were also listed as part of the existing drive to improve east–west communications and improve access to the enterprise zone.

The investment by PD Ports would be much assisted by the electrification of the Northallerton connection to Teesport, while Network Rail and Transport for the North should recognise the importance of Darlington station as a gateway to the wider area and include its development in their forthcoming plans. The combined authority should incorporate the future of the local airport into its plans for the area.

Finally, I recommended a number of items to build on the cultural, artistic and environmental strengths of the area – including an announcement that would prevent all sewage discharges that threatened the water quality of the Tees within twenty-five years.

In the end, it was my proposal to establish a development corporation that was to prove one of the most contentious of any policies I had put forward in any of the high offices of state. I was, at that time, based in Greg Clark's department and by good chance, he had been brought up in Middlesbrough. He saw the virtue of my proposals and was supportive from the outset. He was not, however, the Secretary of State who had commissioned my report. The Treasury had secured the appointment of an official receiver, and a combination of Treasury officials and those directly responsible in the Department for Communities and Local Government were adamant that the proper response was to sell off the most attractive parts of the site in order to repay the outstanding debt owed to the Thai banks.

I argued that such a fragmentation of the site into different ownerships would destroy the opportunity for comprehensive redevelopment. I felt strongly that it was utterly unacceptable that people who had run this business into the ground should be allowed to gain by the piecemeal disposal of the viable bits of the site, leaving someone else to clear up the mess. This was cherry picking at its least defensible. The best outcome would be to persuade SSI to agree to the transfer of the whole site, unencumbered by any charge, to the new mayoral authority in return for some of the profit, if any should eventually emerge.

Conditions were deteriorating, costs rising and a royal funeral in Thailand had diverted attention. I took the case to Anna Soubry, a minister of state under Sajid Javid, who supported my contention, which enabled me to proceed with the preparation of the necessary papers. Officials made one final attempt to frustrate my plans and produced legal advice to indicate that their proposals were the proper way to proceed. I refused to accept this advice and, in the end, Sajid determined the matter in my favour.

The development corporation project became the government's official policy, which I helped to negotiate with Sue Jeffrey, leader of Redcar and Cleveland Council. In February 2016, I wrote to her setting out the three options: to press ahead with a body, financed by government, covering the site itself; to announce an intermediate body, within the context of the Mayoral Development Corporation, covering the 4,000 acres; or to go straight to a more site-limited development corporation. There was growing pressure from local MPs and I was due to visit Teesside later that week when I hoped to announce a decision, a timing complicated by an impending knee operation that would put me out of action for a month. I strongly recommended the second option, which I described as a remarkable and high-profile opportunity to serve the interests of Tees Valley and its people. With her support, I was able to make the announcement as planned on 20 February 2016. It was widely welcomed, with the proviso that the final judgement would depend on the speed of implementation.

During the discussion of the earlier plans for a development corporation, it was Greg Clark who suggested that rather than establishing an Urban Development Corporation, it should become the second Mayoral Development Corporation. The first had been announced by Sadiq Khan in 2015 as the Old Oak and Park Royal

Development Corporation on the outskirts of London. At the time, I had thought this to be an interesting adjustment, furthering the devolution agenda to which we were committed. Years later, issues about accountability were to emerge from the differences between this new model and the original, in that the mayor could appoint themself both as chairman of the combined authority and, at the same time, the development corporation, thus blurring any accountability issues between the two organisations.

My report received front-page coverage in the *Northern Echo* and *The Gazette*, and they added their commitment to campaign to bring jobs and prosperity to the area. Sajid himself was particularly generous and said he 'would personally stay on top of this and make sure we follow through'. Significant support came from the chancellor of Durham University, who offered the research experience of their facilities where appropriate.

I announced the appointment of eighteen directors to the board of the Mayoral Development Corporation in late 2016. I also announced that six of them would serve as non-executive directors of an intermediate body to help ensure that the philosophy and vision of the projects were consistent. Sue Jeffrey; Paul Booth, chairman of the LEP, Steve Gibson, a prominent businessman and chairman of Middlesbrough Football Club; Jane Turner, vice-chancellor of Teesside University; Sir Alan Cockshaw; and John Baker, the ex-HR director of SSI, made up this monitoring group. This team was carefully chosen to secure the best outcome for the site as quickly as possible – they were used to decision-making and expected to reach decisions collectively only after careful analysis.

Of particular importance to me was the appointment of Alan Cockshaw, the former chairman of AMEC, a large engineering company. I had worked with him through two previous projects, which would prove of great value to his new colleagues. The first was the regeneration of the Hulme Estate in Manchester, his home city, followed by the restoration of Manchester city centre there after the bomb in 1996. By great good fortune, Alan had good relationships with the Thai banks involved, born of earlier dealings with them, which helped to ensure that any negotiation with them proceeded in an orderly manner.

The first election for the mayoral authority took place on 8 May 2017. A glance at the area would have made Sue Jeffrey, the Labour candidate, the odds-on favourite, so it was a great achievement that Ben Houchen, the Conservative candidate and the group leader on Stockton-on-Tees Borough Council, secured a majority of just over 2,000 on a low turnout.

His campaign was focused on a pledge to nationalise and rejuvenate what was then called Durham Tees Valley Airport. He struck a £40 million deal with The Peel Group in December 2018 and the airport was rebranded as Teesside International Airport when it came into public ownership in January 2019. It was losing £40 million a year but was seen as a considerable area for development, which is underway. In that same month, the South Tees Development Corporation announced that 1,420 acres of land had been acquired from Tata Steel.

Ben Houchen's efforts have not been without controversy. The board members of the South Tees Development Corporation (STDC) were soon replaced. After the first mayoral election, Houchen became chair of the STDC and Sue Jeffrey remained on the board as leader of Redcar and Cleveland Council. After her defeat in the local council elections, she was replaced by Mary Lanigan, who had been elected as the new leader. Shortly after, Jane Turner and John Baker were also replaced. The other three remained and were involved in the complex and fraught negotiations that were to follow.

There were two key issues for the STDC to decide on: how to consolidate the site and where the money was to come from to tackle the restoration programme. The board took the strong view that, as the costs would be borne by the public sector, any long-term gains should accrue to the benefit of Teesside and its people. The concept of a sovereign wealth fund was favoured to ensure that the unpredictability of political change did not risk its dispersal.

The site of the collapsed steelworks was in the hands of the liquidator, but the three Thai banks still had a charge of around $800 million on the assets. The STDC had to issue a compulsory purchase order to clear up the outstanding claims on ownership and gain control of the SSI assets. Despite many attempts at reaching an amicable commercial agreement, STDC was at an impasse with the banks over the costs of releasing the charge. This stalemate had the potential to delay any progress for many years.

The site was also landlocked by another seventy-acre site owned by a local entrepreneur, Chris Musgrave. Ben Houchen, as mayor and chairman of the STDC, negotiated a deal with Musgrave in which he traded his site for cash and a half share of the STDC. This helped persuade the banks to drop their objection to the compulsory purchase process, which was necessary to acquire their site, in April 2020.

The board was under considerable pressure. The site was costing about £1 million a day to keep safe and the government had cut their initial promise of £250 million to begin the clean-up and building down to £125 million. Musgrave, as part of his deal, contributed the missing £125 million. Quite understandably, there were many questions about these arrangements, but the board, faced with the decision, decided to proceed.

Ben Houchen was re-elected in 2021 with a huge majority and sacked the three remaining members of the original six on the STDC board: Paul Booth, Steve Gibson and Alan Cockshaw. Inevitably, they continued to ask the sort of questions that had been their responsibility when in office but now in public. It was not a happy situation.

The *Financial Times* revealed in May 2023 that a 90 per cent stake in the Teesworks company, which had taken over the vacant steel site, had been transferred to two local developers, Chris Musgrave and Martin Corney. Using the protection of parliamentary privilege, the Labour MP for Middlesbrough, Andy McDonald, accused the mayor of 'industrial-level corruption' and dubious dealings.

Inevitably, there were calls for an inquiry, which I supported, as did Ben Houchen himself. The decision lay with Michael Gove, the Secretary of State responsible. I had an additional interest because the government had terminated the responsibility of the National Audit Office (NAO) to audit local authorities, even though I had created the office for this very purpose, and the NAO had made it clear that they would be able to undertake the task.

Michael Gove chose instead to appoint a panel consisting of Angie Ridgwell, chief executive of Lancashire County Council, Richard Paver, previously the first treasurer of the Greater Manchester Combined Authority, and Quentin Baker, the director of law and governance at Hertfordshire County Council. Their report, published in January 2024, was scathing about the lack of or blurring of accountability between the combined authority and the development corporation and they made numerous recommendations to rectify the position. Despite obvious unease about the lack of transparency, inadequate answers to their questions and failure of communication, they found no evidence of corruption or illegality. I am surprised that the government did not feel that the unanswered questions merited further examination, which the NAO had all the necessary experience to provide.

Looking back, I have no doubt that there was a failure in the governance arrangements that Gove's department should have been aware of and thus prevented the conversion of the mayoral authority into a public–private partnership. Furthermore, the government should not have reneged on its initial promise of a £250 million grant.

Development corporations are designed to serve a public interest in the regeneration of derelict land over the long term. Such bodies should either be directly responsible to government or to an elected mayor, who should not, therefore, be a member. In this case, with Houchen chairman of both the combined authority and the development corporation, it was inevitable that, if anything went wrong, accusations of impropriety would follow. I would be the last person to deny the private sector a role, even in a shared concept, but such a role could have been achieved with a company that was set up for a specific purpose and accountable to the development corporation.

Of all my many visits to Teesside, the most spectacular was an invitation from Ben Houchen to blow up the remains of the SSI site. Before the event – I feel unable to use the word ceremony – he took me on an extensive tour of the work underway. BP, Shell and others, under the net zero programme, are developing a £3 billion carbon capture 800-megawatt plant, which will be followed by a blue hydrogen plant. SeAH, a Korean company, is building a facility 900 metres long and sixty-eight metres tall to assemble wind turbines for the North Sea. Jingye Steel, a Chinese company that owns British Steel, is hopefully building a facility to house two electric arc furnaces and associated infrastructure to recycle our domestic scrap whenever possible.

I remain as confident today as I ever was that opportunities now emerging from the ground are merely the prelude to a transformation that will be regarded as a model of the kind of leadership and process that can turn industrial disaster into thriving activity in healthier and safer conditions.

The net zero revolution will be significant, but the deep-water port that has been built and the substantial availability of land in the surrounding areas will extend the investment profile more widely. I am particularly impressed to hear of the development around the airport – though it still experiences annual losses – and to learn of the recently designated freeport status, plus the modernisation of Darlington train station.

It is now more than forty years since I first stared at the tragedy of urban decline on the banks of the River Mersey. It was an explosion of local ambition, energy and talent that began to reverse the decline. Some thirty years later, it was happening here on Teesside all over again.

Looking out at the remains of the SSI site, I stood with my hand on the button. There was a loud bang and a momentary pause before the cooling tower gracefully fell in on itself, making way for a cleaner, more optimistic future.

Ben Houchen was made a life peer in Boris Johnson's resignation honours list in 2022. He was the only Conservative to win the mayoral elections in May 2024, making him the most senior local Tory politician in the country. Despite the national swing away from the Conservatives, some of which affected his result, he held on with a majority around 20,000, a considerable personal achievement.

Despite the misgivings I have about the management of the South Tees Development Corporation, he has played a significant role in regenerating the area, including the securing of its freeport status. I hope and believe that the site and the area around it will flourish, and the development corporation model will prove its worth in regenerating this often overlooked part of the country.

PART V

EUROPE

CHAPTER 19

THE BACKGROUND

The day of my birth, 21 March 1933, would have caused not a ripple on the ocean of time had it not been for the coincidence that Hitler held the 'Day of Potsdam', which celebrated the opening of the new Reichstag after the federal elections that gave him power, on the very same day. The site was chosen because it was the old centre of Prussia. The date was chosen because on that day in 1871, the first Reichstag of Imperial Germany opened.

Over the nine decades that were to follow I have been a privileged spectator and at times a player on the chessboard of our European history. I recall standing in the kitchen of 1 Uplands Crescent, Swansea, on 3 September 1939, listening to the voice of Neville Chamberlain announce from a wall-mounted radio that 'this country is therefore at war with Germany'. Later, in the same town, I watched the searchlights scan the sky for enemy aircraft as they came over night after night at 9 p.m., which trained our Scottie dog to be waiting at the top of the basement stairs for the family to descend.

I spent the night that ended the Second World War in the Regent Palace Hotel in a room overlooking Piccadilly Circus. I can see clearly in my mind's eye to this day the swirling, delirious crowds packed around the statue of Eros.

As an undergraduate at Oxford, I took the first step towards a more practical involvement. I joined the Oxford University Conservative Association (OUCA). At that time, it had an exceptionally unusual two-tier constitution. The officers were selected by a self-perpetuating social elite of undergraduates based in the Oxford Carlton Club. The members of OUCA themselves had no means to influence the election of their officers and a number of us led the campaign for universal suffrage.

The vehicle for this protest was the separate Blue Ribbon Club, and the cover of its membership card bore three encircled symbols; the United Kingdom, the United States and Europe. The campaign ended when the two organisations merged and the voting system embraced the entire membership of OUCA. The symbolism of that membership card cover remains indicative of the challenges that face the Conservative Party to this day.

I was in Berlin in August 1961 on the night when the Russians closed the Berlin Wall. I wandered around the Brandenburg Gate in the no man's land between Russian submachine guns pointing west and German students singing 'Deutschland über alles' to my rear.

Coming as it did, just sixteen years after the Russians had played a key role in the defeat of Nazi Germany, nothing could have been more indicative of how the world had changed. As my interest in politics grew, particularly at Oxford, I was becoming acutely aware of the unfolding trauma facing the UK. The war had delivered a near-fatal economic blow. The imperial era was moving, often without or beyond our control, to the modern Commonwealth. The Europeans first looked to us as an essential partner – possibly the leader – of a new movement to unite the continent and ensure that two tragic conflicts could not happen again.

The first agreement towards unity, born out of the desire for French–German cooperation, was negotiated by Robert Schuman, the French Foreign Minister. His plan was to coordinate the three industries essential to the conduct of war – iron, steel and coal – so that they could never be used for such purposes again. Jean Monnet, the first president of the new European Coal and Steel Community, envisaged a much wider industrial, social and economic arrangement.

The post-war Labour government had a large majority and was more immediately concerned with the defence implications stemming from Russian occupation of much of Europe. As a consequence, the UK became a leading founder member of NATO.

It was Sir Winston Churchill who proclaimed from the opposition benches in 1946, 'We must build a kind of United States of Europe.' It fell to the Conservative Party, which I was an active member of by then, to articulate the reality of a changed world, to come to terms with it and to create the structures and organisations to make it work.

It is important to understand the agony of the reappraisal of the British position in the world that confronted the Conservatives when we returned to power in 1951. In opposition, there had been a strong team under the leadership of Rab Butler and Michael Fraser in the Conservative Research Department (including Ted Heath, Reginald Maudling, Enoch Powell and Iain Macleod), which had prepared the grounds to transform the domestic political agenda. In practice, it fell to Harold Macmillan to devise a European strategy, sell it to the party and articulate it to the country. It was a message with limited appeal, driven by economic and political reality rather than memories of British imperial history. Macmillan's memories of the Battle of the Somme in 1916 had also deeply influenced his determination to prevent further European conflict. Although there was much division in the Conservative Party, the Commons was dominated by a generation of MPs who had fought in the Second World War – traditionally referred to in the chamber as 'my honourable and gallant friend'.

At this time, there was also a profound and enduring gratitude towards those dominions – Australia, New Zealand, Canada and South Africa – who exercised their independence immediately to enter the Second World War and displayed conspicuous loyalty and bravery in our support.

The rest of the empire had no such choice and were administered through a colonial structure. India, the West Indies and our colonies in Africa also fought with conspicuous gallantry, but the decision to enter the war was ours as the imperial power. In the years after the war, we had to learn hard lessons as we sought to maintain control of remote parts of the world whose inhabitants were increasingly determined to establish their own governments. There were incidents in our record of empire that we all wish had never happened, but it is much to our credit that, from that unpromising imperial background, virtually every part of the empire chose to join the emerging Commonwealth. Regardless, the end of empire necessarily forced the UK to look elsewhere for future alliances – hence the turn towards Europe.

One event finally closed the door on such aspirations. The Anglo-French intervention to recapture the Suez Canal in 1956 confronted Macmillan, as Chancellor of the Exchequer, with an unfamiliar interpretation of the special relationship after the Americans threatened to sell the pound if we did not withdraw our troops from Egypt immediately. Macmillan was a leading member of Anthony Eden's government, which was no longer strong enough to withstand the nationalist pressures across the British Empire.

Following a humiliating withdrawal from Egypt, the government was in disarray for some time. Eden resigned through ill health, to be replaced by Macmillan. He 'emerged' as the agreed candidate, which was the custom in those days. Consultations were held behind closed doors. There was no form of election at all – either to elect a Prime Minister or, as the case may be, a Leader of the Opposition.

Macmillan was all too familiar with the energetic economic performance of the European Economic Community, established by the Treaty of Rome in 1957, compared to our dismal achievements. His attempts to persuade President de Gaulle to agree to our membership ended in failure when de Gaulle vetoed the draft treaty that was being negotiated.

There were serious hurdles to be cleared with our trade relationships, some of them based on imperial preference, others based on gratitude towards the US, but there was also the lurking suspicion that de Gaulle felt a resentment caused by Churchill's apparent disinterest in him during the war. Whatever the difficulties, my generation of Conservatives saw this attempt to create a partnership with Europe as his greatest achievement. Within a decade, Ted Heath had secured his vision and we joined the EEC.

Harold Macmillan rallied the government and went on to win the next general election in 1959. But things went downhill after that; the government lost its way, there were major scandals involving government ministers and Harold himself fell ill and had to resign in 1963.

The system to replace him was still the same and, amid much bitter controversy, Alec Douglas-Home, the 14th Earl of Home, 'emerged' and became the last Prime Minister to have been elected while he sat in the Lords. He held the fort well, but with a general election looming, he had a nearly impossible task ahead. In fact, he almost made it, with Labour securing a majority of only four seats. He resigned as Prime Minister but remained leader of the party. Everyone knew that the system had to change and he stayed on to see it through.

That was the moment when my generation of young Conservatives saw a more optimistic destiny and started to feel the excitement of a new beginning.

The leadership contest that eventually took place under the new rules was the first in which all Tory MPs were able to vote for the candidate of their choice. It came after I had already been selected as the prospective Conservative candidate for Tavistock in Devon, where it was hoped and expected that I would replace the sitting member, Sir Henry Studholme, and reverse the drift to the Liberals in the West Country.

I agonised as to whether I could legitimately express a view about whom I would prefer to take over the party. After all, I was almost certain to be there and Sir Henry would not. I phoned him with a suitable apology for my arrogance and expressed my strong support for Ted Heath. To this day, I have never known whether the silence which greeted my call was disagreement or disapproval. I could not have known then how privileged a role I would be able to play one day.

One memory is worth noting from the early 1970s. I was appointed Minister for Aerospace in April 1972. My family and I spent Christmas in Barbados, after which they returned home while I set off to fulfil an invitation to visit Boeing in Seattle. I was thus the first

British minister to speak in the US about our new relationship with Europe, which was then only days old.

Ted Heath appointed me as shadow Secretary of State for Trade and Industry in 1974 – a position I held until I was moved to cover the Department for the Environment in 1976 by Margaret Thatcher. For the next eight years, Europe was hardly an issue of more than passing interest as far as that department was concerned. In many ways, my relationship with the Prime Minister then was a model of Cabinet collegiate behaviour. Thatcher promoted me; she backed me more often than not. Somewhat to my surprise, she had once told me, as we walked together in the corridors of the Commons, that we were very similar people. I thought it best not to pursue that particular point!

It has been said that she promoted me to replace John Nott as Secretary of State for Defence in 1983 in order to take on the Campaign for Nuclear Disarmament (CND), which had grown apace under the shadow of and then in the aftermath of the Falklands War. While there is no doubt some truth in that, because anyone could see that there were runs to be scored by a robust response to CND, that cannot have been the whole reason. When she tracked me down in the first week of 1983, as I was with my family in Tobago, she expressly promised that the appointment would continue after the election. The move was as much the acknowledgement of my reputation as a cost-cutting, number-reducing quango culler as for any anti-CND campaign skills that I might have.

Earlier in this book, I have outlined the coincidences of history that placed me in a significant observation post from which to experience and participate in many of the events that drove the desire to replace the bloodshed that had characterised so much of European history with a more rational agenda – dialogue, compromises and peace. I spoke on the same subject to the American Chamber of Commerce in London shortly after resigning over the Westland affair in 1986. The speech was called 'An alliance, not an empire'. I did not get the feeling it was particularly well received. My experiences as Minister for Aerospace in the 1970s and as Secretary of State for Defence ten years later had exposed me to the challenges facing this country and Europe itself in the context of industrial competition.

My years in the Ministry of Defence transformed me from a private entrepreneur to a minister wrestling with the nation's defence priorities, its industrial base and the ability to afford a coherent, rational policy. This dilemma was most effectively exemplified with the arrival, one day in 1984, of General James Abrahamson. He was in charge of Ronald Reagan's policy to build an impenetrable wall to destroy any missile attempting to penetrate it, for which he had a budget of $29 billion. In popular parlance, it was known as 'Star Wars'.

At first glance, it was a perfectly understandable initiative. If the enemy threatens to destroy you, how can any government with the resources to counter that threat fail to do so? But there were consequences. The enemy must now try to defeat that defence and may be more inclined to attack. Certainly, the perceived enemy will attempt to find a way through or round that defence and in the past that has always succeeded. The impenetrable castles of old were put to siege; the Germans bypassed the Maginot Line in the First World War. By the same token, no enemy will ever believe that any weapons system is purely defensive. The ability to press a button in California and destroy a car 7,000 miles away containing a wanted terrorist derives from the same technological capability.

The prospect of a satellite space war had moved a step closer, but

I was the Secretary of State for Defence with a Cabinet responsibility for the wider British self-interest. I listened carefully to Abrahamson's exposition of the scale of his resource and, in particular, to the role he outlined for our participation. He was able to offer a partnership to Heriot-Watt University in Edinburgh in a field of advanced technology where the university was a world leader. My reaction as I listened was immediate. The general is out across the world visiting centres of excellence in technological advance with similar offers of partnership. This must lead to the biggest transfer of technology to America's industrial base in history. How can any nation of our size and resource ever expect our companies to withstand such taxpayer-led competition? The answer can only be found in a closer relationship with European research expenditure.

My involvement in the House of Commons during my last four years as an MP was limited, sitting as the backbench MP for Henley 1997–2001. The party was changing, particularly in its attitude towards Europe. William Hague, Iain Duncan Smith and Michael Howard, the three leaders of the party during this time, all represented the Eurosceptic wing of the party.

Even in my constituency there were activists. Vocal branch meetings were increasingly attended by members unsympathetic to the beliefs that I held. Along with Tim Sainsbury, I did what I could to finance the organisation Conservative Mainstream, with the active help of former Chief Whip Tim Renton and John Major's former parliamentary private secretary, Graham Bright. Conservative Mainstream was in many ways the extension of the pressure group that Peter Walker had created, Tory Reform Group. If there was a purpose and a personality involved, it was to keep in existence an infrastructure for Ken Clarke and his supporters in the party and the Commons.

I had always found William Hague an admirable and talented colleague. I was delighted when he was elected to take Chris Patten's place as chancellor of Oxford University. Certainly, he is an orator of outstanding ability – an increasingly rare breed in modern politics. I intervened once in the House of Commons while he was Leader of the Opposition, during a statement on Europe, when I posed this question to Tony Blair:

> Would the Prime Minister recognise that this country, which has proudly defended its sovereignty for 1,000 years, has been told by every Conservative Prime Minister since the late Lord Stockton that we would enhance that sovereignty and our power and influence by drawing closer to Europe? Some of us still believe what we were told and followed the House of Commons whipping procedure at that time.
>
> Will the Prime Minister recognise that his statement – which is a marked step forward in the intention of the government to join a successful single currency – stripped of its party-political rhetoric will be widely welcomed in areas of society way beyond his political party? With that in mind, and given that the conditions entrenched in his statement have to be fulfilled before a successful application is made, will he recognise that that will be possible only if there is an all-party grouping to lead public opinion on the matter? Above all else, will he give the House a categorical assurance that he will lead that all-party alignment?

The increasingly Eurosceptic tone of the Conservative Party in the late 1990s shaped my thinking about how the issue of sovereignty has dominated European debate for over fifty years. Some still think of Europe in purely economic terms – the common agricultural policy, the single market, its new currency. But this is only a part of it. The reality is that Europe is far more about the collective sharing of sovereignty. Why is shared sovereignty central to the European vision? It is because it is the surest way to increase Europe's collective security, influence and affluence. The post-war vision was of a unified Europe from which military conflict was banished. This vision was underwritten by the generosity of the US's Marshall Plan and the creation of NATO.

The European Union remains a work in progress, but the way ahead is clear. Churchill would certainly have grasped the symbolism. More than that, great historian that he was, he would have realised that Britain has never stood apart from continental Europe. Until Boris Johnson became Prime Minister, every one of his predecessors since the late 1950s has – sometimes with enthusiasm, sometimes reluctantly – believed that it was in Britain's interest to draw closer to Europe. Until Brexit, I firmly believed that no nation state ever has or ever will act against its own self-interest. Certainly, Churchill would have believed that.

Whatever the immediate challenges caused by the war in Ukraine, energy crisis and immigration, Europe's economies are immeasurably stronger and more stable than could have been imagined when the union was created. Nearly sixty years of peace has left Europe with an extraordinary asset base: world-class infrastructure, design, technology, brands and skills. Increasingly, across Europe, its citizens enjoy and expect standards of provision and services every bit as good and sometimes better than those here in post-Brexit Britain.

So, what should we tell our children about our other special relationship – that with the US? Is it a concept more frequently accepted on the east coast of the Atlantic than the west? Or perhaps a nostalgic memory born of a shared threat from Nazi Germany and the then Soviet Union? Or just one of many special relationships that the US enjoys across the globe? Or is it something more?

I think that the relationship that exists, whatever it is called, is based on a presumption of shared values. The rule of law that protects human freedom. The right of all to grasp their chance in life. The right of races and religions to live in tolerant equality. The right, in Lincoln's immortal phrase, for there to be 'a government of the people by the people for the people'. It is because we believe in these things, because we share a common language with which to communicate those beliefs, that we presume a deeper partnership. At great moments in our history, with the exception of 1940, that faith has been abundantly fulfilled. It is to the advantage of both countries that that should remain the case.

CHAPTER 20

BREXIT

The battle for the leadership of the Conservative Party after David Cameron's sudden resignation led eventually to the election of Theresa May. At the time, I was a member of the National Infrastructure Commission, chairing a group to regenerate 100 of the worst estates, leading a commission to investigate the opportunities for the development of east London, on both sides of the Thames to the coast, and I had recently received an invitation to join the Secretary of State for Wales in looking at the possibility of a barrage across Swansea Bay. There was no agreed time commitment and I received no salary or expenses, except for the payment of half the cost of my car and the provision of a driver. It was a position that many ex-ministers would have embraced with enthusiasm. This was not just a question of writing the odd article or addressing the pressure groups and think tanks that surround Whitehall. This was the day-to-day moving and shaping of real government initiatives.

During the referendum campaign, Theresa May had campaigned to remain. I had read her speech carefully before the vote and I remember that, of its eight pages, there was, perhaps, half a sentence with which I felt uneasy. On one of the overarching issues of our time, it seemed that we were on the same side. I therefore completely failed to understand how she could now begin to negotiate our departure from the European Union, in direct contradiction to what she had said she believed a matter of weeks earlier.

I had never met May, but as one who had turned down the offer of the Home Office in 1990, I was all too well aware of Iain Macleod's private warning to me that the Home Secretary's job was the graveyard of politics. May, however, had displayed the professional skill to survive there with none of the 'upsetting the applecart' experiences so frequently endured by many of her predecessors. That required a political nose and experience that talked of professionalism to me. I could not wholly accept the view that she had achieved it because two – however talented – special advisers protected her back from the world of reality.

Her elevation to No. 10 coincided with a serious loss of momentum for the devolution agenda. George Osborne, as Chancellor, had driven that momentum; he had made available a pot of capital funding, top sliced from housing, transport and skills, amounting to £2 billion per year to be continued for six years and distributed by competitive negotiation to the mayoral authorities. That source of energy in the Treasury was not to outlive George himself, while the spending departments reclaimed the money he had hypothecated from them. Whitehall's attention turned to the European structural funds and their replacement. These were smaller than Osborne's single pot. The Europeans had always intended that this source of supply would be devolved to appropriate local organisations.

In February 2017, I wrote for the *Mail on Sunday*, arguing that Theresa May should put the Brexiteers in charge so they could not argue that 'the wrong people' were delivering on the result. I also argued that the fightback should start right away:

> My opponents will argue that the people have spoken, the mandate secured and the future cast. My experience stands against this argument. I have had my share of opposition politics. I first became an MP in the 1960s when Harold Wilson was Labour Prime Minister. Our duty, we argued, was to oppose. Oppose who? The Government of the day with its popular mandate. From day one we used our parliamentary votes to challenge Bill after Bill despite its clear presence in the Government manifesto. Of course, we usually lost as the popular elected majority prevailed. But not always.

I reminded readers that, a month before the EU referendum, Nigel Farage said if the Brexit campaign lost by around 52 per cent to 48 per cent (in the event, it won by precisely this margin) it would be considered 'unfinished business' and he would continue to press for a second referendum to reverse the result.

As time passed, a fundamental point became clearer. Under David Cameron, we had been led by a Prime Minister committed to making a success of the European agenda. Under May, we were heading for the exit. I was no longer in sympathy with the government in which I was self-evidently a participant. It was almost inevitable that something had to give.

The precise issue was about parliamentary control and whether Parliament should have a final say over the outcome of the Brexit negotiation. I decided that I would have to vote in favour of Parliament having a final say. I knew the risks. It was obvious that, if I were to be punished, it would be seen as a totemic sacking *pour encourager les autres*.

The fact that the hard-line Brexiteers had been able to vote indiscriminately and frequently against three-line whips in the House of Commons over many years would not save me. Cameron had allowed Brexiteers to campaign as they believed during the referendum. On balance, I took the view that I would probably not be fired, but I was fully aware of the risk and I was totally sure where my personal obligations lay.

I spoke in the House of Lord debate on 7 March 2017, where I reminded peers that I had believed, since I first joined the Conservative Party in 1951, that 'Britain's national self-interest is inextricably interwoven with those of our European partners' and that I deeply regretted the outcome of the referendum. I welcomed the fact that May had decided to 'get on' with the disengagement process and appointed several senior Brexiteers to her Cabinet. But I set out why I did not accept that the result of the Brexit referendum would last for ever:

> I must make it clear that, in accepting the mandate to negotiate our withdrawal from the European Union, I do not accept that the mandate runs for all time and in all circumstances – 48 per cent of our people rejected that concept last year. They have the same right to be heard, as I hope so many of us recognised in those long years of opposition in another place.
>
> We now face a protracted period of negotiation. No one has the first idea what will emerge. No one can even tell us what governments in Europe will be there to conclude whatever deal emerges. No one can say with certainty how British public opinion will react to totally unpredictable events. To give just one example, I am told that it took 240 regulations to introduce the single market in the late 1980s. I remember the resentment that caused, particularly to small- and medium-sized companies. I understand that it may take 1,600 regulations to unravel more than forty years

> of closer union – and no one can say how the vital small- and medium-sized sector of our economy will react to the circumstances that it will then face.

Having outlined my concerns about the Brexit process ahead, I set out why I supported Lord Pannick's amendment to ensure that Parliament would have the final say on whatever Brexit deal was negotiated:

> Everyone in this House knows that we now face the most momentous peacetime decision of our time. This amendment, as the noble Lord so clearly set out, secures in law the government's commitment, already made to another place, to ensure that Parliament is the ultimate custodian of our national sovereignty. It ensures that Parliament has the critical role in determining the future that we will bequeath to generations of young people. I urge your Lordships to support the amendment.

After the result, I set off for Wiltons with my wife for dinner. This was a familiar journey. We first dined in Wiltons in the early 1960s before we were engaged and had done so many times over the years. We had not yet ordered our first course when a waiter told me that there was a phone call and would I be kind enough to return to the House of Lords, where the Chief Whip wished to see me. Anne and I duly returned and I encouraged her to join me as we met Lord Taylor of Holbeach. He had a job to do and I can only record my impressions of the interview, which are not based on anything that he said. It seemed to me that he was acutely embarrassed at what he had been ordered to do. It turned out he had disagreed strongly with the policy of singling me out and actually had argued firmly with the powers that be that I should not be removed from the five government roles that I then held.

He had not prevailed, but there were straws in the wind. He told me I had not lost my membership of the Conservative Party and that I should continue to sit on the front bench reserved for ex-Conservative Cabinet ministers in the House of Lords. His behaviour was exemplary and so continued until he gave up the job after the election of Boris Johnson. Six days after John Taylor had carried out his instructions, Theresa May wrote to me on 13 March 2017 to thank me for my recent and past service in government and explained her reasons for sacking me:

> I am sad that this important contribution had to come to an end following your decision to vote against the Government on the European Union (Notice of Withdrawal) Bill, but I know that, with your many years' experience in Parliament, you understand why that must be. The people of the United Kingdom voted to leave the European Union in a referendum supported by both Houses of Parliament and they look to Parliamentarians in both Houses to respect and deliver that result.

In response, I wrote back to Theresa May to explain in further detail why I disagreed with her approach to Brexit:

> You say in your letter that I will understand the necessity to end that relationship. Here we disagree. In the referendum campaign it was recognised that so deeply held and so divided were the views on both sides that members of the Cabinet and other ministers were free to argue and vote against the government's European policy without sanction.

In my speech I made clear that my vote neither held up nor denied your ability to trigger Article 50. Indeed the urgency about which we heard so much at the time seems in the event somewhat diminished. My only vote was designed to give the House of Commons a second chance to enshrine in law a commitment you yourself had already given to allow Parliament a vote on any Brexit deal. The Commons declined the advice of the Lords and I and most Peers accepted the position.

I have repeatedly said you have every right to end my relationship with the government. The simple fact remains that you have changed your mind since the excellent speech you made in the referendum campaign arguing that we should remain in the European Union. I have not.

The post-Brexit freedoms to enable the better governance of our country did not seem to have penetrated the inner workings of the Conservative Party. A letter informing me that I had been ejected from my membership of the Carlton Club was rapidly followed by a letter from the club's deputy chairman expressing the hope that I was well and hoping to see me back in the club very soon!

Even more bizarre was a round robin letter I received from Boris Johnson after he became Prime Minister in 2019 asking me to rejoin the party. In it, he said that over the last few days it had fallen to the Conservative Party to transform our country fundamentally and permanently for the better, and they needed my help to do that. Nobody seemed to have noticed that I had recently donated £1,000 to the Scottish Conservative Party, the only sane section of the party left!

There followed what was for me, in many ways, a rerun of what happened after my resignation from government in 1986. I became a focal point of media interest in the anti-Brexit campaign. The invitations flooded in and I was back on that same media circuit that had saved me from oblivion all those years before.

• • •

The path to Brexit was a dishonest one, and there are plenty of culprits who stoked Eurosceptic fires.

First, the newspaper owners with deep personal convictions. Rupert Murdoch, owner of *The Times* and *The Sun*, and Conrad Black, owner of the *Daily Telegraph*, neither of them British citizens. There is also Paul Dacre, editor of the *Daily Mail*. Between them, they had much of the printed media at their disposal, as well as a prominent television channel. All must share responsibility for the many falsehoods that appeared in the newspapers they controlled or edited and in the ceaseless propaganda they poured out in their efforts to persuade their readers to vote for Brexit.

Second, Boris Johnson. He succeeded me as the MP for Henley when I stood down in 2001. At first, we had an excellent relationship. During his selection process, he made many of the members laugh by claiming that I was the Lion King. He went on to become Mayor of London, winning elections twice in what is by nature a Labour city. He claimed to stand for the principles of moderate, open conservatism that spoke to many of the ideals I had campaigned for and our relationship remained good.

On the question of Europe, Johnson was all over the place. He had made a name for himself in the 1990s as the *Daily Telegraph*'s Brussels correspondent, writing silly stories about the EU that frequently bordered on lies. When it came to the referendum, he did not even know himself what he believed. Johnson had drafted two separate articles ahead of the campaign, one advocating remaining in the EU and the other recommending that we leave! He plumped for the latter for the simple reason that he calculated that this would give him the best chance of succeeding David Cameron. He then played a decisive role in the campaign to leave the EU.

The third divisive figure was Nigel Farage, who left the Conservative Party in 1992 over the Maastricht Treaty and gradually morphed into a populist Eurosceptic, becoming involved with UKIP, then the Brexit Party and currently Reform UK. After eight attempts, he was elected to the House of Commons in 2024. He receives over £1 million annually from his media activities, a significant advance on the thirty pieces of silver which Judas Iscariot received for his efforts.

UKIP's breakthrough in the 2009 European elections, coming second in a major election for the first time in its history, followed the 2008 financial crash that drove down living standards and prompted a great desire for change. Years of unbroken austerity in the run-up to the referendum gradually fed this hunger for change. The Brexit campaign exaggerated it and diverted attention from the deep and long-term economic problems we still face by exploiting the age-old prejudices of racism, immigration and populist nationalism. A cauldron of simmering discontent was heated and stirred with emotive, but meaningless phrases such as 'getting our country back', 'ending rule by foreigners' and 'preventing bureaucratic measures being imposed by unelected civil servants in Brussels'.

When it came to the 2016 referendum, the holding of which I felt was a grave mistake, the Remain campaign was conducted in the wrong way in almost every respect. It was too negative and it left unchallenged the fact that too much had already been conceded to the Eurosceptics in the Conservative Party who cherished an idealised vision of the future without having any clear detail of what it would look like or how to create it.

The Leave campaign, meanwhile, was strikingly dishonest, stirring up dissent by claiming on a poster displayed nationwide that Turkey was about to join the EU, thus allowing millions more migrants to come to the UK. That was a direct and palpable lie; as long as we remained members, we had a veto on whether to agree to any new applicant joining. This brazen falsehood was repeated by a member of the government on Andrew Marr's politics programme on the Sunday before the vote, on the same day as the poster appeared. Then they claimed that the NHS would receive £350 million a week extra if we left the EU and that Britain would hold all the cards in any negotiations for trade deals after leaving. Boris Johnson threw in his lot with all of this, reiterating and regurgitating all the lies that led to the momentous vote to leave the EU.

After the result, David Cameron immediately resigned and Johnson pulled out of the subsequent race for the Conservative Party leadership after he was stabbed in the back by Michael Gove, another prominent Brexiteer, who declared that he was not fit to be Prime Minister.

Thus, Theresa May succeeded Cameron and followed my suggestion, written in the *Mail on Sunday* days after the result, that she should appoint three senior Brexit supporters to get on with the job: Boris Johnson, David Davis and Liam Fox. If we had to do this, I thought, it would be better to get it over quickly and end the uncertainty, thus avoiding the additional chaos that a vacuum would entail. The presumption was that, as they had argued so strongly to leave, they would have worked out what had to be done.

It rapidly emerged that they had no such plan; it had all been empty rhetoric, bones bare of any flesh, tossed to a frustrated crowd. Davis and Johnson eventually resigned when May sought to inject some reality into the situation.

In an interview with *The Observer* in March 2018, I posed the question, 'Why is it that after eighteen months since the referendum, we have not got any closer with these issues? The answer is simple: because no one has got any answer about how to do it.' I also articulated my view that the case for re-examining the Brexit question was growing stronger as May struggled to find a deal:

> The downsides are becoming more evident as time passes. We have had a serious devaluation of the currency. We have turned ourselves from the fastest growing to the slowest growing economy in Europe and we have made a complete Horlicks of the Irish border. I am totally with the view of Tony Blair and John Major that this matter has got to go back to parliament and possibly to a referendum or a general election.

Later that year, I signed a statement with, among others, Dominic Grieve, the former Attorney General, calling for a second referendum to reconsider the Brexit question. We warned that the Conservatives risked alienating a whole generation of younger voters and we might cease to be accepted as a serious party of government:

> To do this, we must listen to and engage with their concerns on Brexit. They voted overwhelmingly to Remain in the European Union in 2016 – and since then have become even stronger in their views. Since the referendum, nearly 2 million young people are now of voting age. Of those in this group who are certain to vote, an astounding 87 per cent support the United Kingdom staying in the European Union. If we do not hear their voices, who could blame them for feeling excluded and powerless on this most vital issue. The truth is that if Brexit fails this generation,

> we risk losing young people for good. Our party's electoral future will be irrevocably blighted.

Dominic has been a stalwart ally through all this and has recently taken my place as one of the presidents of the European Movement.

As Parliament failed to deal with the Brexit question, I became increasingly involved with the People's Vote campaign for a second referendum. I spoke at one of their rallies in March 2019 at Parliament Square, where I recalled my experience of growing up as part of the post-war generation who said, 'Never again.' I told the thousands of assembled activists:

> I dismiss with contempt the image of us as an isolated island wrapped in a Union Jack, glorying in Churchill's famous phrase, 'Very well, alone then.' I was there. Our army evacuated, our cities bombed, our convoys sunk. Churchill did everything in his power to end this isolation. He offered France a political union if they would fight on. He begged the Americans for help. It only came after Hitler unbelievably declared war on the United States. He embraced Stalin's Russia when colleagues urged him to spurn it. 'Alone' was never Churchill's hope or wish. It was his fear. It was this experience that changed history.

I recalled how Harold Macmillan told British people the truth about the emergence of the empire into the Commonwealth, building on that historic relationship as he sought another destiny for us and applied to join Europe. I added how our accession to the EU led to Margaret Thatcher's pivotal role in the creation of the single market. She insisted on our being at the table with France and Germany. She would have been appalled to see us excluded.

This contrasted with Theresa May trying to secure a Brexit deal that could be sold to the hardliners in Parliament, her dash across the channel, begging bowl in outstretched hand, an interview, a lengthy meeting of our former partners from which she was excluded, a 'take it or leave it' offer. I added, 'That is what the Brexiteers have done to our country. It is a national humiliation, a disgrace, made entirely in Britain.'

I argued that, even if Parliament had passed Theresa May's deal, it would be a terrible outcome:

> Any deal that Parliament can now agree will inevitably be the lowest common denominator of reluctant compromise. This is no way to chart a nation's future. One way or another, the people must decide. They must be free to vote to remain. We are here today on the right side of history.
>
> In a shrinking world of global terrorism, international tax avoidance, millisecond communication, giant corporations, superpowers, mass migration, climate change and a host of other global threats, our duty is to build on our achievements, to maintain our access to the corridors of world power, to keep our place on the stages of the world. What cannot be in doubt is our responsibility to our young generations to pass on to them a country richer, more powerful, safer than that we ourselves inherited. Our partnership with Europe is that destiny.

As the Conservatives continued to blunder towards a disastrous Brexit and the wheels came off Theresa May's government, I advocated that in the 2019 European Parliament elections, voters should back the only party committed to a second referendum, the Liberal Democrats. In an article for the *Sunday Times* in May that year, I wrote: 'I cannot, with a clear conscience, vote for my party when it is myopically focused on forcing through the biggest act of economic self-harm ever undertaken by a democratic government.'

I continued my involvement with the People's Vote campaign with another rally in Birmingham in July 2019, days after Boris Johnson had succeeded Theresa May. Her government had collapsed after successive efforts to pass her Brexit plan had failed. Johnson completed his transformation into a hardliner, intent on damaging the national interest by pushing through the most unforgiving exit deal that would ruin our economic and trading relationships. I told the audience that I recognised there were many traditional Conservative supporters present who felt similarly strained by the Brexit process:

> I have only one voice, one experience, one set of historic memories, one philosophy to bring to the debate. That is a Conservative voice. I have fought in every frontline political confrontation of the past seventy years. I have fought under the guidance of every Conservative leader since Sir Winston Churchill at the 1951 general election. This is not the background from which I would ever have expected to vote Liberal Democrat in the recent European elections.

I noted that some 5 million Conservative supporters voted to remain in 2016. Many of them felt disenfranchised with Johnson's accession to the leadership, which I said had 'injected a new simplistic approach, a new ruthlessness, a new urgency into the debate':

> Across the world, the British tradition of tolerance forged in heated debate in the mother of Parliaments is recognised and respected. British law protects equally the richest and poorest of

citizens of the United Kingdom and visitors from overseas. Each of us is equal. In the last few days, something has changed.

Cabinet has been stripped of all balance, all debate, sworn to an extreme interpretation of the 2016 referendum, bound to articulation based on unfounded and reckless optimism, unrealistic assertions, defended by evasion and bombast, blind to the world in which we live.

The delusion of Brexit forces its proponents into ever smaller circles and ever deeper holes. It is as though our leaders have already cut themselves off from the leaders of the European Union and the rest of the world.

At that time, it was clear that both Parliament and the public were opposed to a no-deal Brexit, while the European Union was opposed to ripping up the Withdrawal Agreement. I predicted what would happen later that year in the general election, when Johnson would be taking on Labour's leader, Jeremy Corbyn:

> I do not stand before you tonight to claim that we have won the war against the folly of Brexit. What I do say is that with every passing day our chance of winning gets better. There may yet be a general election.
>
> An election where the bogey of Jeremy Corbyn will be wheeled out in the traditional 'Reds under the beds' campaign. Redder Reds and bigger beds. This will be the last throw of a campaign that has run out of any credible arguments for its own case. All the polling evidence supports the view that a Corbyn victory is incredible.

Over the summer of 2019, Parliament sought to take control of the Brexit process from Johnson to ensure that a no-deal Brexit was avoided. The People's Vote campaign was increasingly gaining momentum while Johnson sought to push a slightly modified version of May's Brexit deal through Parliament.

I spoke at one final People's Vote rally in Parliament Square in October 2019 about 'the language of the mob' that Johnson was using about the prospect of a second referendum. 'Europe, in my lifetime, has seen the price you pay to regain control from the mob,' I said. While Johnson said that it was time to 'get Brexit done' and later lied to the Queen over proroguing Parliament, in order to prevent further debate about his deal, I insisted that we should reject this cavalier approach to Brexit, buried in a general election:

> 'Let's get Brexit done' is the latest attempt to frog march us where we don't want to go. It is the greatest deceit of them all. Brexit is not a decision taken for a Parliament or for the next decade. It is a creeping paralysis, where yesterday's nostalgia distorts tomorrow's opportunities. The very existence of our United Kingdom now hangs by a thread.
>
> Brexit will not bring us together. It is the wedge that will drive us apart.
>
> Europe, our largest home market, will embroil us in years of detailed negotiation. Every decision will now be decided by unanimous votes of the remaining twenty-seven members.

In the final words of the final rally before Parliament was dissolved, I paid tribute to the energies and passions of those who had come together to try to stop this disastrous harm happening to our country and those who were campaigning for a better future:

> You have come from all over the country. From all parties and

none. All generations, every class and creed. You're British and proud of it. That is the heart of the matter. Pride in our history, our traditions, our culture, commits us to the partnership of modern Europe. Our voice has echoed across the centuries in a very different Europe. A Europe of bitter nationalism. A Europe of deep religious divide. A Europe of tyranny and bloodshed. We have helped to create a Europe of peace.

A Europe where national pride and loyalty can be pooled in a shrinking world to enhance the power and influence of us all. In coming today, you are marching into history. Not the history of yesteryear but the history of tomorrow. Do not lower your sights. Do not avert your gaze. Look straight. Look up, march on.

Unfortunately, my prediction of Brexit buried within a general election came to pass. Faced with the unpalatable choice of Johnson versus Corbyn, the country held its nose and voted Conservative, returning the party with an eighty-seat majority – its largest since 1987. Although Johnson seized on this as a mandate to deliver his hard, extreme form of Brexit, the issue was far from settled. Opinion polls soon showed that a growing number of people thought leaving the EU was a mistake and that many would favour rejoining.

In the run-up to the 2024 election, Susan Williams, the Chief Whip in the Lords, rang me on behalf of Nick True, the Leader of the House of Lords, and herself to offer the return of the Conservative whip. I knew them both well. Nick had worked as my desk officer in Conservative Central Office in the late 1970s and as leader of Richmond council, where Haymarket's head office is located. Susan was a member of the policy group which David Cameron had set up and I had led and whose report began the party's journey to devolution and local mayors. Our paths crossed when she was our leader of

Trafford council from 2004 to 2009 and later when she held various positions in subsequent Conservative administrations. I suggested that we put the invitation on hold until after the election. I did not want to embarrass them if I was involved in any controversy over Europe during the campaign. In the event, I was pleased to accept their offer. It seemed important to me that pro-Europeans should remain in the party, in order to hasten the day when it remembered the history it had been part of under every post-war Prime Minister until the Brexit referendum.

Although there was to be no second referendum, I am proud to have played a part in opposing this national tragedy, including serving as president of the European Movement from 2021 until 2024. Brexit may have got 'done' in 2019, but I believe it is inevitable that one day, Britain will return to its historic place at the centre of Europe.

CHAPTER 21

THE WAY BACK

Predictions are a risky business in politics, but it is clear that, for the next five years at least, our relationship with our European neighbours will be largely determined by Sir Keir Starmer, following Labour's landslide victory. He will not, of course, be free of constraints in how to handle the legacy of Brexit, despite his large number of MPs. Our colleagues in Europe will be briefed by their embassies here on the wider mood throughout this country. Our national media will provide a barometer of public opinion. The European Commission, the European Parliament and national governments will not want to be caught up in any rerun of the 2016 referendum. Any proposals to modify the terms of our departure are most likely to be attacked by the Brexiteers in the Conservative Party as well as by other right-wing groups as a sellout, a betrayal of our national interest.

The referendum and subsequent general election in 2019 both took place in the context of a prolonged period of frozen living standards with the consequential electoral thirst for change. Added to this were the anxieties created by the apparent lack of control of illegal immigration, as emphasised by a daily flow of arrivals across the English Channel in small boats.

Given those challenging circumstances, it only required people with total contempt for the truth – and a strident tone of voice – to claim repeatedly that our problems would all be solved if we simply got back control of our borders, scrapped a web of foreign-imposed regulations and prevented foreign judges interfering in our ability to govern ourselves. As the years have passed since the vote, the case for revisiting our relationship with Europe has grown ever stronger.

Politics can be a lonely place, particularly if there comes a moment when you know within yourself what you must do, at whatever cost to yourself or your career, because either your conscience or your experience tells you that it is right. Most of the public seem to think that we politicians are only in the business for what we can get out of it. The corrupt and occasionally criminal actions of the few, which are inevitably highly publicised when they are exposed, confirms them in that belief.

But most politicians, wherever they sit in Parliament, are not like that. The vast majority of MPs are decent, honest men and women. Certainly, many of them have ambitions for high office as well, but it is also the knowledge that in some small way they can contribute to a wider sense of national purpose that motivates them.

That is why I determined that, if the outcome of the referendum was a decision to leave, the fightback must begin immediately, however long it might take to restore our European relationships. I remembered clearly that the campaign against our membership began the day we joined, was pursued relentlessly and eventually achieved its purpose. Therefore, we had to display that same determination and the stamina to sustain the fightback in the years ahead.

Eight years after the referendum, the Conservative Party has been through four Prime Ministers – Theresa May, Boris Johnson, Liz Truss and Rishi Sunak – and few are willing to actively defend Brexit.

The constant cries from the Brexiteers that they have been betrayed are already well worn. Their argument goes that they have been frustrated by the civil service, the BBC and the so-called 'blob'. They say they need more time to prove the benefits of having left. Yet the problems that Brexit has brought upon the country have destroyed many political careers and exposed the personal flaws of those involved. Johnson's career ended in disgrace when a select committee with a Conservative majority came to the unanimous view that he had lied to the House of Commons. Truss came and went in forty-nine days, having disastrously insisted on a reckless Budget that crashed the economy.

Sunak restored some sanity but was overwhelmed by frozen living standards and rising illegal immigration. He had coped well as Chancellor during the Covid pandemic and the energy crisis prompted by the war in Ukraine. But when it came to the 2024 election, he was squeezed by Nigel Farage's Reform UK, which had held back its populist fire against Johnson in the 2019 election. He also faced an aggressive push by the Liberal Democrats, who took swathes of seats from the Conservatives in their traditional home counties strongholds – including my former constituency of Henley, which the Conservatives lost for the first time since 1906.

The party faces a huge challenge now to pull itself together and set about regaining the respect and trust of the electorate, thus bringing those Tory supporters who have abandoned us in droves back into the fold.

In the first draft of this chapter, I wrote that the party should unite behind the new leader. If I had left it at that, I would have ignored the world as it is and as was so clearly demonstrated in the recent election.

One of the most striking aspects of the 2024 election campaign was how the issue of Brexit was almost completely ignored by both Labour and the Tories. That was deeply dishonest of both of them. I described the subject as 'the elephant in the room' when I wrote an article for *The Independent* saying that almost all of the key issues needed to be debated within the context of the UK's relationship with Europe:

> Both major parties are afraid of losing votes to the hard right. Labour needs to rebuild its red wall while the Conservatives run scared of Reform … The state of our economy, defence and environment, the need to level up our society, control immigration and restore Britain's standing in the world. None of these issues can be honestly addressed in isolation from our relationship with Europe. Yet Europe is the no-go area.

I highlighted how many of the grave challenges facing Britain in 2024 were all linked to the issue of Brexit:

> Why cannot the two major parties debate immigration in the round? The boats contain just 5 per cent of those who might or might not be sent to Rwanda. They are a small part of the near 700,000 net immigration figure – the real elephant in the room.
>
> Until we consider the consequences for our farms, care homes, hospitals and universities of culling the numbers, all the talk of change, the constant assertion of 'plans' amount to little more

than platitudes blowing in the wind. Whatever we decide to do, we need to work more closely with our European neighbours, who share our experiences and consequent tensions.

It was obvious that Labour and the Conservatives should be discussing a closer defence relationship with Europe. Platitudes don't have much firepower. The world around us is becoming ever more unstable and dangerous, and there is little that Britain can do alone about famines, droughts and conflict forcing millions of people around the globe from their homes.

From the Conservatives, we had brave talk of turning a corner, of a plan working. But how can we seriously believe we can significantly improve our economic situation alone, after severing our connections with our largest trading partner and nearest neighbours? How can we build a Silicon Valley here if, for years, we cut ourselves off from European research and can only return to the table as a supplicant? Our companies must compete with American and Chinese companies, which are technologically underpinned by huge defence and space budgets. Yet no one was willing to have this difficult conversation. That remains the dilemma for the new Conservative leader Kemi Badenoch.

On the other hand, the new Labour government is showing a few welcome signs that they are open to taking some pragmatic steps to right the harshest wrongs we have suffered by cutting ourselves off from Europe.

I suspect that Keir Starmer will choose areas where we can move closer to Europe but which do not stir up the anti-immigrant vote. The first and most obvious area is defence and security. The summit at Blenheim Palace in July 2024 showed that the change of Prime

Minister has started to foster some goodwill between the UK and its European allies, but that is only the start. The UK and Europe itself need to do much more.

The only realistic threat to Europe's security that might involve us is from Russia, and this may have to be faced with or without American support. That is not to suggest that there are no other circumstances in which British troops could be involved. It is only to say that it is not possible to conceive of any other realistic threat today, whereas in 1940 the enemy was at the Channel.

Donald Trump's rhetoric is a throwback to the 1940 'America alone' tendency, when his party forced Democrat President Roosevelt to promise not to enter the war. The US only came to support Europe after the attack on Pearl Harbor in 1941, with Hitler declaring war on the US a few days later. I have much praise for what has been called Pax Americana, but Trump's return to power in January 2025 might be a game changer.

We are more likely to preserve the NATO alliance intact if Europe is seen to be doing more to protect itself. An initiative that seems to me long overdue – but nevertheless practical – would be to offer to merge our forthcoming defence review into a wider review of European defence. I had some experience of coordinating pan-Europe defence, including the formation of the European Space Agency, which gave us satellite leadership in that organisation. We are part of the European defence system within NATO, but there is a multiplicity of defence budgets there, which are spent principally to meet the needs of national armament and equipment manufacturers rather than in a coordinated way following an overall strategic European defence appraisal.

The US and China each have one coordinated budget and

procurement system, which delivers the economies of long production runs and the benefits of coordinated research programmes. These, in the case of the US, flow through to Silicon Valley where vast sums from the space and military budgets enrich the industrial strength of the private sector.

Security today has to be based on sharing power in the face of a threat. Do we really want to go back 100 years to the nation states of Europe, when generations of young people were sent to die because politicians could not resolve their differences peacefully?

It does not have to be like this. We have seen the benefits of trans-European contractors in the production of Airbus. That grew from the initial seeds sown by the Schuman Declaration in 1950.

There should be a realisation of the need to replace national procurement strategy with a European procurement strategy. NATO has delivered beyond every expectation, but the very success of the stability it has given us has diminished any urge to drive the process further. There are huge prizes to be won from more effective coordinated procurement – though it would be controversial, as most other major changes have been.

This would have to be politically led to have any chance of success. In negotiating the Eurofighter Typhoon deal in 1983, I came face to face with the real world. The French had negotiated a project based on the interests of their manufacturers. The British were excluded. I renegotiated that deal with Germany, Italy and Spain, which, to my regret, excluded the French, who thus proceeded alone with their Raphael project. History has now repeated itself, with a Franco-German-Spanish project to replace the Typhoon, leaving Britain to pursue a partnership with Italy, Saudi Arabia and Japan for its own replacement. I do not question the desirability of those two latter countries as partners, with their financial resources and ability to influence the scale of orders, but this is an industry-led concept. I cannot reconcile our defence interests with supply lines dependent on an unpredictable Middle East and an industry on the other side of the world. The Ministry of Defence must have been asleep on the job.

Our defence interests should not be negotiated by the narrow economic self-interests of our contractors. Defence strategy must be determined by governments. A European-wide review would start with the leaders of those countries with significant defence industries. Later, the rest of Europe could be offered procurement deals to bring their budgets into the coordination.

The same argument applies to other threats. Take global warming and climate change, for example. Environmental pollution does not recognise national frontiers. Europe is among the richest continents in the world. We need to coordinate and lead by example. There is a cost, of course, but it is better than the alternative.

We can work better together by capitalising on the younger generation's support for Europe. We must use every opportunity to keep it that way, especially by rejoining youth movement programmes to keep our young people in touch with Europe. I was much heartened to learn that the Starmer government is considering just such a scheme. It is the same argument for the research sector. If we can combine our budgets, then that enriches us all. Our scientists know this and want us to rejoin European programmes, including Erasmus.

The supposed benefits of Brexit are almost non-existent so far. The miracle trade deals that were supposed to compensate for the loss of access to the European market have failed to make even the slightest difference to the trade lost. None of the benefits promised so lavishly to our farmers have materialised, while much of the pain, having been delayed until after the election, is yet to come. The UK will be forced to adjust to whatever changes the EU makes in order to keep our access to the European markets, but we shall have no way to influence those changes. This issue has also now become obscured by the government's inheritance tax policies.

Contrast our current situation with that facing Margaret Thatcher, who dispatched Lord Cockfield to Brussels to ensure the UK's influence was central to the formation of the single market in 1985 when he became a European Commissioner. The UK's interests were protected then because we were at the table. Now we are not. In the years to come, we will need to negotiate some form of involvement, if only in a consultative role. We will have to consider what happens if we have access to third countries on EU terms – if Europe changes those terms, do we have to change as well?

During the pandemic, many Brexit supporters claimed that it was only because we had left the EU that we were able to develop and distribute the vaccine more quickly than others. What few realise is that the AstraZeneca jab was developed by a British company in Europe under the rules of the European Medical Agency. If we had remained in Europe, we could almost certainly have persuaded the rest of Europe to fit in with our timetable. And as a result of Brexit, that agency has now left London and moved to Amsterdam.

There have been no benefits for the City of London either. It was not just the domestic British market that gave our financial institutions such strength and influence; it was our dominance of our time zone within the European market. That dominance is now seeping away as companies shift their staff elsewhere in Europe and companies are choosing to float elsewhere, especially in the US. The finance industry is moving people abroad. The only good deregulatory news is that the cap on financial city bonuses has been removed to enable huge increases in top pay. Not quite the levelling up that was promised!

There is a similar need for coordination and cooperation in dealing with the huge technology firms, which have a profound influence for good as well as for bad. There is an urgent need for regulation and there will be an acrimonious debate about whether the UK is strong enough to take them on alone. It seems to be common sense to create – or join in – some suitable European grouping; this would not need to involve rejoining the EU.

The same applies to the joker in the pack, the knottiest problem of all: illegal immigration. The reaction to the riots in the summer of 2024 presented a wonderful opportunity to turn that page. Many more people took to the streets to defend the rights of immigrants than to support the thugs. I expressed the same thought when I addressed the Conservative Party conference in 1983 about our ethnic minorities: 'They are Black, they are British, they live here, they vote here.' The conference cheered me to the echo.

We should come clean and admit that the challenges of preventing illegal immigration are going to increase. We have to find a way to control our borders, but our borders are Europe's borders too! Those seeking to cross the Channel in small boats are not French. They come from all over the world, so any honest appreciation of the difficulties involved must include the recognition that the small boats are just the daily illustration of a much larger problem.

The overwhelming majority of our legal immigrants are here to fill essential gaps in our health and public services, to provide staff for our burgeoning hospitality industry or to contribute much-needed funds by studying at our universities. No one should underestimate the public outcry that will follow if any controls are too tight. Most immigrants are here legally, but what remains unacceptable is the inflow of those that arrive outside the law.

This problem, in fact, affects our European neighbours much more seriously than it does us. In 2023, some 29,000 illegal immigrants crossed the Channel; in the same year Italy was confronted with over half a million crossing the Mediterranean and the Aegean in boats.

It is surely common sense for us to join forces with the rest of Europe to protect and police all our borders together. We should also recognise the root cause of the problem, which is the contrast in living standards revealed to the four corners of the globe by the ever-present internet. The internet represents the greatest vehicle for world awareness that has ever existed. In real time, in the most remote impoverished corner of the world, people can see the standard of living here.

We should recognise that, where the domestic conditions in their countries make it possible, the right solution is to send the illegal immigrants back with the clear message that they must apply to come in the correct, legal way. In countries where such conditions clearly do not exist, we should consider creating some new form of Marshall Aid with other European nations facing the same problem and coordinate our aid programmes to create better conditions in those countries. Then we can together coordinate and negotiate appropriate repatriation schemes, such as the UK now has with Albania.

None of this will be easy. We must also face the harsh reality that many of these people are escaping from civil wars, famine and corrupt regimes or come from countries or communities for which we have special responsibilities – Hong Kong and, for the limited number of people who worked for us, Afghanistan.

It is not, as Donald Trump alleged, rapists, criminals and thugs who risk the hazardous journeys to get here. It is mostly young men, enterprising, energetic and ambitious, hungry for prosperity which they can share with their families. The UK is a particular magnet, not only because they may have relatives here but also because English is often their second language.

We must win this argument, and that calls for the collective voices of all who care to speak out, as we saw on our streets in the summer of 2024.

I am over ninety-one and I have listened to many of the more rabid racist outbursts again and again. A glance at the wider world will show you that there are communities tearing themselves apart as a consequence of just this sort of language.

Look at Donald Trump's words about Mexican refugees, look at the treatment of the Uyghurs in China, the Rohingya people in Burma, the tragedy of Gaza and Lebanon and the carnage in Sudan. There is a common theme, a perception that anybody slightly different is a threat – foreigners and would-be migrants alike.

Nigel Farage and his so-called Reform Party are not new phenomena. They just represent a particularly nasty strain of racism and the politics of hate that was seen here in the 1930s, then reared its ugly head again in the 1960s and now is evident across Europe and the US.

In the early 1960s, I came up against it during my involvement in the hotel and employment businesses. I saw the Smithfield meat market porters march to Enoch Powell's tune in 1968. It is often forgotten that Ted Heath kicked him out of the shadow Cabinet and, shortly afterwards, the Conservatives won the next election. No serious Conservative today should ever dance to this tune.

There are no simple solutions to these most complex of problems.

When I started in politics, there were grown-ups in charge, taking evidence and willing to listen before reaching consensus on a policy for the future. Now one of our major challenges is how to take a class of social media-drenched politicians, who commit themselves day by day, tweet by tweet, to follow some fashion or fad simply to gain some instant short-term popularity, and get them to think ahead in terms of six months, a year, five years, a Parliament or perhaps even a decade. We need leaders who are willing to find the levers and language to tackle this most difficult of challenges ahead.

There is a wider battle to be fought in the rhetoric about Europe, but we must start with practical, pragmatic ideas about how to change our society. All the proposals I have suggested could be done right now, though the right would no doubt howl with rage.

However, the sad fact is that none of these things alone will move public opinion by the time of the next general election. There will have to be a credible plan which shows the way to a general sense of well-being, based on rising living standards. What I cannot foresee is how long it will take the Conservatives to find a leader capable of leading the party back to power from the centre ground.

I do not see anyone who is willing to put their head above the parapet and say what is becoming increasingly obvious: Brexit was a catastrophic misjudgement. It was a grave act of national self-harm and it must be reversed as soon as possible. Public opinion is moved, by and large, by one thing, and only one thing. That is the way people feel about the pound in their pocket. If they are feeling well-off because the economy is growing, they have more cash to spend on what they want. They vote for the government of the day because they don't want the other side to disrupt it. If, on the other hand, they are feeling disgruntled, they will vote for change.

In the absence of anyone from my party willing to make the case for closer ties with Europe, I hope that Keir Starmer's Labour government will begin to take some of these sensible, pragmatic steps to take the UK back where it belongs. He appears to have started with the most important step, to reset relationships at a personal level. He will have no problem within the Foreign Office. Our ambassadors know well that dialogue is where their trade excels. In their daily work, they will carry the message to their contacts that there is a new mood. Ministers should deliver the same message and make it their responsibility to establish cordial relations with their opposite numbers. This might serve a wider purpose of equal importance in that many of the public services on the continent work more effectively than those here and we should find out why.

I have referred to many examples here where closer cooperation is there for the taking. The government should take heart from the realisation that many of the steps suggested are of minimal interest to the wider public. The body of law that Maragret Thatcher did so much to establish when she pioneered the single market is the framework that makes civilised life desirable. Eight years ago, we were promised a bonfire, but not so much as a single wisp of smoke has served to stimulate our economy. For those who wish us to repair our ties with Europe, we need to stop shadow boxing and go on the attack. Ask the Brexiteer zealots for detailed drafts of any regulation changes they wish to see and then expose them to the howls of British companies who would then suffer the consequence of lost trade. Or, as bad, the warnings to our health, the environment and safety that such a bonfire could produce.

Instead, there is a clear case to be made in private and public about the economic reality we face. This is where the case for reversing Brexit must start; it has made us poorer and voters are increasingly recognising this.

I am not oblivious to the challenges ahead in winning this argument. We are a European power and our history is the history of Europe. The Romans, before they consolidated with their neighbours and became Italians, inspired our religion. The French were responsible for much of our social framework that exists today; they developed the monasteries and built the cathedrals. Our history is of the great battles on land and at sea, as we fought with our European neighbours to acquire empires overseas. We treasure our classical architecture, inspired by the work of Palladio in Northern Italy. The music we play and the pictures in our museums are more the work of European artists than British.

It is only the cult of the narrowest of nationalism that tries to bury all this history and replace it with slogans designed entirely to inflame the basest instincts of tribalism. We have always been a European power. That is who we are and that will never change.

ACKNOWLEDGEMENTS

I set out to write this book curious to know what had happened to the initiatives I had set in place during my seventeen years as a minister. In many cases, sufficient time had passed to make judgements based on facts. I remain indebted to Sam Sims for the commitment with which he researched the evidence and drafted an early text. The project was delayed because David Cameron brought me back to the corridors of power, but I picked it back up again after I was sacked by Theresa May in 2017. In 2023, I asked Sebastian Payne to help me complete the task and update the autobiography I had published in 2001. I am most grateful for the energy and professionalism that led to the draft that Biteback agreed to publish. Caroline Michel, my agent, deserves my gratitude for her help and advice. To this must be added my admiration for the contribution of Catriona Allon in her role as editor.

I cannot name all those who have given me advice and improved my memory of events they shared with me, but I want them to know of my profound gratitude. There are, however, three people I must name. Tracy Rodger has been my personal assistant for twenty years. She has been invaluable in the coordination of both the book and my relationships with so many people, plus the achievement of actually getting the job done. Alan Kemp has been always on hand with advice and comment since we first met in the Ministry of Defence in the late 1980s. He brings an important contribution: he tells me what he thinks even when it is not what I want to hear. And Michael Mates first entered my life as a member of the select committee that investigated the Westland affair. He has been a good friend ever since and has brought an eye for detail to this story and a generous devotion of time to its telling that has proved invaluable.

Finally, I must thank my wife Anne for putting up with the mountains of paper all over our home. Any day now they will join the rest of my papers in the Bodleian Library.

INDEX